International Politics of HIV/

D1078421

The HIV/AIDS epidemic is one of the most catastrophic phenomena that has impacted and will continue to impact people's lives in Sub-Saharan Africa, influencing all aspects of society. Today around 29 million people are living with the disease in the region.

This book examines the global governance of the HIV/AIDS epidemic, interrogating the role of this international system and global discourse on HIV/AIDS interventions. The geographical focus is Sub-Saharan Africa since the region has been at the forefront of these interventions. There is a need to understand the relationship between the international political environment and the impact of resulting policies on HIV/AIDS in the context of people's lives. The book points out a certain disjuncture between the governance structures and the way people experience the disease in their everyday lives. Although the structure allows people to emerge as policy relevant target groups and beneficiaries, the articulation of needs and design of policy interventions tends to reflect international priorities rather than people's thinking on the problem. In other words, it is argued that, while the international interventions highlight the importance attributed to the HIV/AIDS problem, the nature of the system does not allow interventions to be far reaching and sustainable.

Offering a critical contribution to the understanding of the problems in HIV/AIDS in Sub-Saharan Africa, this book will be invaluable to students and researchers of health, international politics and development.

Hakan Seckinelgin is a Lecturer in International Social Policy at the Department of Social Policy, London School of Economics and Political Science. His research interests include international organisations, social policy, civil society and HIV/AIDS in Sub-Saharan Africa.

WITHDRAWN

LIVERPOOL JOHN MOORES UNIVERSITY
Aldham Robarts L.R.C.
TEL. 0151 231 3701/3634

LIVERPOOL JMU LIBRARY

3 1111 01249 4553

International Politics of HIV/AIDS

Global disease – local pain

Hakan Seckinelgin

Routledge
Taylor & Francis Group

LONDON AND NEW YORK

First published 2008
by Routledge
2 Park Square, Milton Park, Abingdon, Oxon OX14 4RN

Simultaneously published in the USA and Canada
by Routledge
270 Madison Ave, New York, NY 10016

Routledge is an imprint of the Taylor & Francis Group, an informa business

© 2008 Hakan Seckinelgin

Typeset in Times New Roman by
RefineCatch Limited, Bungay, Suffolk
Printed and bound in Great Britain by
TJ International Ltd, Padstow, Cornwall

All rights reserved. No part of this book may be reprinted or
reproduced or utilized in any form or by any electronic,
mechanical, or other means, now known or hereafter
invented, including photocopying and recording, or in any
information storage or retrieval system, without permission in
writing from the publishers.

British Library Cataloguing in Publication Data
A catalogue record for this book is available from the British Library

Library of Congress Cataloging in Publication Data
Seckinelgin, Hakan, 1969–
    International politics of HIV/AIDS : global disease—local pain / Hakan
Seckinelgin.
        p. ; cm.
    Includes bibliographical references and index.

ISBN-13: 978–0–415–41383–1 (hardback: alk. paper)
ISBN-10: 0–415–41383–4 (hardback: alk. paper)

ISBN-13: 978–0–415–41384–8 (pbk: alk. paper)
ISBN-10: 0–415–41384–2 (pbk: alk. paper)

    1. AIDS (Disease—Africa, Sub-Saharan. 2. AIDS (Disease)—
International cooperation. I. Title.
    [DNLM: 1. HIV Infections—Africa South of the Sahara. 2. Health
Policy—Africa South of the Sahara. 3. International Agencies—Africa
South of the Sahara. 4. International Cooperation—Africa South of the
Sahara. 5. Policy Making—Africa South of the Sahara. WC 503 S444i 2007]

RA643.86.A357S43 2007
362.196′979200967—dc22
2007000377

ISBN13: 978–0–415–41383–1 (hbk)
ISBN13: 978–0–415–41384–8 (pbk)
ISBN13: 978–0–203–94615–2 (ebk)

ISBN10: 0–415–41383–4 (hbk)
ISBN10: 0–415–41384–2 (pbk)
ISBN10: 0–203–94615–4 (ebk)

To Damien

Contents

Acknowledgements

It would have been impossible to write this book without the contribution of people living with HIV/AIDS, within the context of the disease and those people who are trying to do their best to help them. I am deeply indebted to a large number of people, who wanted to remain anonymous, in a number of countries who were happy to share their lives' experiences with me. Time and again I was humbled by the willingness of people to talk and discuss their conditions independent of the great problems they face on a daily basis. I was regularly told 'No problem, we'll talk to you. At least you can tell people what we think so that they can understand what our lives are like.' Also, thanks are due to those who work in international organisations and non-governmental organisations. The book would have been incomplete without their openness and interest in discussing their work with me. I also thank the following for discussing some of the ideas which are developed in the book with me: Jacquie Rubanga, James Deane, Laura Leonardi, Luciana Bassini, Pierre Claver, Betty Nabinye, Deo Nyanzi, Warren Nyamugasira, Moses Matou, Rebecca Mukasa, Stephen Ochieng, Joseph Semujju, Brigitte Quenum, Shalita Steven, John Rwomushana, Shirley Baker, Prisca B. Chitomfuna, Alison Cook, Margaret Kalane, Andrew Kiptoo, Miyanda Kuunda, Mariola Mierzejewska, Valencia Mogegeh, Malebogo Monguakekse, Karabo Mongwaketse, David Mugo, David Mukuyamba, Kennedy Mupeli, Bawani Mutshewa, Simon Mutonyi, David Chizao Ngele, Vuyisele Otukile, Divya Rajaraman, Michelle Marian, Schaan, Exhilda Siakanomba, Tumie Thahane, Walter, Otis Tamfumaneyi and Maryla Wiesniewski.

The research leading to this book was supported through various sources. The initial field research was supported within the Global Civil Society Year (GCSY) book project with funding from the Rockefeller Brothers Foundation. I thank Mary Kaldor and Marlies Glasius for their encouragement at the time and continued support for the research through the years. The intellectual forum that they nurtured around the GCSY has provided an important forum. LSE's annual staff research/travel grants were used for large parts of the field research. I thank also the Suntory and Toyota International Centres for Economic and Related Disciplines (STICERD) at LSE for their Small Grant in spring 2005 that facilitated a part of the field research.

Initial ideas forming some of the chapters were presented in a number of workshops organised by BISA Poststructural Politics Group. I thank the organisers Jenny Edkins, Maya Zehfuss and Louiza Odysseos for these opportunities and all the participants for their helpful comments. I was fortunate to take part in the LSE Philosophy Department's Ph.D. Research Methods Seminar in the 2006 summer term. I am grateful to Nancy Cartwright for inviting me to jointly organise the seminar series on 'Evidence and HIV/AIDS'. Chapters 4 and 5 were greatly improved as a result of many discussions we had in the group. I also thank the group members Jacob Bjorheim, Maria-Elena di Bucchianico, Damien Fennell, Jeremy Howick, Sara James, Nisrine Monsour and Fernando Morett. The encouragement and support of colleagues and friends in the department of Social Policy, LSE, was very important to sustain the research over a long period of time. Particularly I thank Gill Bridge, David Lewis, Eileen Munro, Wendy Sigle-Rushton, Peter Townsend and Gail Wilson. Also, I have benefited greatly from discussing many of the ideas with successive cohorts of students enrolled in the department's master degrees in Social Policy Planning in Developing Countries and NGO Management over the last six years. They have always been very enthusiastic and engaging. Many of them have become friends. Particularly I thank Leanne Bayer, Fiona Wilson, Marissa (Wilkins) Hoffman, Hulda Ouma, Jo Nicholls, Rachel Parker, Lynda DeGuire, Nicola Cullen, Tisha Wheeler and Gavan O'Sullivan. I would also like to thank Leanne Bayer for her warm welcome to Burundi and for the long discussions we had on many aspects of developmental life and work.

I also want to thank Heidi Bagtazo, Harriett Brinton and Amelia McLaurin at Routledge, and Helen Moss, for their support in this project. I thank three anonymous referees who commented on the proposal. Their insightful comments were much appreciated.

Finally, I must thank Damien Fennell. I owe him a great deal. In discussions with him through the years many of the ideas in the book were clarified and improved. He also read many drafts of the manuscript and his comments no doubt improved the argument. More importantly, his support during the research and writing-up periods was all-important for me to keep going. For all these reasons and more, the book is dedicated to him. Of course as always the responsibility for the shortcomings of this book remains mine alone.

Some of the ideas which are developed and expanded in Chapters 1 and 2 were initially introduced in the following works: H. Seckinelgin (2004) 'Who can help people with HIV/AIDS in Africa? Governance of HIV/AIDS and civil society', *VOLUNTAS: International Journal of Voluntary and Non-Profit Organisations*, 15: 287–304, and *Global Governance: A Review of Multilateralism and International Organizations*, 11(3). Copyright © 2005 by Lynne Rienner Publishers, Inc. Used with permission. The initial ideas informing the discussion in Chapter 2 were also expressed in Hakan Seckinelgin (2006) 'Multiple worlds of NGOs and HIV/AIDS: rethinking NGOs and their agency', *Journal of International Development*, 18: 715–27. An earlier version of Chapter 5 appeared as Hakan Seckinelgin (2006) 'Civil society and HIV/AIDS in Africa: the use of language as a transformative mechanism', *Journal of International Relations and Development*, 9(1), March, reproduced with permission of Palgrave Macmillan.

Introduction
Global disease versus local pain

This book is about the impact of international organisations and their HIV/
AIDS-related policy frameworks in Africa on people infected, affected and
living in the context of the disease. It has three central arguments. One, there
emerged a global governance of HIV/AIDS through the convergence of
international policies developed by the international organisations. Two,
while this policy convergence provides the resource base for interventions, it
does not reflect on its own impact in the way people experience the disease.
This is partially related to the structure of international organisations and the
way ordinary people are incorporated into the debates within them, and
partially to the fact that international interventions do not only provide help
and manage the process of policy making and implementation but also constitute their own subjects and relevant domains of policy with which they
engage. In other words they institutionalise particular relations and actors as
relevant for their interventions. Three, the construction of subjectivities as the
object of the international policy interventions creates an anomaly for people
who experience the disease within their socio-cultural and economic contexts.
In the process of institutionalisation they become patients or risk groups that
are in turn objects of medical knowledge. In this way the experience of the
disease as a social phenomenon is transformed into solely medical experience
as constructed by the international expert knowledge. Thus, in relating to the
disease and the policies people face a set of dilemmas in relation to the
available subjectivities that can or cannot be relevant for their everyday thinking. This situation, it is argued here, presents an important challenge for
policies, and most importantly questions their relevance for the issues at
hand. Furthermore this questioning is also about whether the existing international regime or governance of HIV/AIDS is an appropriate mechanism to
deal with the issues in multiple contexts across Africa.

There are a lot of studies and published work looking at HIV/AIDS in
various African contexts in order to understand the spread of the disease or
the efficacy of policies. There is little reflection on the mechanism through
which policies are developed and implemented. Given the ongoing international focus on HIV/AIDS and on Africa, it is imperative to reflect on
some of these international mechanisms. In this sense the book is different

from many others. Although it is based on research in various African countries on people's experiences of the disease, it utilises these to look at the international organisations and the relevance of the governance structure that has emerged. Rather than positioning itself in order to comment on what people living with and in the context of the disease should do, it reverses the analytical lens on to international actors and their practices in the context of the pandemic. In this reversal two things are obtained: (a) the international policy process is linked with the context of implementation within which people experience both the disease and the policies and (b) more importantly people's experiences are employed to question and analyse the position of international actors.

On 6 April 2006 the *Washington Post* newspaper carried an article on 'How AIDS in Africa was overstated' which was reporting the conclusions of new research published in the *Lancet*, a British medical journal. The research disputed the accuracy of the United Nations Joint Programme on AIDS (UNAIDS)' estimates of HIV/AIDS in Africa. This article was followed up by an editorial in the same newspaper on 10 April 2006 on 'Assessing AIDS'. The editorial argued that as a result of the discrepancies between the recent research highlighted in the article published on 6 April 2006 the credibility of the United Nations would suffer. Here the main target within the UN system seems to be UNAIDS. The editorial points out that UNAIDS has been complacent about the inaccuracies in its statistical reporting for what seems to be a political expediency to keep the global AIDS coalition together in addition to keeping the funds coming for HIV/AIDS interventions in Africa.

In this they refer to 'frustrated experts' who are unhappy about UNAIDS' generalised intervention policies and were suggesting more targeted intervention strategies for particular risk groups. The inaccuracy in the statistical reporting is taken to be a watershed for deciding what to do with the HIV/AIDS pandemic in Africa. The editorial in a decisive tone says that, 'now the organization appears to have published dubious AIDS data', certain policy priorities within the HIV/AIDS field promoted by UNAIDS need to be questioned. It points out that the credibility of the UN matters less than 'the reaction of health officials in poor countries and donor agencies' who have been pointing out that, while there is an underfunding in this field, AIDS is overfunded in comparison to other diseases. And it moves on to suggest that 'Prolonging the life of an HIV-positive adult is expensive and difficult; preventing malaria with low-tech mosquito nets may be more cost-effective.' The editorial ends by the suggestion that, out of this debate prompted by the dubious statistics on AIDS, HIV/AIDS will still emerge as a high-priority policy concern as 'it tends to strike poor countries' skilled urban people, leaving behind a generation of orphans and puncturing hopes of development progress'.

I want to use this particular case of HIV/AIDS discussion in an influential newspaper in the United States to open the introduction, as it captures issues and tensions that are in the centre of the international HIV/AIDS debate. They include the accuracy of available information, the knowledge claims of the experts, the role of donors, and policy priorities particularly focusing on treatment. The editorial raises important questions about the overall international AIDS perspective. It highlights the role of certain actors, the importance of certain policies and the way they can be implemented, as well as the politics of knowledge. The editorial can also be seen as setting the boundaries of what is seen as relevant to discuss in this area. However, in doing this it not only emphasises certain actors' role in this policy arena and their funding concerns but also presents an acute problem immanent in these discussions in relation to the role of people infected and affected by the disease in multiple socio-economic and cultural contexts across Africa. Typical in its approach to HIV/AIDS in Africa, in the editorial people who are infected and affected are conspicuous by their absence from the discussion. As some of these issues are the focus of the book in front of you I want to briefly look at this editorial to see what sorts of boundaries are highlighted in it. I will look at two issues: (a) the question of statistics; (b) the question raised about treatment.

The main theme of the editorial on the statistical problems is a good place to start. The structure of the argument is as follows:

> The statistics presented by UNAIDS are not accurate. The new research indicates a much lower level of HIV/AIDS in countries (though it is still high in southern Africa).
> Therefore, UNAIDS is unreliable.
> As a result the policies advocated by the organisation need to be reconsidered to reflect the state of affairs highlighted in the new research.

There are several issues here. One, the argument illustrates the difficulties involved in both collecting and understanding the data, and understanding this fact within the larger international fora. Two, the relationship between statistical analysis of the state of affairs and relevant policy orientations provides the justification for policy change. Here the knowledge base informing the need for change is located with the outcomes of the new statistical information. Three, by linking UNAIDS' overestimation to generalised policy implementation, it also implicitly assumes that if the statistics were correct then UNAIDS' policy approach would have been correct too. In other words the justification for the scope of the policies on both accounts would depend on a certain measurement of what is happening that is represented in the statistical information. Here, on both sides their positions are justified on considering this information as the basis of their knowledge claims in relation to the state of affairs in Africa.

Both sides are trying to justify a certain position by relying on a certain kind of knowledge claim that is demonstrated through potential robustness of various statistical approaches. Thus, while there are differences in terms of considering what needs to be done, they seem to agree on the methods of how to know about what the state of affairs is. It is in the latter consideration that the typical absence of African people's voices is evident. The conditions of people are assumed in the statistical representation of the disease, and individuals are considered significant or not implicitly in the general statistical discussion of whether there was a generalised disease. This absence of people's voices can be observed in different aspects of the discussion, for instance in the implicit eminence of the expert knowledge on both sides of the debate. Even if we assume that UNAIDS statistics are accurate, the link between high numbers and the generalised policy interventions is based on the interpretation of experts and their understanding about what needs to be done. In the same way there is no explicit justification for the editorial's move from the claims of inaccuracy to the contestation of the policies other than relying on the views of 'frustrated experts'. Here the important issue is on the question of whose knowledge matters in thinking about what needs to be done in relation to HIV/AIDS. Implicit in this is the ordering of different kinds of knowledge claims for policy decisions.

Another important aspect of this editorial is the content of its policy suggestion. It juxtaposes malaria versus HIV treatment. It acknowledges that HIV/AIDS is an important issue among discrete risk groups while there are other diseases impacting people's health that are not focused under the present international funding priorities. Here the editorial seems to be critical of the policies that are initiated in a number of countries in Africa to roll out treatment. Of course, it ignores the fact that having malaria does not increase the person's likelihood of becoming infected by HIV while people with HIV can be made more vulnerable for malaria, in particular if the immune boosting treatment is not available. Implicitly, the concerns expressed in the either–or logic seem to be unrelated to HIV or malaria and their impact on people *per se* but more related to cost-effectiveness for those who are funding these interventions. This is underlined by the suggestion that it is 'expensive to keep people alive'. While a certain general commitment to help people is evident, the parameters of this help are based on its cost-effectiveness for the funders rather than people's evident needs and, of course, people's right to health. This is a critical point in that it demonstrates whose views and concerns matter most. Although the editorial points out that the views of public health officials in countries and donors are considered to be important, clearly international donors are given higher priority. Similarly UNAIDS' position presents a serious concern or sensitivity to the donor perspectives. The justification of generalised intervention policies is related to high prevalence rates suggesting a generalised epidemic in various countries. However, on balance there seem to be serious challenges to these interventions and to their community reach. Therefore, a number of questions arise: Can the generalised interventions be seen as a way of keeping the debate in the public eye? Does this approach provide incentives for the donors who are also interested in maintaining their developmental concerns as the focus of their involvement?

The tension in this area is also related to a certain fatigue among both donors and the international community as a result of not observing substantive changes in the way the pandemic has been developing independent of the existing interventions. In some ways the editorial is also a reflection of this fatigue.

The debate I sketched out in relation to the editorial raises a number of questions in relation to the role of various actors in HIV/AIDS but also in relation to the new policy interventions such as treatment: Is this a global disease? If it is, why is HIV/AIDS a global problem? What is the relationship between expert knowledge and people's experiences of the disease? Who decides what is the best way to deal with the pandemic? What is the role of people living with the disease in the policy making? Are national governments prepared to deal with the pandemic at multiple levels of prevention, treatment and care? Is treatment the magic bullet? Can these interventions be sustainable in the long term? How long can people be on treatment? Many of these questions are in the centre of the concerns in relation to whether the HIV/AIDS pandemic has been adequately addressed so far and whether the existing intervention frames will have an impact on the future of the people living with the disease. They also highlight the complexity of the people's experiences and the kinds of questions that they will ask to see whether their needs are addressed in the existing policies or not. There are several quick responses to these questions. One can easily argue that the responses to these questions follow a model response: 'generally no and rarely yes'. The reason is always located within one of the questions too. While the importance of these questions is clear to everyone, the timeframe to develop coherent and in-depth responses to them does not fit in the emergency timeframe within which policies are developed. It is argued that we don't have time to think and develop the research we need to save people's lives now. It is of course true that people living with the disease need urgent support. However, this should not be an impediment for thinking about whether we are really saving lives in the long term and whether the existing interventions will be sufficient for the future that is built on what is being done today. In other words, research and reflections on what has been done until now, that is producing basic knowledge, should not be considered as a mutually exclusive exercise with addressing the immediate needs of the people today. This logic has also influenced the style of research that can be produced in this field. In other words, the relationship between the way HIV/AIDS is perceived and the impact of this perception on social research is an important issue.

Most research is medical and most social research is linked with civil society interventions and conducted to inform particular policy implementations. While this is important, as it gradually becomes more technical-outcome oriented it has a limited scope that does not include questions of policy frames and assumptions that are leading the research and policies. For instance, it is not rare to hear from the international policy actors that *the problem with HIV/AIDS is about how do we technically fix the implementation problems or how do we scale up smaller projects. It is not about looking at whether we have the right ideas or not. We don't have time to theorise.* This no doubt introduces an important time constraint on potential research whereby a timetable for policy process and implementation determines the extend to which research can be in-depth and searching. Furthermore, research becomes focused on policy evaluation rather than looking at whether the policies and actors who are producing them have the appropriate understanding and knowledge to justify what has been proposed and in most cases applied and also whether there are important actors missing from the picture. Here I don't want to dichotomise these positions; my aim is just to point out that there is a certain character to the existing social research in this field. Clearly policy evaluation is an important process but assessment of certain knowledge claims and their appropriateness for warranting a policy are also central.

The occurrence of this either–or logic itself requires research to understand what the impact is of existing international policy processes dealing with HIV/AIDS in this manner. This would consider the way the disease is conceptualised, which then informs the production of particular policies to address the problems faced by the people in the context of the pandemic. This approach also needs to be contextualised within the field of policy implementation, for it is central to understand how far such conceptualisation of the disease and the subsequent policies inferred from this are relevant for people living in the multiple socio-cultural and economic contexts. These considerations need to look at the questions of: How do actors in the international environment consider their role? Do they consider their own impact? How do they use knowledge as evidence for their interventions? What is the impact of these on the way people engage with the disease in diverse contexts? Of course, we come full circle; responses to some of these questions are demarcated by the funding concerns and the extent to which there is a long-term commitment to multi-layered support for HIV/AIDS interventions. This is a timely consideration given that the disease is still expanding its grip while new financial resources are pledged and more internationally focused interventions are proposed. It is, therefore, imperative to understand the relationship between the international policy environment and the impact of its policies on HIV/AIDS in the context of people's lives.

There is no doubt that research pointing out such impact is extant. Most research in this field argues that there is an important role played by international actors in this field at multiple levels (Whiteside 2006; Campbell 2003; Poku 2002). The role of international organisations such as bilateral donors and intergovernmental organisations is analysed in terms of their funding support and the rapidity of their response to the pandemic. Here, most research recognises the existing constraints on international organisations due to the nature of these actors. In this, civil society groups and their interventions are also closely observed. In particular the role of civil society actors is highlighted in the interventions within resource-poor contexts. The impact of these organisations is focused by looking at funding provided by the international actors or by looking at the potential for scaling up civil society interventions. More critical perspectives also look at the appropriateness of interventions and actors such as civil society organisations for long-term HIV/AIDS interventions. The literature recognises the existence of political will as demonstrated in international policy documents and discussions at the global level. This is juxtaposed with the more lukewarm political will demonstrated by the lack of public debate in many African countries. In other words the global political discussion is taken to be leading the debate. I argue that, while the international interventions highlight the importance attributed to the HIV/AIDS problem, the nature of the system does not allow interventions to be far reaching and sustainable. Although the structure allows people to emerge as policy-relevant target groups and beneficiaries, the articulation of needs and design of policy interventions tend to reflect international priorities rather than people's thinking on the problem. Arguably the bulk of existing literature and research takes the African context as the analytical category within which this disease needs to be addressed. As a result the international system and mechanisms that are developed in it are taken to be external factors trying to help people with the disease by intervening in this context. There are several reasons for these interventions: to provide technical assistance and to create policy in order to help people in this context to overcome the constraints that are identified around gender, socio-cultural limits of behaviour, governance and economics. Arguably here one observes a certain attempt to deal with *their* problem, African problems. Thus, the impact of this conceptualisation and the impact of actors working in it on the people living with the disease becomes opaque.

The book aims at understanding the way international policy makers impact people's lives in the context of HIV/AIDS. It does not aim to provide a compressive survey on global AIDS issues or provide a description of the general state-of-the-art information about HIV/AIDS. This is on the one hand due to the fact that statistical information is generally contested, as we have seen, and the scientific information on HIV/AIDS and areas such as treatment are constantly changing. On the other hand it is also due to the existence of this kind of general information-based material in the literature (Epstein 1996; Barnett and Whiteside 2002, 2006). In this book, I am interested in understanding the mechanisms that are mediating the relationship between international actors and people living with the disease and producing a certain common sense about the policy environment that is taken to be *the* context of HIV/AIDS in various socio-cultural and economic contexts within which people experience the disease in Africa. The questions I posed earlier in relation to the international organisations are relevant for this discussion. They point out the fissure in the global system that has emerged in the last decade to deal with the global disease HIV/AIDS. In this, the common language of 'global disease' has been an important reference point for international policy actors. Mechanisms that have constructed this system are the grounds of producing a certain relationship within which experts emerge as the dominant figures, people living with disease and their contextual experiences disappear to re-emerge as statistical information, the agency of certain actors becomes prioritised for policy interventions, and a certain knowledge base demarcates what can be done. In this sense the international system, or the governance system, on HIV/AIDS not only manages but constitutes the agency of certain actors in the relevant domains of policy. It is important to question this process and the common sense it produces from the perspective of infected and affected people who are living with the disease in multiple contexts in Africa. At the end of the day it does not matter whether policies work, or not, for the interests of policy organisations; it matters a great deal whether policies work for the people.

Now I will look at the question of the globality of HIV/AIDS. Is this really a global disease? If it is, in what sense is it a global disease? Looking at these questions is important to understanding the particular path and the context within which HIV/AIDS polices have developed. The past experiences in relation to other diseases and public health problems create particular ways of dealing with the new challenges. In his study on varied responses to AIDS in industrialised countries Peter Baldwin argues that the responses to the occurrence of AIDS varied among different developed countries. This variation was related to the established public health procedures and the way individual socio-cultural contexts historically conceptualised this kind of diseases (2005). Baldwin's argument has relevance for the international context and the way it has conceptualised HIV/AIDS. No doubt international policy context has a particular way of conceptualising and dealing with epidemics that reflects the past experiences. The way HIV/AIDS is conceptualised as a global disease is linked with this international context. This in turn has implications for people living with the disease in multiple socio-cultural and economic contexts.

The largest international health organisation, the World Health Organization (WHO), has suggested that TB, malaria and HIV/AIDS are the major cause of suffering around the world, while the developing world is the location for most of these sufferings. The WHO has begun to relate the lack of health to poverty and to underdevelopment. In the early 2000s, the then Director-General of the WHO, Dr Gro Harlem Brundtland, asked 'why global health is now starting to come into focus as a serious political issue' (Brundtland 2001: 1), to which she suggested two main answers. First, she argues, is 'the realisation of our common vulnerability to diseases in a globalised world', and 'the growing body of evidence linking ill health and the slow progress of economic development' is the second reason (Brundtland 2001: 2).

Although both of these reasons articulated by Dr Brundtland are reasonable, they give clues about the problematic nature of the general attitude that is symptomatic in the intergovernmental organisations in relation to diseases.

Considering these diseases as if they were just emerging as political issues or considering them under the new global awareness of common risks is missing the point that most communicable diseases have been global for a long time. Particularly in the case of malaria and TB this statement highlights a certain historical amnesia. This idea that diseases are becoming political implicitly suggests in this instance that, as developed states and international organisations are becoming much more involved in this area, diseases are constituted as a matter of politics (see Woods 2006).

History and people's sufferings matter. The political change implied by the WHO is *a reality*; however, the direction of this change is not only based on, as suggested, the realisation of global vulnerability and disease-induced poverty at the international level. Some of these diseases have spread and constantly influence people's lives as a result of political and economic considerations at both the national and the international level. Diseases and public health considerations are always linked to political concerns. In the case of HIV/AIDS I would argue that the increased dissatisfaction of people suffering from this disease in the early years has been very clearly located in the debate into the politics of health around the developed world.[1] In this instance the lack of resources and care available in the system turned HIV/AIDS into a political question for many people well before it was recognised in the way in which Brundtland discussed the issue.[2] However, the question here is a different one: whether Brundtland's articulation can be seen as responding to a demand coming from the people in the developing world, or whether it is more about the position of an intergovernmental organisation that conceives the world through top-down understanding of events. By posing this question I am questioning the location of people in the discussions of the global disease HIV/AIDS. The divergence between Brundtland's suggestion about the changing nature of this politics and my articulation reflects the changing location of people in thinking about health. In the latter, people take an active role and initiative in describing their needs and the appropriate health interventions while in the former people are integrated into politics only as patients, or as target populations, that are suffering from a disease. Their individual needs depending on their socio-political conditions are subsumed under the medical characteristics of a disease whereby the essential needs of a patient are universally described. In other words the ecology of a disease overrides the needs of a patient deriving from his/her social ecology.

The concern about the people has become an important issue, as evident in the increased civil society activity across the globe. Of course, bringing people into international policy-making processes is a difficult challenge. Typically for an international organisation, the WHO, for example, has responded to this change by creating new communication avenues with civil society actors. In 2001 the WHO formed its first WHO Civil Society Initiative, headed by Eva Wallstam. One of the reasons for this move according to her was the advocacy role of civil society demonstrated in the process leading to the People's Health Charter in the People's Health Assembly in Dhaka 2000

(IFMSA 2001). The Assembly was a civil society initiative to bring people into the debate, as they suggested that 'Governments and international organisations have largely failed to reach this goal [health for all], despite much rhetoric' (TWN 2002). The advocacy work convinced the WHO to target through this new initiative 'to strengthen mutually beneficial relationships between WHO and civil society organisations (CSOs)' (IFMSA 2001: 3). This is also stressed by Brundtland from a wider perspective: she suggests that 'we [WHO] cannot expect there to be a single entity in control, directing others with military precision ... the work will be taken by a variety of groups' (Brundtland 2001: 3).

However, a tension remains in these relations, as there is a danger of considering politics, *pace* Brundtland, only in relation to the changing institutional politics of the WHO and other international organisations' interests, and the inclusion of new organisational forms, such as civil society groups and non-governmental organisations (NGOs), into the global governance of health reflected in these interests, while people's politics is a reaction to the entire relationship between health and this historical process (Chandhoke 2002). Thus what is political can be in excess of any organisational form that is taken to represent people in civil society (Chatterjee 2006). In other words, if the inclusion of civil society into the global politics of health means only to use these organisations in dealing with a global disease, the people, their particular needs and the way their claims are negotiated will once more disappear from the discussion. But this does not mean that their politics ends; it becomes neutralised at the level of international policy-making processes (Farmer 2003). Therefore, in order to resist the imminent depoliticisation, it is imperative to understand the essentially political nature of diseases and the historical path that has created the present globalised conditions. In this the path which has constructed HIV/AIDS as a global disease and its implications can be observed.

Owing to the existing logic of considering international processes as external to what happens in public health in Africa, there is a danger of obscuring the international socio-political mechanisms of producing particular forms of understanding to deal with the diseases around the world (Wendt 1999; Price-Smith 2002). This needs to be challenged. The historically implicit exclusion of people from the health debate needs to be addressed, as this process produces the discussions of emerging diseases and spaces for the participation of people by way of civil society. A historical analysis will argue that diseases have always been global in various forms that were political and it is the politics of the past that has created a certain outlook for considering the global nature of HIV/AIDS at present that in turn produces particular outcomes for people infected, affected or living in the context of the pandemic in Africa. The next section will present the way the global politics of health has evolved.

History of globalised diseases

This section aims to give a summary account of the long history while establishing the construction of the modern path to the global politics of health at present. It is possible to consider the impact of the relationship between diseases and the processes of globalisation under three headings: (a) the spread of diseases from one location to others through means of people's travels, (b) the relationship between various medical traditions to deal with unexpected diseases, and (c) the ascendance of a particular understanding of medicine and its impact on the diseases. In reality these three paths are mostly merged and have shaped each other according to the socio-political contexts. Although various stages of the globality of diseases in this analytical framework essentially refer to different logics of globalisation, it is the cumulative historical experience created by each stage that ultimately informs global health politics. The talk of globalisation in the first stage is related to the logic of discoveries and encounters with the *exotic*. The second stage relates to the logic of permanent settlement of Europeans in the newly discovered geographies. The third stage in this process is about the logic of colonialism. The aim in each stage is to demonstrate the larger concerns inbuilt through the historical process in the globalisation of diseases and medicine.

The spread of the diseases

The great discoveries of the globe by Europeans from the fifteenth century onwards not only opened up new horizons for people and opportunities to get rich and win souls but became a conduit for the unintended spread of new diseases around the world. Although many infectious diseases were part of everyday life in geographically isolated populations, the increased human contact created new grounds for these diseases to take hold of large communities in their wake. The expansion of extended human contact, through travels and settlements in Africa, the Americas and Asia, facilitated the spread of diseases such as yellow fever, smallpox, syphilis, cholera, plague and many other fevers around the world. The changing natural environment made travellers, settlers and the natives of newly discovered geographies vulnerable to many diseases. It was not only those directly exposed but also those located within the larger geographies of empires, such as the Spanish and Portuguese empires, who became vulnerable to *new* diseases.

The spread of smallpox in Brazil and Mexico, for example, can demonstrate this situation. The trans-infection of populations was experienced in the immediate aftermath of the discovery of the Americas. The smallpox epidemics recorded from the late fifteenth century onwards in the New World were directly related to the European conquests. The epidemics lasted until the end of the slave trade between Africa and Brazil in the early nineteenth century (Alden and Miller 2000). Climatic conditions such as drought and resulting famine might have been instrumental in the spread of the epidemics;

it is clear, nonetheless, that the disease itself was introduced as a result of the workings of the Portuguese empire. These global interests in sustaining sugar plantations in Brazil with imported African slaves created a direct relationship, and thus a pathway for smallpox, between Central Africa, where smallpox had been observed as an epidemic, and Brazil, where the pristine native population created the right conditions for long-term spread of the disease (Alden and Miller 2000: 208). The importance of smallpox in creating a 'a demographic catastrophe' in Mexico is also emphasised (McCaa 2000). Clearly, the wide-ranging networks allowed the introduction of smallpox. In a similar fashion it is suggested that syphilis, which spread through Europe after the discovery of the Americas, was transported to India in due course by Portuguese travellers. Syphilis seems to have arrived in Europe immediately after the discoveries of the Americas in the 1490s and spread through Europe. This spread travelled very fast to India in 1498, Canton in 1504 and Japan in 1512 (Boomgaard 1996: 49) with the European journeys to the East. Some of the diseases, however, made the journey back to Europe. Plague is considered to have originated from Asia and cholera was considered to have travelled to Europe from Goa, where it was an epidemic from the mid-sixteenth to seventeenth centuries (Pearson 1996: 23).

It is clear that even in a limited fashion looking at specific infectious diseases, which caused havoc around the world in the past, presents us with a rather dynamic picture of intensification of the impact of infectious diseases as more and more people become introduced to new geographies. This is not to say that these diseases did not exist before; it is clear that some of them were endemic diseases to particular locations. The point is that the movement of people brought the movement of diseases with it. The rapid expansion of smallpox, cholera, plague and syphilis demonstrates the logic of encounter. The diseases were either introduced to a location or carried back to countries where travellers were coming from.

Medical traditions

The relationship between people and diseases is one of the important junctures between human beings and the nature within which they live. Similarly, this relationship manifests a path on which the former attempts to make sense of the latter in such a way that people can live better lives. The medical traditions around the world, in some ways, are attempts to make sense of human beings' location in the larger natural environment. Although there are many medical traditions such as Chinese, Indian, Islamic and Western, there has been a long process of influence and exchange of knowledge and ideas among these traditions. Particularly in the time period starting with the great discoveries, the diseases were not the only phenomena that were travelling, but medical practices and understanding among various traditions also became exposed to each other in a much more unmediated manner. On the one hand the European practitioners had to make sense of local diseases for which there were believed to be local remedies. On the other hand the local healers had to understand the newly arrived European medical procedures such as bleeding. In other words, this was the period of observation, trial and innovation that eventually spread to the entire extent of the vast mercantile networks.

In the case of dealing with smallpox in Brazil, Alden and Miller suggest that, towards the end of the eighteenth century, the method of inoculation had emerged as the effective way of dealing with the problem. The initial usage of the method, however, derived from elsewhere; inoculation was used by 'some Africans and the technique spread from Turkish sources to England', and British slavers used the method in the Atlantic slave trade before the Portuguese were convinced of its usefulness (2000: 218). In Goa, the Portuguese encountered the local medical tradition and on many occasions fused Western and Indian medicine in order to solve problems. Of course, what is being considered to be the local knowledge in Europe according to Pearson was already a fusion of 'Latin, Arabic, Greek and Hebrew knowledge' (1996: 21). Armed with this medical knowledge and understanding the Europeans experienced the newly encountered diseases such as cholera and malaria in India. Considering that Europeans were settling in new regions, it was natural for these people to be curious about the way locals dealt with these diseases. As a result some of the medicinal drugs local to India were sent to Europe (Correia-Afonso 1990). It is also noted that some medical surgery techniques followed the same route and travelled to Europe (Patterson 1974). The history of the establishment and expansion of the Dutch East India Company (Verenigde Oostindische Compagnie – VOC) documents the existence of the extensive medical cross-fertilisation that took place in the East. The company 'during the 18th century had, on average, some 250–300 surgeons in Asia, of whom slightly over 100 could be found in the Indonesian archipelago' (Boomgaard 1996: 43). It was this strong medical involvement and establishment of clinics around the VOC factories that created the impetus for communication with the natives. Boomgaard suggests that several medical drugs, as a result, became global in the sense that they travelled through the mercantile networks and were used to cure similar diseases around the world. One such cure, for example, was *radix China* – China root from Goa used against syphilis through a wide geographical area from Java to Europe (1996: 49).

Although it is possible to argue that the outcome of these cross-fertilisations in terms of medicine is unclear, they suggest that, with the expansion of wider human contact through the networks of Western travellers, settlers and missionaries' medical knowledge became a negotiated and tested substance. Once people from both sides were convinced of certain medical techniques or remedies, the techniques or remedies became widely amalgamated with the existing practices or some of these were transported throughout the vast geographies. Arguably, as the Europeans were becoming more settled in new regions and established their health systems such as hospitals and clinics, a relationship between the existing local knowledge was established. Medical practitioners from all sides observed each other's practice and began to negotiate their compatibility (Boomgaard 1996). It is the idea of the Hippocratic tradition that the importance of local medicine for endemic diseases is central for cure that allowed a curiosity-based consideration of various traditions with some equality. It is the combination of this perspective and the socio-political understanding of relations with already-existing social structures that gives us the logic of settlement. The logic assumes a certain level of equality between settlers and the locals. It was through this logic that medical substances from the East were introduced to Europe. Clearly this was to change rather rapidly in the eighteenth century owing to both the changing medical understanding in Europe and the changing political outlook.

Therefore, it is possible to consider medicine as something which has been global for a fairly long time. It is also possible to argue that medicine was something that was negotiated. The networks within which diseases and their medical knowledge become globalised in the sense of being spread to wide geographies are important. Another aspect of the juncture between diseases and their global character presents itself through the manifestation of such networks during the period of colonisation in the nineteenth century.

Politics of medicine

The changing conditions of colonialism throughout the eighteenth century and in the nineteenth century coupled with the changing perceptions about the nature of medicine and diseases had gradually altered the relationship between medicine and its globality. The nature of the relationship is related to the logic of colonial projects. The process gained pace as the political nature of European involvement was transformed from being related to maritime trade and trade posts to the establishment of the next phase of colonialism based on the establishment of overseas territories (Hobsbawn 1987). The sense of curiosity for local medical knowledge and practice that had accompanied the concerns for their lives began to leave the Europeans. They became much more concerned with their long-term survival in what is described as the 'fiercely malevolent tropics' (Arnold 1996: 7). This mode of thinking differs from that of the previous period in the sense that there was a major attempt by the colonising powers to deal with infectious diseases that were widely killing the Europeans such as malaria, cholera and sleeping sickness. The purpose of the medical concerns and the political expediency of colonialism had manifested itself as a merger between two sides: 'for European doctors in the nineteenth century, tropical medicine and military medicine were nearly synonymous' (Curtin 1996: 99). Towards the end of the nineteenth century the focus on tropical diseases reached a high point culminating with the founding of tropical medicine as a separate medical study area in Britain. Arguably not only is the idea of tropical medicine a part of the colonial project but it also helps to maintain the conditions of the colonial projects. Many young British doctors became interested in tropical diseases while serving in the British colonial project either as members of the Army in India or in the West Indies, or as members of administrative offices such as the Imperial Chinese Custom Services, like Patrick Manson, who at a later date became the founding father of tropical medicine (Haynes 1996: 218). Haynes argues that the research in these environments aimed to 'advance the mission of empire and establish Britain's reputation as a leader in a medical-scientific speciality' (1996: 219). It is these arguments which demonstrate a change in the way diseases and medicine were becoming global as a part of the expanding colonial empires, above all the British, but also according to Osborne the work of the French physicians in the colonies was usually 'influenced by military or paramilitary agendas' (1996: 82). It was also related to projecting and protecting the power of the colonisers.

However, it is not correct to assume this was only happening on the basis of military might. It is reasonable to suggest that the development of a particular understanding of tropical medicine based initially on increased engagement with sanitary sciences and then the acceptance of the germ theory of diseases in Europe also contributed to the expansion of globality of medical practices throughout the colonies. On the one hand, the sanitation, Armstrong suggests, was meant to differentiate between anatomical and environmental spaces (Armstrong 1993: 396) whereby the traditional environments were more and more questioned, particularly by missionaries trying to demonstrate that African traditions were *unhealthy* for individuals. According to Butchart, for example, it was out of the sanitary divide that the image of Africa as 'dark with barbarism . . . [and] savage customs' grew (Butchart 1998: 75). On the other hand, it is the success of finding out about the causes of malaria through germ theory that opened the next stage. It bolstered the methodological shift from 'diseases in the tropics', whereby the entire space within which a disease occurs is considered in dealing with it, to 'tropical diseases', in which particular diseases are singled out and attempts are made to solve them on their own, such as malaria (Worboys 1996: 199). The implication of this switch has been important, as it meant that it was possible to eradicate single diseases through a focused effort. Considering the possibility of again eradicating a disease by controlling the environment within which the *singular* cause of the disease can be found suggested that the colonial authorities were in a position to decide which diseases to engage with as discrete areas. This approach then become commonplace in the imperialistic interests in Africa. Those diseases threatening the health of administrators and the military and the health of those natives who were working for the profit of colonial empires became the target of medical interventions.

In an attempt to solve the sleeping sickness disease in Congo, the Belgian government, for example, focused on northern Congo, as it was related to their interests in the rubber industry, but it was a way of dealing with the diseases in a vertical form (that is top-down and focused directly on the cause of a disease without considering the larger context) and by moving people to other areas they spread the disease to the rest of the region. In order to increase the efficiency of the mine workers who were suffering from unsuspected mental conditions, workers were exposed to 'the experimental chambers and heat tolerance tests' where they were put naked to simulate the conditions in the mines for the observation of medical officers (Butchart 1998: 93). Arnold suggests that 'non-whites continually informed the western understanding of the tropics and of the tropical diseases as clinical objects, as sources of epidemic danger, as sick or "shrinking workers"' (Arnold 1996: 8). There is no doubt that this attitude has changed, while a mentality related to top-down control of patients in a disempowering manner has lingered on.

In other words, the past is a narrative of expanding diseases and solutions for those diseases that are relevant to the concerns of colonial powers without much reference to the stories of people and their needs and interests. The crucial component for a medical problem to emerge as a global disease seems to be related to its perceived impact for the global aspirations of international actors. A similar link is also true for the disappearance of certain diseases from the public discourse. Arguably the declining medical focus of the West on malaria and other tropical diseases despite large numbers of people suffering from them can be related to the end of colonial interests. Also, it is true that the colonial legacy still remains in the politics of global diseases in the form of vertical health policies. Farley argued that twentieth-century medical effort in the third world was an 'imperial tropical medicine' in terms of the definition and imposition of policies and the consequent 'non-involvement of the indigenous population' (Farley 1991: 13–30).

The changing logic of global relations clearly influenced the way disease and medicine are thought of, from an earlier position of trying to understand the local perceptions of disease and medicine to a much more top-down and dominating perception where claimed knowledge of the Western expert has become non-negotiable. This gradual change also reflects the changing power relations between those colonialists and local people. It is in some ways a change whereby local people have become populations to be managed for the greater interests. How far is this kind of globalised understanding of disease and medicine relevant for HIV/AIDS as a global disease today?

The relevance of the historical process is in the way HIV/AIDS is characterised as global and the subsequent policies developed to deal with the disease. In this process the logic of that period, discussed above, as it pertains to the medicine, to the position of local knowledge, and to production of interventions and the position of international actors, still applies. The vertical-health policies of the colonial period were a reflection of vertical socio-political relations. Today we still have vertical-health policies that reflect a different kind of vertical socio-political arrangements in the international arena that are linked with the colonial history. In this sense when we look at HIV/AIDS as a global disease it is clear that the way the disease is constructed as a global one, together with TB and malaria, follows a certain international interest that is expressed, by international actors, this time in the vocabulary of developmental interests in post-colonial Africa. The integration of vertical-health policies within the structures of developmental interventions that have developed since the 1950s creates important questions about the impact of these on target populations, particularly once they are disaggregated at the level of people's everyday lives in particular contexts in Africa. Discussions of global HIV/AIDS contain a set of knowledge claims to deal with the disease in target populations with the implementation of policies developed by the experts at the international level and delivered by actors that are seen as efficient. It is clear that HIV/AIDS issues have become gradually internationalised by the participation of more and more international actors in the policy debates. Through this gradual internationalisation it has also become a domain of specialised expert knowledge, that is, ostensibly medical knowledge. Therefore global for HIV/AIDS seems to suggest a dual process of internationalisation and within that medicalisation.

Another aspect of the global here is linked with the particular form of politicisation of HIV/AIDS issues. Since Brundtland's statement HIV/AIDS has indeed become a global political issue. The best evidence for this can be seen in 2005 when a year-long number of political and civil society events focusing on Africa and problems of Africans climaxed in the summer around the G8 meeting in Gleneagles, Scotland. The civil society activities around the Making Poverty History campaign, demonstrations against the G8 and the global series of concerts, organised by Bob Geldof and Bono, taking place at the same time and commemorating the original Live Aid concert were attempts to put Africa and *African problems* in the centre of the global political agenda. In all this, HIV/AIDS was positioned as one of the most important problems, where centrality of increased funding and of treatment across Africa was highlighted. Most of these activities were also supported by the international political elite, including the British prime minister, Tony Blair, who had also chaired a high-level Commission for Africa. In some sense there was an important convergence between civil society and the political actors to deal with the poverty in Africa. It was a moment in time where the concept of global disease, global politics and global solutions seemed to make sense as international leaders and people across the world were focusing on one set of issues. While arguably in 2005 Africa was very much in the media, or as the unfortunate BBC programme title suggested *Lived on the BBC*, the general attitude towards understanding the problems in general and HIV/AIDS in particular has not changed. All are considered from a certain analytical distance. In most public events Africans were absent, and there was no clear understanding of what people in different parts of a vast continent were thinking about the way they were portrayed in many of these events. A set of generic African problems was presented and people elsewhere asked to help them in their struggles. In other words, what is conceived to be African problems, and HIV/AIDS in particular, is still, on balance, considered independently of the international context within which these problems are produced.

In the process, HIV/AIDS has become a global political and public issue while those who are living with the disease are marginalised and have become an abstract target group for global help.

So, if we consider what makes HIV/AIDS political in this scenario, it becomes clear that the global 'Western' activism and its targeting, as demonstrated in 2005, the leaders and political elite of the developed world are constituting the politics of this global disease. This not only suggests that the disease became global according to the interests of certain powers in the international context, but also bolstered the activities of transnational civil society in the developed world as the voice for the poor independently of considering whether they have any local voices participating in these international activities. Furthermore, it points out that if international actors manage to get enough money they can overcome these problems in Africa. In other words it established the public and experts in the developed world as the agents of change in Africa, while Africans were discussed as a population with problems. In this manner the conceptualisation of the disease and the way it has been tackled are directly located within the international policy context.

The research that informs this book began with a basic query on the discrepancy between a gradually increasing international focus on HIV/AIDS in Africa and the lack of substantive progress in relation to the state of affairs in people's lives. I was interested to see what people are thinking about the situation and the policies that are attempting to help them. To this end interviews with various actors (people living with the disease, people affected, civil society actors, international NGOs, international donors, local policy makers, doctors and local carers) in six countries (Botswana, Burundi, Lesotho, Rwanda, Uganda and Zambia) were conducted. These interviews were mostly semi-structured and open-ended. There were also many group discussions and opportunities for participant observation. The research took place at various times between December 2001 and July 2005. Thus, it was possible to observe the impact of emerging policy mechanisms that were implemented. The focus of the book came out of this research. Over time, concerns have emerged about internationalisation of the problem and medicalisation of people's experiences, two important areas through which international organisations are functioning. Also, within this civil society has become a dominant actor. This was clear from the perspectives of international organisations as well as from the people's perspectives. However, it was clear from the latter's position that the impact of this dominance was not always obvious.

The research is directed by three simple interlinked questions. Following Bent Flyvbjerg these could be stated in a general form as: where are we going, is this desirable and, if not, what should be done (Flyvbjerg 2001: 60)? The first question puts emphasis on the idea that understanding future direction requires a contextual analysis of the present to connect what has happened, where we are now and what is being targeted. The second question asks about the desirability of what is proposed at present. In terms of HIV/AIDS, it looks at the governance structures dealing with the problem within which needs and policies are/should be located. Therefore the idea of desirability is linked to the people who are in need whereby according to their needs a policy or a given governance structure should be desirable or not. Here, this will mean juxtaposing the people's needs and actors who are trying to respond to them. Finally, the last question explores tangible alternatives to what is on the table, doing this with a certain ethical concern as expressed in 'should'. This ethical position or direction is derived from the analysis provided by the previous two questions. In other words, a decision about what needs to be done needs to look at the context and then think about tangible options. These methodological moves are central to the argument of this study. The aim is not to provide a descriptive mapping of what is happening within the international organisations and within their internal negotiation processes. To do so would limit the analysis within a particular discipline of international relations with its organisational/political interests in the international organisations. The aim is to link international organisations and their policies with the implementation field of these policies where people experience both the disease and the policies. It is possible to articulate a position which would consider the disease as a global political issue and would try to address it at a global level. However, another disciplinary approach would construct the disease as a local problem, as the disease is experienced under localised conditions by people whereby people in different locales have different experiences of the disease. While both analyses might provide insights to what is happening, the experience of the people demonstrates that the disease is neither global nor a merely local phenomenon. It is located in between these processes which are interacting with each other at multiple levels. Therefore, in order to understand this link and the way they influence each other, mechanisms that are instrumental in expanding the scope of international policies and thus the reach of international organisations need to be analysed. This analysis requires a multi-disciplinary perspective and multi-layered approaches to enable an understanding of the complex situation within which HIV/AIDS occurs and is experienced by people. This approach also requires the research to bring forward people's experiences to question the knowledge claims and policies devised by the international actors.

The book begins with an Introduction in which it argues that, while HIV/AIDS has become a concern for global politics and politicised through the activities of wide-ranging civil society activities in the global arena, people still experience the disease in particular localities under particular socio-cultural and economic constraints. The relationship between this global aspect of the disease and its experience in particular contexts needs to be looked at from the perspective of those people who are the target of the global *endeavour* to overcome the impact of the disease. Then the book is

LIVERPOOL JOHN MOORES UNIVERSITY
LEARNING SERVICES

divided into five chapters and a conclusion. Chapter 1 presents a way of looking at the international HIV/AIDS policy environment within the policy process continuum. It argues that, although there is a multiplicity of actors and ways of thinking about HIV/AIDS, gradually a certain governance of HIV/AIDS at the international level has emerged. It takes this emergence process as a form of institutionalisation within which stakeholders in the debate are positioned and constructed according to certain power relations that exist in this context. Then in Chapters 2 and 3 two processes, institutionalisation and medicalisation, are focused on to understand how they function and what the implications are of their functioning. In the latter part of the book, in Chapters 4 and 5, I look at two mechanisms, knowledge claims and the policy language, through which the institutionalisation process becomes productive in the domain of policy implementation; thus people living within the context of the pandemic become objects of this process. It is with this analysis that we can observe the impact of the international policy process on people and on the disease. The conclusion brings together the theoretical implications of the book's argument with the policy implications. Throughout the book italics are used to bring people's views and comments into the discussion and highlight the relationship between policies and their experience by people.

1   Governance of HIV/AIDS

The HIV/AIDS epidemic is one of the most catastrophic phenomena that has impacted and will continue to impact people's lives in Sub-Saharan Africa. According to UNAIDS in December 2005 an estimated 40.3 million people are living with HIV. Around 25.8 million of these are living with the disease in Sub-Saharan Africa. In 2005, 3.2 million people contracted HIV (UNAIDS 2005a: 2–3).[1] The epidemic is generalised largely in eastern and southern Africa, influencing all aspects of society. It also seems to be intensifying in southern Africa (UNAIDS 2005a: 4). In addition, there are predictions that estimate a steady increase in the infection rates in the years to 2010 in many countries. This includes western Africa, where numbers at present are not as high as in other parts of Africa. These terrible numbers do not reflect lack of attention. Far from it, the problem has been given importance in the international development and aid policy agendas for the best part of the last ten years. International funding for interventions has been gradually increasing for the region. This has been boosted by the Bush administration's US$15 billion pledge to 12 African and two Caribbean countries for HIV/AIDS interventions over five years from 2003. The aim is to support treatment and prevention in the designated countries. Despite controversy over its focusing on abstinence as a prevention method, the funding presents a major contribution to the global attempts. Considered in relation to projections of UNAIDS, which forecast a US$3.07 billion requirement by 2005 for Sub-Saharan Africa in order to provide care and support for those who are in need, the US contribution is of considerable importance. It is at this point that the question of internationalisation of the policy frameworks that gives a global outlook to HIV/AIDS becomes important. To analyse this, the chapter first looks at the process of internationalisation and how this process has created a governance system for HIV/AIDS policies. Here, the aim is to unpack the role of governance structure in influencing the behaviour of particular actors. Then it highlights some effects of this system as expressed by people who are targeted by the policies.

The existing policy intervention models channel funds through diverse policy actors. These typically include governments, non-governmental organisations, community groups and private sector groups. Arguably, existing intervention channels and actors have not been as productive as expected or hoped. This is demonstrated in a report by the Global HIV Prevention Working Group (GHPWG). The report points out an important problem, the problem of reaching people who are in need. It suggests that in general fewer than one in five people have access to basic HIV prevention programmes. In terms of Sub-Saharan Africa, the report argues that 'only six percent have access to voluntary counselling and testing (VCT) and only one percent of pregnant women are able to obtain access to treatment to prevent mother-to-child transmission' (GHPWG 2003: 2). What conclusions should one draw from this?

It could suggest that (a) there has not been sufficient sustained and focused support, both politically and financially, as most of the interventions require such steady and constant support, and (b) actors that are initiating these interventions have been unsuccessful in engaging with large parts of the infected and affected populations to change their behaviour. These two conclusions are linked. For example, one might assume that if a were solved then b would be too. In this way, the US contribution could be seen as a way of bridging the gap discussed in the GHPWG report. The financial input could allow programmes to be scaled up to address the needs of people within a larger population. However, while addressing (a) is central, it is questionable that (b) will automatically follow as a result. If this alternative logic is correct then there is a danger of putting large funding into ineffective policy intervention structures that will not produce satisfactory results at the end of a given time period. This in turn may have long-term consequences for the sustainability of the programmes created. For example, funders might become reluctant as a result, and people infected and affected might become disillusioned in relation to behaviour change. To determine which logic is correct, therefore, it is imperative to look at the existing mechanisms of policy implementation rather than to assume that once finances are in place things will improve. Indeed, contributing factors to the depressing gap discussed in the report may even be related to the characteristics of agents that are considered to be the most effective channels for policy implementation. If this is the case, it indicates a severe problem for the international policy actors in understanding what needs to change in the existing system to achieve desired goals.

Internationalisation

The internationalisation of the debate can be looked at through a gradual institutionalisation of the HIV/AIDS issue in the intergovernmental organisations' agenda through which the issue became an important part of the international political debate. By looking at responses to the disease in various country contexts it is also possible to discern an earlier internationalisation process based on the image of the disease as a Western problem. I start by briefly commenting on this as the first phase of internationalisation.

The internationalisation of HIV/AIDS, of course, did not mean the emergence of the disease in the South for the first time. The disease had been in the South from its onset and the way it had been considered was influenced by international discussions. However, a different kind of influence emerged at the end of the 1990s which was related to the perception of the disease through the gaze of medical science and international politics. Before the second wave of internationalisation, the image of AIDS and its context was of a Western homosexual disease. This was promoted by the media where available in developing countries. This early association of the disease with homosexuality created problems for various countries at the onset of the epidemic in the South. The early identification of patients in developing countries resulted in a very limited response from public policy quarters. The response largely amounted to branding the disease as a foreign import from the West confined to high-risk groups such as gay men or the denial of the existence of AIDS altogether (Treichler 1999: 99–126; Farmer 1993: 111). Since it was possible to deny the existence of homosexual identity in certain cultures, the public authorities were able to be inactive in relation to HIV/AIDS, considering it an alien problem. The impact of initial and sustained opposition to certain prevention methods, in addition to the disbelief in such a complex disease among traditional communities by various faith groups, hindered the possibility of early interventions. As a result, respected community leaders had to take on the burden of talking about living with AIDS as a possibility and not a cause of hopelessness. Archdeacon Zebulon Mung'esi of Bunyole, Uganda, talked about AIDS in his family (Whyte 1997: 216). At national level, in Uganda for example, Revd Gideon Byamugisha was the first practising priest in Africa to declare his HIV positive status publicly to educate people about the disease. At the international level there was the intervention of President of Zambia Kenneth Kaunda in 1987 who announced that his son had died of AIDS and demanded his fellow leaders around the world and in Africa in particular engage with the AIDS epidemic with an open mind (Foster and Lucas 1991: 38). While the inaction of African governments was clear from the First International AIDS Conference in 1985, where no African government was present, Kaunda's intervention was a turning point for some African countries. It also highlights a central difference between people's reactions and the way subsequent internationalisation has influenced the debate. While in the developed world people with HIV/AIDS took the initiative and forced governments and drug companies to provide what they needed, in the South AIDS was articulated by outsiders rather than by people living with it.

This also influenced the nature of local activism and the reluctance of governments to engage with AIDS. At the time, the problem was addressed by and large by existing religiously based groups and services and some international non-governmental organisations (NGOs) already working in the affected countries. One of the first groups to provide services was the International Family Planning Agency, which locally distributed a manual on лıDS (Harper 1989).[2] In addition, international funding agencies got involved in funding HIV/AIDS-related programmes, for example USAID and the Canadian International Development Agency (CIDA) supported prevention and sensitisation work in Senegal from as early as 1985. Actions of these groups focused on informing people about the disease and generally talking about prevention methods. Although the immediate reaction to the disease in 1984 was to ignore it as an alien homosexual problem, towards the end of the 1980s governments were pressurised to engage with the disease (Ford 1994: 89). As the second phase of internationalisation emerged, funding from international sources created many local NGOs and supported the continuity of local initiatives. In some countries already-existing NGOs and community groups provided the grounds for international interventions.

In the late 1980s international organisations gradually came to accept HIV/ AIDS as an international problem. In this internationalisation of the debate, actions of individuals and their groups made a considerable difference, such as the already-mentioned intervention from Kenneth Kaunda in 1987. Another important intervention was by Dr Halfdan Mahler, the then director of the WHO, who in 1988 stated that 'many people at first refused to believe that a crisis was upon us. I know because I was one of them' (Panos Institute 1988). Activist groups also played an important role in opening up the international fora for people with AIDS (PWAs)' participation in the debates.

These perspectives were supported and stimulated by individual experiences of medical professionals coming from developing countries. Dr Jonathan Mann was one such professional. He became a central figure in the debate, making a case for a comprehensive global approach to the epidemic that incorporated concerns for the developing world. For him it was clear from his experience in Zaire as directing officer of the Centre for Disease Control (CDC)-led project to follow up 'early cases of the disease in Europe that involved Africans' that the disease was an important social issue on a global scale (Mann *et al.* 1986). Arguably it was the political activism in the developed countries which pushed the disease into the international political frame of mind. As the awareness of the scale of the disease emerged through the activism of people working in various contexts and their lobbying in the WHO, this stimulated the debate to create a space for discussion and to create a mechanism for international interventions. These attempts toward internationalisation of the response to the epidemic were built on time spent in convincing professionals of the WHO that the epidemic was influencing people in the developing countries and was not only an industrialised-country problem based on gay communities (Gordenker *et al.* 1995: 42).[3]

The international debate was also created through the intervention of both the Northern activists and informed discussions provided by medical professionals experiencing the diseases in developing countries. The support subsequently provided by the WHO to host international conferences on AIDS provided an important global space for people to come together and discuss emerging issues and medical advancements around AIDS. The meetings early on involved only medical professionals, health specialists and policy-related participants. Patients were not considered to be relevant participants. Gradually these international gatherings were pushed to open themselves up to include people with AIDS too. It was in 1989 that ACT UP with its counterparts in Canada stormed the Fifth AIDS Conference in Montreal. It was the first time PWAs were in such fora. 'PWA Tim McCaskell grabbed the microphone and "officially" opened the conference "on behalf of people with AIDS from Canada and around the world"' (ACT UP). In other words, activism was spilling over the national borders and creating international links among activist groups from across the globe. Groups such as GMHCs and ACT UP were providing know-how for civil society action in this area (Watney 1994). The activism in these areas allowed PWAs to assert their right to participate in discussions that were central to their lives. This was an important challenge to both the medical profession and intergovernmental organisations. Arguably these events and activists' interventions were also part of the internationalisation process that was crystallising around the issue of HIV/AIDS and PWAs globally. The main source of this expansion into the global was the values and beliefs people – PWAs – held in relation to feeling solidarity with others who were suffering from the same disease, in addition to simply giving their pain a voice. However, the global perspective beyond this deeply rooted camaraderie quickly turned into international institutionalisation.

In 1987 the WHO established its Special Programme on AIDS, which later became the Global Programme. Around this time Perez de Cuellar, the then secretary-general of the United Nations, brought the issue to the General Assembly and called AIDS 'a global conflict' (Gordenker *et al.* 1995: 41). From 1987 onwards, under Mann's directions, through the Global Programme on AIDS (GPA) the WHO played an important role; NGOs were considered to be partners in this move. The GPA has become the focal point for communication between intergovernmental policy discussions and NGOs that have already moved to work with people on HIV/AIDS in the South. Its approach was 'medically and epidemiologically driven and adopted a short term and conceptually limited fire-fighting perspective' (Barnett and Whiteside 2002: 74). The GPA became a specialised agency in 1996 called the United Nations AIDS Programme. Its mandate is to coordinate the UN system's response to the global HIV/AIDS crisis. UNAIDS replaced GPA as a much more visible face of the response of international organisations and it has also become a knowledge centre with its Geneva offices on HIV/AIDS. Arguably it has inherited GPA's model where ready-made policies were produced based on best-case medical interventions for behaviour change implemented in various countries. The internationalisation process became even more intense in the late 1990s, culminating in a special meeting of the UN General Assembly (UNGASS) in June 2001 to discuss HIV/AIDS. This is generally seen as an important turning point for HIV/AIDS. The meeting and its final declaration set HIV/AIDS right in the centre of the international political debate as a global concern. It was also at this UNGASS meeting that creation of a global funding mechanism for HIV/AIDS was envisioned. Subsequently malaria and TB were added to the mandate of the organisation and it was entitled the Global Fund to Fight AIDS, Tuberculosis and Malaria. The organisation acts as a financial instrument rather than an implementation agency, with its budget funded by international donations from individual states. It has introduced several interesting structural innovations as an international organisation. The changing attitude of the international fora also reflects a gradual change in the perspectives of the governments of industrialised countries. This is important, as intergovernmental organisations became highly influential in the health policies in the developing countries.

In the meantime another process also influenced the internationalisation process and strengthened the motivations that were behind new international organisations such as the Global Fund. The announcement of the possibility of multiple drug therapy in the Eleventh International AIDS Conference in Vancouver held in July 1996 brought hope to people with AIDS. Around 15,000 scientists, activists, politicians and representatives of pharmaceutical companies (particularly those involved with drug trials) came together to discuss new developments. According to accounts of the conference, the event took place in an uncharacteristically optimistic mood despite voices to keep things in perspective. One such voice was Dr Peter Piot, head of the newly created UNAIDS, who warned that '[T]here is hope, yes, but let's not exaggerate. Let's not switch from very dark pessimism to hype and over-optimism so we will have a hangover within six months or a year' (Piot 1996). As a poster in Britain in December 2001 rightly noted, 'No One Has Been Cured'; however, the disease in developed countries has become a treatable (HAART) chronic disease which does not influence people's everyday lives any more in the way it did before. The possibility of keeping people alive by controlling their immune system with the use of a combination of drugs revolutionised the debate. By providing a new way of tackling the disease in developed countries, it provided a renewed hope for people living with the disease. One of the most important complications of the new situation, however, was the cost of multi-drug therapy. It is this aspect of the new situation which has proved to be an important hurdle for people living in developing countries in particular. The high cost of the drugs created a situation in developed countries where treatment was incorporated into the medical system. In contrast in developing countries treatment has remained unavailable and interventions are kept to prevention and care. A case of *drugs for us, condoms for you*. The possibility and conditions for treatment provision in developing countries have highlighted a number of international issues and cleavages which are still at the centre of the debate, as discussed earlier, in the Introduction.

The production costs of multi-drug treatment meant that the hope presented by the new technology was out of reach for most developing countries. This fact immediately positioned the big pharmaceutical companies that produced the drugs, and thus were very protective of their patent rights, and activist groups in many countries at loggerheads. The latter were arguing that benefits from these medical innovations were everyone's right independent of the interests of the big pharmaceutical companies. This situation also strained the relations between governments that were attempting to protect big industrial interests, such as the US, and AIDS activists who were trying to help people in Africa once they realised the benefits of treatment. Here, we have the internationalisation of treatment and treatment activism. In this process there were many actors that were trying to make drugs internationally available to those who were in need. These included medical professionals, international NGOs, governments and international organisations. It was clear that there had to be a number of new initiatives to support access to the drugs. In 1997 'France launched [the] French International Therapeutic Solidarity Fund (FSTI) to pilot treatment projects in Francophone Africa' (D'Adesky 2004: 20). And in 1998 the UN established its Drug Access Initiative, which was then run by activist groups such as the Health Global Access Project. Some of these initiatives were attempts to provide funding for purchase of drugs to make access to treatment possible without breaching patent rights. However, the scale of the problem in developing countries required faster and wider availability of cheap treatment than was available at the time. Initially Thailand and Brazil and then South Africa argued for generic drugs to be produced and utilised within their own countries, arguing that generics be made available to whoever needed them. This was encouraged by the decision in February 2001 of an Indian generic pharmaceutical company, Cipla Ltd, to provide AIDS combination drugs to frontline groups like MSF for US$1 a day. In this way a new stage in the efforts to tackle the disease was begun.

While treatment had become a possibility for people in developing countries, it also made treatment with generic drugs a major component of international trade discussions and disputes. In particular this occurred within the ongoing discussions on the World Trade Organization's trade-related aspects of intellectual property law.[4] The provision of generic drugs was also supported by international activists such as Médecins Sans Frontières (MSF) and Health Action International. In May 1999 they organised a conference together with Consumer Project on Technology (CPT) entitled Increasing Access to Essential Drugs in a Globalised Economy Working Towards Solution. At the end they issued a statement to officials of WTO, the 'Amsterdam Statement', that called 'for health to be made a priority at the WTO Seattle negotiations and demanded a balance between the rights of patent holders and the rights of citizens in intellectual property rights regulations'.[5] Furthermore, the statement called on the WTO to create a Standing Working Group on Access to Medicines which would look at the conflict between access to medicine and patenting rights and develop ways of operationalising the existing WTO regulations. Among its list of recommendations two are particularly important: 'compulsory licensing of patents (under Article 31 of TRIPS)' under emergency circumstances and 'allowing for exceptions to patent rights (under Article 30 of TRIPS) for production of medicines for export market, when the medicine is exported to a country with a compulsory license'.

The pressure on pharmaceutical companies to reduce their prices to make drugs available was mounting. One way this emerged was as a joint initiative in 2000 by the UN system (UNAIDS, WHO, UNICEF, the UN Population Fund and the World Bank) and five big pharmaceutical companies (Boehringer Ingelheim, Bristol-Myers Squibb, GlaxoSmithKline, Merck & Co., Inc., and F. Hoffmann-La Roche – joined later by Abbott Laboratories in 2001 and Gilead Sciences in 2004). This was the Accelerating Access Initiative (AAI), which aimed to provide discounted drugs for HIV/AIDS-related illnesses to the least developed countries based on country GNP. The aims included to 'accelerate sustained access to and increased use of appropriate, good quality interventions' and to 'strive to reach significantly greater numbers of people in need through new alliances involving committed governments, private industry, the UN system, development assistance agencies, non-governmental organizations and people living with HIV/AIDS' (Noehrenberg 2004). AAI engaged with countries to develop the national plan for the possible interventions while also negotiating with pharmaceutical companies to conclude supply agreements (UNAIDS 2002b: 5–7). In order to coordinate various stakeholders' involvements a new UNAIDS Contact Group on Accelerating Access to HIV/AIDS Care and Support was created in June 2000 (UNAIDS 2000b).

While the formation of AAI had been discussed, the disputes on importing generic drugs climaxed with a court case between big pharmaceutical companies and South Africa's Treatment Action Campaign in April 2001.[6] The possibility of cheap provision had changed the nature of the debate, as can be seen, for instance, in the Harvard Consensus Statement on Antiretroviral Treatment for AIDS in Poor Countries of April 2001, signed by 148 academics. It provided parameters for making antiretroviral therapy immediately available to poor countries, while at the same time providing for carefully controlled clinical trials to be conducted in order to determine the best practices for providing HIV therapy in resource-poor settings. Included in the statement was a detailed cost estimate for delivering antiretroviral therapy as well as a proposal for how this treatment could be financed by resource-rich nations. The statement was the first authoritative declaration on the possibility of using available technology and resources in developing countries. It also called upon wealthy countries, in partnership with poor countries, to establish a global HIV/AIDS Prevention and Treatment Trust Fund to provide both the scientific and the financial leadership to make antiretroviral therapy available in the areas of the world hardest hit by the epidemic. Its importance lay in using 'existing and developing infrastructure, such as networks that have been developed for directly observed therapy' for TB and mother-to-child HIV transmission. Furthermore, the statement located the debate into a moral framework, noting, 'The disparity in access to effective treatment between wealthy countries and developing countries is neither scientifically nor ethically justified at this time' (ibid.: 4). This challenged the international political framework and the pharmaceutical industry by making the treatment issue central to the global debate. The timing and the content of this intervention were very important, particularly in terms of the civil society action against pharmaceutical companies in South Africa of April 2001. It indicated solidarity with the Treatment Action Campaign while providing scientific and moral justification for further action.

It was in this climate that the UN General Assembly meeting on AIDS convened in New York in June 2001. The outcomes of the meeting can be seen as attempts to deal with some of the problems by reiterating the international political commitment. The funding problems surrounding treatment and overall HIV/AIDS-related interventions motivated the proposal for the creation of the Global Fund. However, the meeting could not solve one important disagreement on the prioritisation of either prevention or treatment. At this stage, this debate had a particularly negative impact on Africa, as treatment procedures were seen as too complicated to be implemented in resource-poor contexts. In 2001 one particularly unfortunate statement to this effect was by Andrew Natsios, Director of USAID in 2001. He suggested that Africans could not keep the time to administer HAART regimens: 'They do not use western means to tell time. They use the sun. These drugs have to be administered in certain sequences' (Attaran *et al.* 2001). The refusal to provide treatment on the basis of an assumed inherent weakness in people from Africa almost relocated the debate back to the early nineteenth-century moral framework. Although this statement was discredited immediately, the sentiment it expressed lingered on until the Barcelona AIDS conference in 2002, where several groups presented examples of treatment success in resource-poor countries (Farmer *et al.* 2001).

By this time the issues raised by the Amsterdam Statement were creating problems, as pharmaceutical companies were still keen to protect their patents through the WTO mechanism. The issues were taken up at the WTO Doha meeting in November 2001, which issued a ruling allowing for compulsory licensing to produce generic drugs in developing countries for emergency health problems such as AIDS, TB and malaria. However, they did not resolve the second issue raised by the Amsterdam Statement on producing generic drugs for exporting, arguing that countries would have to acquire technology to develop generics under compulsory licensing within their own countries. This problem still persists, since the US refuses to engage with the debate. Of course, given the resource constraints in many African countries the possibility of producing a domestic generic drug industry raises many further challenges.

The internationalisation process that has been sketched here is a process of bringing the debate and policy responsibilities under international organisations. Moreover, in the same process a certain professionalisation of international activism occurs, owing to the nature of the policy process, but also because, as HIV/AIDS has become much more of a chronic disease in the developed world, activists have become professional actors. This internationalisation process is a part of the emergence of HIV/AIDS as a global disease whereby the process itself is seen as contributing positively to tackling the disease, in contrast to the earlier period of internationalisation of a negative image. However, arguably not all see the process in a positive way. Paul Farmer and his associates argue that 'the response of the affluent countries and their institutions – from aid agencies, non-governmental organisations, and the pharmaceutical industry – has been insufficient (the death toll and increasing HIV incidence are the most eloquent rebuke to contrary assessments)' (2001). Reflections of Jonathan Mann on this issue seem to be portentous. He argued in 1999 that:

> it is now acceptable to think and live in isolation; people in the rich countries can receive treatment with whatever the latest and best science can provide; the North has resumed its limited, 'charity based' approach to international assistance against AIDS ... the biomedical research established can pursue its course with diminished attention to pressing societal needs.

Also, while the international process has motivated a lot of changes and the emergence of international coalitions and organisations, it has embedded ways of thinking about HIV/AIDS within the international HIV/AIDS community of experts and activists. In addition, resources are still provided within what Mann calls a 'charity based framework'. Paula Treichler argues that this mode of engagement took the form of 'a First World Chronicle' (Treichler 1999: 99; also see Watney 1994). It suggests that the epidemic in developing countries was articulated through the vision of the developed world around their interests and priorities. Here, by interest and priorities I don't mean a self-conscious effort for enrichment but rather that the policies are based on the perspective and assumptions of those who are part of this international process.

International perspective

The internationalisation of the disease has also brought with it a certain way of understanding and looking at the disease. This can be observed in the international policy discussions or in the documentation produced on HIV/AIDS by the international organisations. In this section I look at two documents that reflect the state of understanding within the policy environment: the UN General Assembly Resolution and the 2002 UNAIDS report on the state of the epidemic. The UNGASS's final resolution 'Global Crisis –

Global Action' not only set out the road map for policy interventions for dealing with HIV/AIDS but has also established a global initiative for funding countries that are in need. Since its release the document has been adopted as the reference point by many countries for their funding arrangements and for the creation of many national AIDS councils in Sub-Saharan Africa. Therefore it should be considered as a document which has focused attention on the issue and the major problem areas within it. Both the meeting in New York and the document are generally considered to reflect the international political will to support people in their fight against the epidemic. In other words, the UN process relocated the debate to a global political level as a central agenda item which has since dominated many international political forums such as the G8 meetings and the meetings of the World Trade Organization.

The document recognises prevention as the mainstay of the global response, with care, support and treatment seen as necessary parts for the effectiveness of such a response. The importance of vulnerable groups such as women and children is recognised. Characteristically, the document is a statement of understanding and of guidelines for future action without detailed analysis of how its goals can be achieved. Nonetheless it provides a political momentum for future action. The focus of the document also reflects the prevailing common sense before Barcelona 2002, which centred on the possibility of effective treatment delivery in developing countries. Up to this point most resources targeting developing countries focused on prevention. According to one eminent international group, early on they were only motivating and focusing their Southern partners, and those groups they were funding towards prevention-related activities. They did not see treatment as a feasible option in the developing countries. However, after 2002 there was a strong shift in the other direction. International actors have since focused on treatment at the expense of prevention. It seems that addressing both was not considered financially feasible. Of course this either–or logic creates problems, for example focusing on treatment does not influence the increasing infection rates. As a result, UNAIDS is now trying to bring prevention back as a central focus (2005a, 2005b).

One of the important consequences of this refocusing towards treatment can be seen in the increased global funding for HIV/AIDS interventions. There has been a clear increase in the contribution of developed countries for these efforts. Overall funding rose from US$198 million in 1998 to US$3.5 billion in 2002 (UNAIDS 2002b: 32). According to the estimates of the Global HIV Prevention Working Group, developing countries themselves contributed US$1.7 billion of private sector input to affected households and to domestic governments' expenditure, with the rest provided by international donors.[7] The overall total of the foundations' contribution is estimated to be US$200 million in 2002 (UNAIDS, 2002b: 340).[8] Another part of this funding increase related to the newly established organisation, the Global Fund, which became operational in 2002. Since then, 52 countries have pledged to contribute US$8.6 billion to its budget. However, by April 2006 only US$4.4 billion of this had been paid (Global Fund 2006). After five rounds of distribution, 57 per cent of this went to support HIV/AIDS-related interventions. And in terms of geographical distribution, 55 per cent of the funding went to Sub-Saharan Africa (Global Fund 2006).

Another consequence of this refocusing has been the setting of clear stakeholders in the fight against the epidemic: governments, bilateral donors, civil society, the private sector, international organisations, community groups and people living with HIV/AIDS (PLWHA). This list is a commonly used one. The classification of actors is recognisable from many other documents in this area. Typically, they represent these groups as engaged in dealing with the disease. Policies initiated to bring these groups together are considered under the multi-sectoral interventions rubric. According to the UNAIDS report on the global HIV/AIDS epidemic 2002, 'it has become commonplace to include multiple ministries, as well as representatives of civil society and other development partners in high-level political coordination structures' (UNAIDS 2002b: 176). This model is also replicated in many national AIDS councils in the region, such as in Uganda, Botswana, Malawi, Kenya, Namibia and Zimbabwe. The same report states that these multi-sectoral attempts are 'key to building capacity within civil society and enabling people and groups to be active participants, rather than passive targets of, programming' (UNAIDS 2002b: 178). It then goes on to emphasise that this is an important characteristic by outlining the role played by civil society 'in advocacy, participating in policy and programming design and implementation, and in the provision of services, especially at the community level' (UNAIDS 2002b: 178). These intentions and the actual increase in the numbers of NGOs lead many to view civil society as revitalised or created in some cases. Indeed it seems to have convinced most of the international multi- and bilateral donors to focus on civil society and to channel their funding towards their activities.

Consider the World Bank's Multi-Country AIDS Program. It is putting 50 per cent of its funding directly into the civil society sector. Many other funding bodies, such as UNAIDS and DfID, require strong civil society participation for the dispersion of funds into country programmes. One of the review criteria used by the Global Fund to assess the soundness of an application for its funding is that a proposal 'enables the development, strengthening and expansion of government/private/NGO partnership'. The role of civil society actors is recognised along with the effectiveness of their work. According to the Global HIV Prevention Working Group, 'the reversal of the AIDS epidemic can happen if proven prevention interventions are used in combination and brought to scale' (GHPWG 2003: 1). The proven methods – implicit in the report – are that 'combination prevention uses a range of science-based strategies, from encouraging delayed sexual activity to condom promotion, from voluntary HIV counselling and testing to programs for injecting drug users' (GHPWG 2003: 1). Furthermore, it also establishes the importance of policy reforms in education and elsewhere as central for dealing with gender inequalities.

These initiated financial and institutional changes and the clear political support for particular interventions and agencies that is expressed in most international political arenas set out an overall framework which has underpinned the nature of international activities in this field.

Governance

The internationalisation process and the policy which are observed in the gradual development of international organisations and coalitions dealing with HIV/AIDS should be seen as a governance structure. The disease, as discussed earlier, is considered a global problem. In this, the globality of the disease is related both to its occurrence in multiple country contexts across the world and to the international policy context which provides the institutional support for interventions across countries. This *globality* locates policy formulations into a certain *global* context whereby *global* intervention policies are to be supported by *global* funding with *other resources* formulated accordingly. Alongside this formulation process, certain practices for coordination, communication and implementation are established as a particular language game.[9] This understanding of the global process surrounding the HIV/AIDS pandemic is very much in line with Leon Gordenker and Thomas Weiss's definition of global governance as:

> efforts to bring [a] more orderly and reliable response to social and political issues that go beyond capacities of states to address individually. Like the NGO universe, global governance implies an absence of central authority, and the need for collaboration or cooperation among governments and others [who] seek to encourage common practices and goals in addressing global issues.
>
> (Gordenker and Weiss 1996: 17)

Following Gordenker and Weiss, the concept of governance articulated here focuses on governance as a process of developing common aims and practices. It allows one to look at the impact of this process on its intended target field. This markedly differs from, for example, the common parlance promoted by the World Bank that focuses on promoting governance issues through a good governance agenda which ties largely with 'increasing popular participation, reducing poverty, and improving project performance' (Nelson 2000). Using this concept, the Bank attempts to achieve its developmental aspirations through initiating policies to change governance-related practices in developing countries. In contrast my concern is with a particular governance system that is discussed critically by looking at it as an agent that influences the form of interventions and practices. It fits well with Elke Krahmann's definition of governance as 'the structures and processes that

enable governmental and non-governmental actors to coordinate their interdependent needs and interests through the making and implementation of
policies in the absence of unifying political authority' (2003: 331). Although
this definition allows one to overcome a certain conceptual confusion about
the idea of governance by focusing on, in general, a fragmented process
involving various actors, it is in danger of setting out an image that is too
comfortable. The important imbalances among actors trying to coordinate
their interdependent interests have important consequences for the policy
outcomes and the way governance is constituted through the process of negotiation. Thus, in this process the idea of power is critical, power which is
exercised through the everyday practices of negotiation and project management among various actors. These practices set out the concepts by which the
problems are perceived. In other words, they constitute the organisational
subjectivities of various actors. Therefore, here, governance of HIV/AIDS is
considered to have an impact both on the way policies are articulated and on
the actual outcomes as experienced by people. From this perspective, the
agency of particular actors such as civil society organisations or NGOs
within the governance structure can be articulated, while an assessment of
the impact of actors on each other and on the disease also becomes possible.

Thus, the international policy environment as it pertains to HIV/AIDS will
be considered here as a particular 'practice of governance' that looks at the
forms of governing put into practice (Tully 2002: 538). James Tully argues
that these forms include:

> the language games in which both governors and governed are led to
> recognise each other as partners in the practice, communication and
> coordination of activities; to raise problems and propose solutions;
> and to renegotiate their form of government, including languages of
> administration and normative legitimation.
>
> (Tully 2002: 539)

In this sense, the concept of governance here does not just consider policy
makers as exercising power to manage the disease as a technical issue. It also
considers the productive process of the relations and context within which the
HIV/AIDS field is constituted as a policy intervention domain. In this, the
practices of governance set out the institutional arrangements, decision-
making processes and the capacity for implementation within the context.
They also constitute the agency of certain actors and relevant domains of
policy, a result of which, for instance, is that people with the disease are
constructed – in a way independent of their everyday lives – as patients to be
governed in a particular domain, that of the international HIV/AIDS policy
as produced by certain languages and technologies. Considered from this
perspective, HIV/AIDS governance is a set of complex inter-constitutive relations which creates legitimacy for certain actors, including civil society actors.

Governance context

The definition of 'governance' used above differs from a rather technical and instrumental usage common in recent years among the leading multilateral and bilateral organisations involved in development. It is related to the emergence of new thinking on development based on comprehensive development frameworks and Poverty Reduction Strategy Papers (PRSPs). In these developmental approaches the idea of governance includes altering public sector management to initiate greater citizen participation, to ensure government accountability and transparency of public policy in order to be able to move on achieving higher goals of development. It is from this perspective, for instance, that the role of civil society has become pronounced. It views the increased number of civil society activities as an indicator of an increasing citizens' voice and a way of meeting demands for public accountability and transparency. This perspective was born of two processes: the changing perspectives in international development within which there has been an ascendancy of civil society actors as partners, and the internationalisation of HIV/AIDS whereby the first generation of AIDS activists have been replaced by professional international activists. Arguably the two processes have reinforced each other in creating a much more professional civil society activism which is also technically competent to be a part of the international discussion. Thus, civil society is incorporated into the governance structure.[10]

This incorporation process is evidence of practices that create a particular way of governing the international HIV/AIDS policies and interventions. The role played by civil society organisations (NGOs and community groups) at present in the HIV/AIDS epidemic can be analysed in relation to the general governance of the disease, 'practices of governance'. It allows the analysis to take explicitly into account the processes which lead to the establishment or acceptance of a certain system as a governance structure whereby certain influences are institutionalised in relation to the internal processes. In this way the activities of those actors that are a part of the governance are maintained within the parameters of the system. This way of looking at the processes takes into account the conceptual feedback which is created for the agency of the actors such as people living with the disease on the ground, who are the focus for development initiatives and HIV/AIDS interventions.

The perspective applied here follows an understanding that considers governance as 'the forms of reason and organisation through which individuals and groups coordinate their various activities, and practices of freedom by which they act within these systems, following rules of the game striving to modify them' (Tully 2002: 539). The governance structure I am considering in relation to the HIV/AIDS interventions involves international organisations (such as the World Bank and the Joint United Nations Programme on HIV/AIDS – UNAIDS), individual donor countries (such as the US, the UK, Norway, Sweden and the Netherlands) and their aid organisations (such as USAID and DfID), national governments and their existing policy intervention channels and national civil society. At the local level there are community groups and local and international NGOs working with national or transnational NGOs. Although many multilateral and bilateral organisations have individual priorities depending on their particular expertise and mandate, a *de facto* governance regime for HIV/AIDS has emerged. This has been partially facilitated by the establishment of UNAIDS as the coordinating body for UN-related organisations' involvement in HIV/AIDS interventions that are co-sponsored by:

- the United Nations Children's Fund (UNICEF);
- the World Food Programme (WFP);
- the United Nations Development Programme (UNDP);
- the United Nations Population Fund (UNFPA);
- the United Nations Educational, Scientific and Cultural Organization (UNESCO);
- the World Health Organization (WHO);
- the World Bank;
- the United Nations Office on Drugs and Crime (UNODC);
- the International Labour Organization (ILO).[11]

Furthermore, this emergence has been bolstered further by organisational developments such as the Global Fund and by the inclusion of HIV/AIDS as one of the main policy areas in comprehensive development frameworks like the Millennium Development Goals (MDGs). This latter process has also anchored HIV/AIDS policy discussions firmly into the international development policy frameworks with its concerns on decentralisation and privatisation for social sectors.

Within this process actors are attributed roles. Civil society is by and large constructed as a resource category which is to be utilised as an efficient and effective way for engaging with the disease at community level while also serving the logic of decentralised service delivery. In terms of the HIV/AIDS policy context, the role of civil society is to act as a conduit between policy structures and the people. Prevalent in this are a few central assumptions both justified by and justifying the practices of governance. These are: (a) civil society is related to the people and reflects their needs; therefore (b) civil society is effective in reaching people; therefore (c) civil society should be brought more into service delivery; and (d) this increases the accountability and the transparency of governments in line with their development aims and restructuring plans. In this way, on the one hand, the status of civil society within the policy context is considered partly in reference to international policy makers, while on the other hand the idea of civil society in relation to people also has purchase. The problem, however, is understanding the possible impact of civil society and assessing its impact in relation to HIV/AIDS. The governance system assesses this by attributing a certain success to the process by which it relates to people on the ground using the assumed aspirational status of civil society within the policy context. This logic makes civil society appear nearly independent of the global policy context even though it clearly is not only part of this governance structure but also constituted by this structure in its present role as a key agent of intervention. In this the structure locates civil society with people, implicitly posing an intimate relationship between the two. Then naturally, the increased NGO and community activity is taken (or asserted) to be reflective of people's participation in the process of dealing with the disease, one which will ultimately produce positive outcomes. In other words, the response to the question of 'Where are the people?' can be made by pointing out the increased number of NGOs without actually articulating anything about the experience of people in multiple contexts.

Overall these considerations lead to a questioning of the international governance of HIV/AIDS and the way it relates to people infected and affected by the disease. It moves beyond standard thinking about governance as a technical tool that makes 'effective action likely, satisfies donors, responds efficiently and produces observable results' (Poku 2002). By introducing a dynamic theoretical lens, governmentality, policy actors are located in the context of the consequences their actions have for people's lives while also being located in the space within which their agency and the policies they are implementing are articulated. Therefore, the actors such as NGOs can be seen as linking the context of policy makers with the context of needs. However, it also attempts to overcome a general assumption about such actors where images of these actors are articulated based on the assumptions prevalent in the policy-making context, which are independent of their actual organisational characters and abilities. This raises questions about the substantive components and overall assumptions of this governance system. Furthermore, it argues that the governance system not only produces a mechanism to manage a number of actors but also produces its own understanding of the situation. In relation to the state of HIV/AIDS, it creates the *common sense* for the HIV/AIDS policy universe.

Where are we now?

This common sense can in part be looked at through international policy documents. These documents usually balance a positive attitude based on the achievements of the international system with a realism that notes that the hard task ahead is mired with funding and implementation problems. Some of these are perennial problems for HIV/AIDS in the region, such as 'knowledge is not enough, partial measures produce partial outcomes, [and] countering harmful gender norms' (UNAIDS 2002b: 81–4). While not providing direction as to how one might overcome these problems in a given context, the documents typically provide insights about the situation in the region and assess what is happening according to the achievement of internationally decided policy aims. In this there is also presented a sense of success which is based on considerations of further integration of the policy process with the governance structure. This implicit sense then justifies narratives of achievements with the result that an increasing number of international policy implementations in countries reinforce their integration to the international system (see UNAIDS 2005a: 2–6). Of course success here is arguably about the wider implementation of tools and fund-raising efforts rather than the outcomes which these interventions produce.

In understanding the state of HIV/AIDS there are certain parameters that shape the content of our common sense in terms of policy interventions and actors. On their bases, despite the awareness of the problems, the approach of policy making, the implementation process and the confidence for actors involved in them remain the same. Many interventions such as condom distribution, voluntary counselling and testing (VCTs), and mother-to-child transmission prevention methods are taken to be working as tools to influence behaviour change (GHPWG 2003: 36). The institutions for policy implementation, such as governments, the private sector and NGOs and their multi-sectoral partnerships in particular, are considered to be providing a right agency for moving forward. The problems that are presented in these documents are those that relate to funding gaps, scale of implementation, mainstreaming tools/procedures of interventions and educating more people for behaviour change. In short, there is no doubt that the funding and the methods of intervention have constituted the main focus of most of the policy debates in Sub-Saharan Africa. Indeed, from this perspective there are changes taking place. Arguably the changes are *real*, in that they are having an impact on the *everyday lives* of international and domestic policy makers, donors and the implementers of policies.

In contrast, both the general trend of expansion of the disease and the experiences of many people on the ground bear witness to the fact that the everyday lives of infected and affected people remain largely unchanged, particularly with respect to uncertainty due to the doubts on policy sustainability. The perspective on change and success examined in the documents appears to be dependent on the observer's position where the observer is incorporated within the governance system. From the organisational perspective, changes are measured by increased quantities of interventions and funding similar to those of the past, without taking stock of whether what was done produced overall positive outcomes. People's experiences with their husbands/wives, parents, children, friends and neighbours in their homes and workplaces show that what has been assumed to be an effective way of intervening is open to question. These people's perspectives also reveal the special nature of the disease.

Moreover HIV/AIDS and its associated problems keep escalating at an exponential pace. The data sections of the documents show that the epidemic is increasing its hold on many societies, despite claims of declining infection rates in some contexts (see UNAIDS 2005a: 26). On the ground people are still being infected and dying in great numbers. The often mentioned stigma remains a persistent fact of life in spite of the many public information campaigns across Africa: despite the widely available information through many NGO campaigns, a hidden stigma is a reality. While people acknowledge HIV/AIDS publicly, they may not change their prejudicial social conduct against those who have HIV. In addition, millions of orphans are facing a grim future. As orphans they are vulnerable now, but they also risk when growing up becoming a part of the vicious cycle through which the disease is spreading. Despite the efforts put into awareness and sensitisation campaigns, general behaviour change seems to be an outcome that remains to be fulfilled.

What has changed?

According to many infected and affected people and activists working on the ground, there are good reasons for this unchanging state of affairs. Some express it in a direct manner: *We (NGOs) got it wrong. Now we are trying to correct our mistakes.* They argue that the campaigns on HIV/AIDS have suffered from targeting, design and delivery problems; 'scare tactics do not make people change their behaviour' (Bawani 2003). Campaigns are in general context blind and gender insensitive. Moreover, many categories such as 'young', 'orphans' and 'gender' (women) are applied without any understanding of how people in these ascribed categories in fact live. In most cases interventions that appear coherent and targeted from within the international policy domain are produced in an uncoordinated manner with either misleading or contradictory information which creates a certain HIV/AIDS fatigue among people. In the absence of change in their lives as a result of such interventions often people prefer to ignore the messages. In the end many feel that, if they are going to die anyway, why should they locate themselves outside their community by revealing their status?

In other words, experts just talking is not going to help people. Locating how the disease spreads via a particular behaviour makes sense only in a particular community. It is clearly not enough to say HIV passes through sex. We have to understand what sex means and why and how it happens in a given context before starting a generalised campaign for prevention. According to a communication specialist in Zambia, *Communication in this field has been one-sided. Messages were designed according to the suppliers' understanding of the problems rather than the receiver's situation that informs his/her needs.* The communication specialist argued further that *Some of the prevention messages given through their depiction of HIV/AIDS patients isolated these people from their communities. In addition most campaigns carry an implicit moral judgement about sex and the patient which exacerbates the stigma problem.* As a result people refrain from attending clinics or getting condoms. He suggested that *'To say don't do this' also requires us to understand 'why one does it'; otherwise the communication remains one-sided and ineffective.*

This kind of miscommunication is also illustrated by others. In Botswana an experienced peer education specialist, who has been involved with peer education for prevention, argued in an exasperated manner that, *Although peer education is promoted and funded by many donors and is carried out by a great number of NGOs, the efficiency and effectiveness of this policy is highly questionable.* Her questioning was informed by the behaviour of the many people she had trained as peer educators. In her experience, *Though peer educators deliver prevention messages to the participants during workshops, as soon as the workshop ends they revert back to their traditional gender roles and try to and at times have sexual relations with willing participants.* In this, *The male peer educator utilises traditional tools (gestures and postures implicitly understood by the other side) available and comprehensible in the context in order to request sex.* This contradiction, according to her, *is related to the ambiguity of the messages available to the people. They are able to relate to the messages such as having consensual sex or refraining from having casual sex with multiple partners as abstract ideas, but without converting them into life strategies for their social context* (see also James 2002). In other words, awareness is not enough to change behaviour. In most cases it seems a general awareness and subsequent stigmatisation are leading to a hidden epidemic.

According to a Zambian Anglican priest who combines his religious role with social work in one of the compounds in Lusaka, *Despite the wide availability of condoms and awareness of HIV, various help groups have carried contradictory prevention messages, and also were not explicit and did not understand the realities of people's lives.* He noted that, *in order to get people to use condoms, groups created an understanding that using condoms will help you to get rid of the disease.* Therefore, *after using condoms once or twice most of the people either decide that, having used it, they now are fine and have sex as usual, or they see others dying despite using condoms and therefore question why should they use this thing they consider to be dirty.* A combination of misrepresentation and abstract ideas in fact has a negative impact by creating a resistance for other interventions.

In addition, the assumption of a particular impact for particular actors and tools seems to be a common problem in many interventions. This is visible from the strong feelings that were expressed by both infected and affected people in relation to VCTs. They argued that *the assumption behind the testing does not work in reality.* The assumptions suggest that knowing your status gives you courage to choose how you live; you can change your behaviour, not only in relation to sex, but also to your diet and your lifestyle in general. Many PLWHA argued that *this is fine in theory* but questioned how it could be done. In Zambia it was clear that, despite existing law, once status was known PLWHA lost their jobs under false pretences, with AIDS being the real issue. As a result, they lose the income which would allow them to have a balanced diet and an appropriate environment. Subsequently, their family life breaks down, their diet becomes precarious and they live with high levels of stress since they cannot afford medicine or anything else. All of these factors contribute to the spread of the disease in contrast to the assumed choices VCTs purport to enable people to exercise. In short PLWHA cannot control their lives.

Another aspect of this divergence between assumptions about interventions and reality was revealed in Botswana where people who get sick tend to move to the rural areas to be cared for by their families. However, some of these people refrain from revealing their status and carry on having sexual relations.

A PLWHA brought up another important problem related with the treatment issue. He stated that, though they were happy to hear about the funding given to the Zambian government for treatment purposes by the Global Fund, the number of people who would be treated by the amount was far too limited and they did not know how the selection was going to be done. He also added sceptically, *What guarantees that one will be paid for life?*

The problem expressed in this last statement is linked with the larger problem of poverty and the way development interventions have been carried out. Poverty represents the contextual constraints on people's lives within which they experience the disease. Unless interventions are based on an understanding of how poverty and the disease interact, some of the methods discussed above will remain in the abstract and will continue to contribute to the stigma. Furthermore, actors that are intervening need to understand the impact of already-existing development interventions on the disease. For instance, the situation in Zambia's copper belt is exacerbated by the decline of copper mines, and the urban areas which sprang up to accommodate workers are now facing major problems. In these areas it is very hard to find new employment, and the increased necessity for care and support cannot be addressed because the community support links in such contexts tend to be much weaker than is generally assumed. On the one hand if people stay, *there is nothing much to do, with alcohol, boredom and absence of any other work creating a market for sex-work in return for a little to eat, while on the other hand if people go back to their original communities, the disease will increase its grip further in the other parts of the country.*

All of these examples and the many possible others demonstrate that the disease happens within a particular social context: urban, rural, small, large, industrial, in schools, in a workplace and in the family. All of these spaces reflect particular complex gender relations which are constantly played out between inter- and intra-gender roles, providing incentives and disincentives for action. They also bear witness to a certain mismatch between the psycho-social context of the disease and the mechanisms of interventions. The lack of agency among certain policy actors to change behaviour or to sustain a possible change, in spite of extensive involvement in communities, seems to be related with this mismatch. The causes of the ineffectiveness of interventions are related with the nature of the implementing agencies, for instance NGOs, which are constrained by organisational characteristics that are independent of qualities attributed to them by the international governance structure.

Most of the programmes and projects related to the discussed experiences are initiated with government participation funded by international donors and contracted out to NGOs to be delivered. Although many discussions focus on multi-sectoral partnerships whereby governments and the private sector are given high visibility as investors, in most Sub-Saharan African countries these multi-sectoral practices denote NGOs and community groups being contracted in to implement programmes and projects and to deliver services. Though the exact number of NGOs and community groups working under this kind of arrangement in the region is unavailable, for researchers in the field in many diverse countries of the region these organisations constitute the bulk of policy interventions and service delivery actors. Even the Global Fund considers 'an intense mobilization of civil society' is required. This view seems to be taken as the blueprint by many international agencies as well as national policy makers as a way of legitimating the role played by NGOs within the governance structure. As noted earlier this asserts two interlinked processes: (a) the assumed aspirational status of civil society in terms of both closeness to people and its contribution to democracy (influencing the accountability and the transparency of governments) and (b) the role of civil society in the process of decentralisation where it becomes a sector for service delivery. According to UNAIDS, the activism embedded in the presence of non-governmental and community organisations around AIDS is seen as a global force influencing the policy makers (UNAIDS 2002b: 11). It is further noted that dozens of AIDS strategies were introduced through which local community organisations that are playing a pioneering role were brought into partnerships. In this way, NGOs are normalised into the governance system whose norms and language are produced both through the requirements for funding and through the designated service delivery areas available for NGOs within the system. The form of governance implicit in the following language is clear: 'an important role for governments is to clear the way so all sectors of society can contribute to the response' as a participation of 'religious, cultural and community groups or associations, employers, trade unions and non-governmental organisations' (UNAIDS 2002b: 176). This bolsters the role of civil society for national interventions. Considered within the context of Sub-Saharan Africa, it suggests that the response to the epidemic is broadly planned at the international level while implementation relies on a set of fragmented organisations.

Though it is true that new funding is put into the system for treatment in many countries like Botswana and Zambia with the help of the Global Fund, and that some NGO projects are indeed demonstrating positive outcomes, the disease is by and large still expanding its grip on many communities and societies. Furthermore, I argue that the situation on the ground gives us two contexts within which we need to consider the understanding of the present in relation to HIV/AIDS: the context of the policy makers and the context of the people infected and affected. The ineffectiveness discussed above is created by the disjuncture between these two contexts. The former's articulation of the relationship between the two seems to be based on assumptions about people's nature, lives and needs rather than concrete evidence about how people change behaviour and what they need for this process. This is challenged by the latter context, which provides a gaze produced by the experience of people in their everyday lives. It not only captures the fact that the disease is expanding, but also exposes the inherent problems in the governing mechanism for intervening with the disease. In articulating their problems many infected and affected people reveal deep-seated, long-established links between the spread of the disease and values/social norms that are underpinning societal mechanisms preventing people from openly engaging with the disease. Furthermore, they point out the centrality of decades of not-so-successful development interventions on people's lives. These revelations raise doubts over the effectiveness of the methods that are seen as proven in the context of international policy processes. This system is also largely based on existing conventional thinking on international developmental approaches and priorities as they are reasserted through the MDGs. For instance, it is not clear that interpretations using the available numbers of condoms distributed or numbers of people visiting VCT clinics to attribute success in positive behaviour change will ever be appropriate from the perspective of people's lives, as these interventions/*interpretations* do not engage with people's beliefs or try to understand existing mechanisms for change. It also raises questions about the policy implementation channels and the way these are bolstered by the governance mechanism in terms of a legitimating discourse and language implanted through administrative processes.

In summary, in the discussion of internationalisation and governance in this chapter, the aim has been to point out how the HIV/AIDS policy context has been constructed in a particular way. The argument does not suggest that people living with the disease and within the context of the pandemic are not a part of this governance. On the contrary, it argues that they are also incorporated into this system, but in a particular way: one that makes sense to the international policy makers. In this a disjuncture emerges between people as generic policy target groups and people in their everyday lives. This disjuncture emerges where the impact of international policy processes on peoples lives can be observed. The next chapter develops the analysis by looking at the question of how this internationalisation process becomes a governance structure by institutionalising a set of norms as common sense for action in this policy world.

2   Constructing agency in the time of an epidemic

AIDS is named a global disease. It has become one of the indicators for showing that we are living in a globalised world with global risks. Moreover, the consideration of HIV/AIDS as a global problem has resulted in the creation of yet another globalising process: an international policy framework to understand HIV/AIDS. Thus, a global framework has emerged to solve a global problem. In most HIV/AIDS-related international policy documents the importance of civil society is emphasised and the role of non-governmental organisations within it is seen as central for multi-sectoral interventions to adequately deal with the disease (UNAIDS 2002b, 2004a, 2004c, 2005a, 2006; GHPWG 2003). It is within this framework, in the international governance of the disease, that NGOs are taking part and contributing to the fight against the disease. It is also within this international process that their agency is acknowledged. For example the 2004 annual UNAIDS report argues that 'Civil society organisations often have innovative approaches to the epidemic, and can channel funds to communities, augment state service delivery, and monitor national government policies. At the community level, governments' administrative procedures must be flexible enough to include NGOs' (UNAIDS 2004c: 157–8). In this statement the idea of NGO agency follows the available literature on NGOs and on their role in advocacy, service delivery and being flexible. It is in this context that NGOs have a certain agency attributed to them.

This chapter looks at the conditions of this agency and the way it has been constructed within the international policy process. It suggests that by looking at this it is possible to understand the way international organisations institutionalise their norms and values through policies. Also, in this the impact of institutional norms and values on HIV/AIDS in Sub-Saharan Africa can be observed. In doing this the chapter considers NGOs from a sociological context: how they relate to the disease from within the larger international processes. Thus, the chapter moves beyond the conventional thinking in this field that considers NGOs as independent actors whose role it is to bridge the gap between various policy structures and the people, in order to deliver the policies effectively and efficiently. There are two general reasons for this conventional view: the dominance of the discourse of civil society within the development circles in the last decade and the *perceived* effectiveness of NGOs in dealing with localised problems (see Fowler 1988; Edwards and Hulme 1992; and Najam 1999). Prevalent in this are a few central assumptions in the international development field that have been dominant in underpinning this process of institutionalisation of NGOs: (a) NGOs are related to people and/or reflect their needs; therefore (b) NGOs have more effective ways of reaching people; therefore (c) NGOs should be at the centre of service delivery; and (d) as people's organisations they can use advocacy techniques to increase the accountability and the transparency of governments in line with their development aims and restructuring plans. The research following these assumptions pays little attention to the effects of international organisations mediated by NGOs on HIV/AIDS in Sub-Saharan Africa. With NGOs considered as central actors, international organisations are merely considered as external factors according to their technical and resource contributions.

In contrast, this chapter argues that international organisations have important effects in the context and these effects go beyond their assumed benign charitable aspirations (Jepperson 1991: 153). One way of assessing this effect is to look at the accuracy of the agency attributed to NGOs in the HIV/AIDS field within the international institutionalisation process. It considers NGOs as constructed conduits between the international fora and the local context. This institutionalisation process treats NGOs in the field as structurally similar organisations which are exposed to similar pressures.[1] As a result there is a problem of agency for these organisations in relation to their assumed locations within particular socio-cultural contexts, as *local organisations*, distinct from their participation in the international realm. The effect of international institutionalisation processes is evident in the literature on NGOs, which, while providing insights based on countless case studies, is mostly limited to questions of organisational efficiency and effectiveness (see Sahley 1995; Lewis 2001). Unfortunately, apart from a few studies,[2] the socio-political location of NGOs within which their agency is recognised is generally neglected.[3] By focusing on management and organisational issues, as important as they may be, the international institutional location of NGOs within larger socio-political and cultural contexts is taken to be unproblematic. As a result, the contextual conditions of agency related to the emergence of the NGO form as an organisational actor within specific social junctures are neutralised, in general and within the international HIV/AIDS policy arena in particular (Douglas 1986: 46).

This chapter contributes to the ongoing debate from various angles. First, it empirically links the institutionalisation of NGO agency in the realm of international organisations to the field of NGO work in Africa. Thus, it highlights a disjuncture between the assumed agency of NGOs in the international HIV/AIDS policy arena and their actual effectiveness on the ground.[4] It points out the way institutionalisation affects actors that are traditionally considered to be outside the domain of international organisa-tions. It argues that, unless NGOs can have an agency formed in relation to particular people within a given socio-cultural context, assumptions of posi-tive policy outcomes will remain spurious.

Second, by understanding the constitution of NGO agency from the per-spective of institutionalisation it demonstrates how international perspectives create an NGO isomorphism on the ground. It also points out that this move brings an associated 'normative change' for the local groups (Finnemore 1996: 338). In this way it highlights the importance of the power relations that are embedded in the mechanisms of this process (Barnett and Finnemore 1999: 726). The analysis also provides a theoretical basis for understanding an important dilemma in the HIV/AIDS field which feeds into this dis-juncture. The problem is that most international policy interventions are try-ing to address behaviour change-related issues while being constructed at the international level. In order to be able to engage with people in the way they experience the disease, policy makers first have to understand the problems with the assumed NGO agency.

These two steps provide a perspective that is linked with the experiences of people living with the disease in particular countries. The effects of the inter-national organisations are considered in order to understand their impact on the disease in context. In this way the analysis uses the institutionalisation perspective to look at the mechanisms producing these effects. Therefore, the chapter does not provide an analysis of this debate from within international relations, which looks at the nature of international organisations according to the various theoretical schools of this field. One reason for this is the fact that the debate between schools in international relations is methodologically limited within the confines of international relations. There the aim is to consider whether or not international organisations are purposive agents in international relations.

In contrast my concern is the impact of international organisations on people's everyday lives as they experience the disease. This approach connects micro concerns about human well-being with macro concerns expressed in the international organisations.[5] It takes as a starting point Michael Barnett and Martha Finnemore's work that international organisations are purposive actors with power to influence and change other actors' behaviour, where the content of their influence is based on their normative world view with result-ing negative or positive effects on others (Barnett and Finnemore 1999: 726). Moreover, by looking at the agency attributed to NGOs in the HIV/AIDS context from this angle, the analysis goes beyond the limited boundaries of international organisations. I argue that the effect of these international organisations' power can be observed in the way they have engaged with HIV/AIDS in Sub-Saharan Africa through NGOs (Finnemore and Sikkink 1998: 892). In this way the analysis focuses on the mechanism that mediates their impact and the effects of that mechanism. Furthermore, this questions the above-mentioned assumptions that are made about NGOs within international development. Under these assumptions, NGOs are seen as linked to international organisations where the link is only seen as a resource and technical exchange within which international organisations are providers and NGOs are *grass-roots* implementers (Fowler 1988; Farrington *et al.* 1993; Anang 1994; Sandberg 1994; Therkildsen and Semboja 1995; Hulme and Edwards 1997). Another way in which NGOs are linked to the international organisations in the post-Cold War period is by their treatment as appropriate agents for improving democracy and bringing people into contact with political processes through civil society (Hearn 2000; Ottaway and Carothers 2000). Here again, although the agency is attributed within an international context, NGOs as actors are considered independent of this in their democratic roles. In other words they are considered to have a democratic agency in virtue of their constitution.

In both cases the institutionalisation process and its impact are ignored by a focus on what NGOs can do by improving their organisational capabilities. The general outlook of these approaches is NGO-centric. That is to say, what NGOs can do as individual actors with their own aims is disembedded from the social context (Meyer and Jepperson 2000: 106–7). NGOs are considered to have a set of relations with other actors on a one-to-one basis for coordination and management purposes (see Robinson *et al.* 2000). As a result, the field neglects the general understanding of how a set of institutional social relations construct the identity of certain actors, such as NGOs, in particular social processes, and hence their agency. Furthermore, the NGO-centrism also creates a generalised perspective on these relations and on the desirability for the survival of NGOs in areas of social engagement. On the one hand, the institutionalisation process which constructs specific capability for actors based on particular social relations specific to a social context or social problem becomes subsumed under opaque generalities which in the end create an ideal type, a homogenised organisational form, about NGOs and their sociological relations. On the other hand, paraphrasing Meyer and Rowan, this situation also reflects myths (assumptions) about NGOs in the institutionalisation process particular to the international policy arena (Meyer and Rowan 1977: 341).[6]

This chapter addresses these issues in the following way. The first section presents the institutionalisation perspective as a theoretical lens. This is done by discussing Mary Douglas's work. This allows us to rethink the idea of agency as discussed in the second section. The following section then looks at the claims of agency made about NGOs within the international HIV/AIDS policy and at the role of international actors in this that provide the basis of the institutionalisation. The chapter then discusses why this perspective matters for the HIV/AIDS context. This considers the limits of NGO agency within the larger socio-cultural institutionalisation processes which construct NGOs as relevant actors. It argues that rather than having a generic organisational agency NGOs have varied agency depending on the social contexts within which they are located. Furthermore, it concludes that the agency attributed to NGOs in the HIV/AIDS field frustrates engagement with the long-term sustainable changes required to deal with the disease.

Institutionalisation

This section looks at institutionalisation and the way it produces agency in relation to actors' behaviour and capabilities. It looks at institutionalisation by considering the mechanism for agency attribution. To do this, it first takes issue with the conventional attempts to think about institutions that are evident in the literature: the NGO partnership discussion and one of the theoretical rationales provided for this discussion, the new institutional economics model advocated by Teddy Brett. Second, it presents a sociological understanding of the institutionalisation process which allows one to better understand its effects as they are produced in the process.

There are a number of attempts in the literature to address the issue of the institutional location of NGOs. These are usually delivered under the rubric of NGOs' external relations, which are conceptualised at present as partnerships with various sectors. They usually include relations with state actors, funders (the aid industry) and business as well as communities (Hulme and Edwards 1997; Heap 2000). The influence model developed by Martin de Graff is one of the more coherent analytical ways for looking at these relations (de Graff 1987). Also, important emphasis has been put on the NGOs' relations with states. In this a set of frameworks are proposed within which NGOs engage with states which emphasise the impact of state behaviour on the roles played by NGOs (Clark 1991; Wood 1997). However, most of these discussions look for ways and means for efficient and effective coordination of these relations. By looking at NGOs' links in partnerships with states, funders and communities, the institutional process is located into internal organisational management processes. Even critical work such as Sarah Michael's, which looks at the power relations within which African NGOs are located, finishes by looking at how African NGOs can be empowered using mostly internal organisational factors (Michael 2004: 145–63). Overall, these discussions analyse NGOs as independent variables within the institutional environment both at the international and at the local levels. Therefore, the understanding of institutionalisation processes is reduced to inter-organisational relations and the procedures for managing these relations, and to the discussions of capacity building for NGOs to manage these relations (Sahley 1995).

This is an effect of a theoretical position which is observable in Brett's considerations of institutionalism and the role of civil society. It is based on 'three stereotypes which appear throughout development policy literature: the market, the state, and civil society' (Brett 2000: 17). He observes that institutions are 'considered as rules that structure social interactions in particular ways based on shared knowledge by members of the relevant community or society' (Brett 2000: 18). He also states that an institutional perspective provides a wider angle for understanding the relations in society beyond individual interest. It brings a larger organisational perspective which influences individuals' choices by exposing individuals to more diverse motivations for them. In this way he sees institutional rules as a framing set for developing effective organisations. Thus, he locates individual behaviour in relation to a set of institutional imperatives into views that are based on some free and independent individual self-interest (Brett 2000: 18–21). However, in Brett's account the organisations are treated as individual rational actors acting and reacting on their own terms to their environment (DiMaggio and Powell 1991).

Although Brett's argument provides a good opening for a discussion of institutionalisation, it is a very limited attempt. By fixing the sociological context of institutionalisation to a particular tripartite view of the organisational realm it does not provide a space to consider the role of international organisations in a context (Barnett and Finnemore 1999; Onuf 1989: 261–3). Brett has chosen this approach 'because these stereotypes are often considered to be the most important institutional forms of competition, coordination and cooperation respectively' and he adds that 'it is important to understand the ways in which each of these types addresses the basic problems of social organisation' (Brett 2000: 17). This position generates several problems: it ignores the institutionalisation process, that is the set of values and rules, directing acceptance of the idealised tripartite social stratification; and for our analysis of NGOs, although it brings an institutional perspective, it does so within an understanding of sectoral relations which reiterates the conventional, ongoing organisational discussions on partnership and accountability in the literature. Thus, it encourages NGOs to be considered as generic organisational forms for a particular realm within this tripartite division rather than actors as constructed under a certain socio-political process.

Furthermore, this view ignores the fact that its way of seeing the system is an effect of a particular set of socio-political values and norms, or of a discourse.[7] The general neo-liberal development policies provide such a discourse by taking economic growth as their main target, a move whereby organisational forms become independent actors contributing to this aim (Ostrom 1993; Ferguson 1994; Easterly 2002). Brett's perspective provides an important shift in the explanans from individual behaviour based on self-interest to that of an institutional set-up as expressed in an organisational world. However, he moves the level of abstraction without changing the basis of the explanans in self-interest, which now works at the organisational level located within a tripartite ideal institutionalised social division (Moe 1987). This falls short of giving an account of why self-interest is the basis of such a system and also why this tripartite model is taken as the ideal social model. It, therefore, does not say much about the way the activities of these organisations are structured and how norms and values influence their activities. As a result it does not say anything about the power relations constructing

particular outcomes for those who are taking part in a particular institutionalisation process. This approach can only generate discussions that
focus on organisational forms and the rules and norms for procedures of
organisational action, or governance structures (Shepsle 1986; Ostrom 1986;
Williamson 1985).

This is particularly limiting when trying to understand NGOs' capabilities
in the HIV/AIDS context, since this discussion focuses on the ideal model of
an organisation and uses it to get organisations to think about effective procedures or rules for managing themselves (from the perspective of international organisations). In doing this, an understanding is promoted of 'the
end to which their [organisations'] behaviour should be directed' and 'the
means by which those ends' can be achieved (Friedland and Alford 1991:
251). Of course, this leaves unquestioned whether this understanding, based
on a set of procedures and rules, limits what these organisations can think
and do (Friedland and Alford 1991: 243). That is to say, it does not engage
with the effects of capacity building for particular procedures and rules and
what can be done on that basis by these organisations. Moreover, in terms of
action, it deflects interest from concerns about HIV/AIDS to generalised
management issues and capacity-building frameworks. This is not good
enough. Unpacking the way the institutionalisation process constructs and
'constrains' the activities of NGOs requires a dynamic understanding of this
process.

Investigating the institutionalisation mechanism

Mary Douglas's work provides a perspective capable of representing the
institutionalisation process dynamically. In it she uses the term 'institution'
'in the sense of legitimized social grouping' (Douglas 1986: 46). Although
this sounds rather minimalist compared to the more detailed concept of
institution employed by Brett, it effectively locates the discussion into social
processes and tools of legitimation by establishing what can be seen as an
institution. Her position focuses on the entrenchment process of certain ways
of establishing relations as a set of conventions. However, she also notes that
not all conventions turn into 'a legitimate social institution'. This needs a
parallel cognitive convention to sustain it (Douglas 1986: 46). This cognitive
convention, or 'justifying principle', is considered to be outside the grounding
conventions for institutions themselves (Douglas 1986: 46). In this manner
the discussion can engage with the values and rules underpinning and legitimating what is taken to be an established understanding of a social organisation in a given context (Powell 1991: 188–9). In this sense, the tripartite social
stratification can be taken as a convention in creating a capability for NGOs,
while justification for this arrangement is related to the values and perceptions underpinning the emergence of such a stratification which is based on
distinct spheres of social organisation in the first place.

It is these values and perceptions that are considered the source for 'the strategies and cultural constructions employed by individuals' in considering their agency. They 'are drawn from a stock of available discourses (verbal or non-verbal) that are to some degree shared with other individuals, contemporaries or maybe predecessors' (Long 2001: 18).[8] Both Douglas's and Norman Long's perspectives allow us to go beyond the self-interest-based understanding of institutional relations. Clearly, there may be self-interest at play when actors participate in such an institutional relationship and it may tell us why actors participate in this or that process. However, it does not tell us much about the question posed by Douglas, 'Why do you do it like this?' (Douglas 1986: 47). Furthermore in pointing out the values and rules that are related to differentiated socio-cultural repertoires, they allow Douglas's question, in this case for the purposes of understanding NGOs' agency in the HIV/AIDS field, to be responded to by engaging with 'potentially conflicting social and normative interests and diverse and discontinuous configurations of knowledge' (Long 2001: 19). According to Barnett and Finnemore, this orientation brings the relationship between organisations and their environment to bear on what organisations can do (Barnett and Finnemore 1999: 703).

From this perspective of institutionalisation, NGOs appear not as the central reference point (NGO-centrism) of analysis, but as a point of entry to understand a set of relations that create a particular capability for various actors and thus lead to a set of actions. There is no doubt that NGOs participate in the creation of agreed conventions within a process of institutionalisation involving multiple social actors and sites. In this way they become part of the process and contribute to it. But what is presented in the Douglas–Long perspective is the fact that this participation process, which results in some capability attribution, takes place within a set of justificatory norms, values and knowledge claims which allow such participation to occur. This is related to what Douglas calls 'institutions confer identity' (Douglas 1986: 55–67). In doing so, institutions govern from a distance, according to Nikolas Rose, through the guidance provided by language, techniques and tools of governance (Rose 1996).

Douglas provides a coherent understanding for the possibility of such governing. This can be unpacked by looking at the claim that 'to recognize a class of things is to polarize and to exclude' (Douglas 1986: 60). Here, an institutional process clusters things as kinds by establishing what is similar and different. Douglas argues that institutions are similar to theories that are said to confer sameness or distinctness 'by their being held in the embrace of a theoretical structure' (Quine, cited in Douglas 1986: 59). Thus the suggestion is that sameness, or related difference, is not a general attribute but a social construction based on a system of knowledge (or a discourse). In this way it is argued that social analogies used in establishing sameness 'assign disparate items to classes and load them with moral and political content' (Douglas 1986: 63). In this vein those qualities that are generally attributed to NGOs such as flexibility, leadership, efficiency and effectiveness (for example see

Tendler 1982; Fowler 1997) that are used as generic characteristics can be seen within this institutionalised confirmation of identity. Furthermore, this confirmation is also supplemented with moral and political characteristics assumed to follow from these organisations' closeness to the people, taken to be the people's organisations in the processes of democracy.

Here, it is important to note, following Nelson Goodman, that this clustering or confirmation of an identity is very much related with the main values and rules of the confirming process. In Goodman's terms this depends on the cognitive world of 'the world-maker' (Goodman 1978). Douglas considers this process under the heading of 'Institutions do the classifying' (Douglas 1986: 91–109). She suggests that an institutional vision of a world is based on its own values and knowledge claims which are transmitted through processes of systematic channelling of perceptions that form available relational processes for various actors.[9]

The point of this discussion is that individuals or actors participate in diverse realms by making choices through available options regulated by specific systemic categories framing their identity, behaviour and overall agency. This is presented as a dynamic process whereby individuals are able to dream of new ways of being, but where the new way needs to be considered as related to a similar institutionalisation process from a different domain. As Douglas puts it, 'they make new kinds of institutions, and the institutions make new labels and the label makes new kinds of people' (Douglas 1986: 108). In this way, the approach moves on to argue that different institutions use different classifications and therefore that they legitimate different kinds of capabilities. Moreover, the attributed capabilities categorise and classify the beneficiaries of resulting actions according to the discourse of the capabilities. As a result, NGOs determine whom they are dealing with and whose participation they are seeking through these categories.

Barnett and Finnemore follow this framework in analysing the power of international organisations (Barnett and Finnemore 1999: 710–14). In their discussions, the institutionalisation mechanisms articulated by Douglas are linked to the way in which international organisations transmit 'norms and models of "good" political behaviour' (Barnett and Finnemore 1999: 710–13). They also note that it is possible to see an explicit motivation for applying the institutionalisation mechanism because international organisations are 'armed with a notion of progress, an idea of how to create better life . . . [they] have a stated purpose to shape state practices by establishing, articulating, and transmitting norms' to influence other actors' behaviour (Barnett and Finnemore 1999: 713).[10] This can be supplemented by Roland Jepperson's argument that various orders of organisations within a system can function as institutions. He argues that in a multiple organisational system 'primary levels of organisations can operate as institutions relative to secondary levels of organisations' (Jepperson 1991: 146). In this he emphasises that whether an organisation is also an institution depends on its centrality within the system: 'in systems, cores are institutions relative to the peripheries'

(Jepperson 1991: 146). This is central to the ongoing discussion of NGOs within the global governance of HIV/AIDS. In the system, international organisations must be seen as institutions in relation to NGOs which are working at the field level within individual countries. The classification and transmission of norms and activities that can be achieved in this field by various actors are articulated at the international level.

Jepperson's is a particularly useful perspective for engaging with the debates on definitions of NGOs that involves various classifications (Korten 1990; Smillie 1995; Najam 1996; and Vakil 1997). Furthermore the theoretical discussion overcomes the general tendency in the NGO discussions to attribute a certain sameness to NGOs in general, and to developmental NGOs in particular, across the board by relying on overemphasised organisational characteristics.[11] In this way NGOs can be seen as the products of a set of relations between environmental conditions that are instrumental for motivating various forms of organisations around particular issues such as HIV/AIDS. It suggests an argument that various definitions have differentiated institutional locations with important implications for NGO capabilities and resulting action.[12] Furthermore, it brings an understanding of power within a system that informs the organisational outlook of NGOs. In the end, an actor will act according to the framing provided by the institutional context. Note that this is not about how NGO management can balance various relations and decide on its own rationality; it is about how its rationality is influenced/constructed under a particular value system.[13] This, however, does not mean an immediate negative disempowerment for NGOs, since as Jepperson argues 'all institutions simultaneously empower and control' (Jepperson 1991: 146). Thus, analyses of the appropriate agency for interventions in the field in relation to NGOs within the HIV/AIDS policy environment need to be seen as a social construct produced within a particular socio-political and cultural process.

Agency

In the previous section I outlined the way the institutionalisation process functions as the environmental condition for organisations. It argued that this process is mediated through the setting out of objectives and means of achieving them for organisations that are located within a system. Furthermore, it is suggested that international organisations can act as institutions for other organisations insofar as they frame and maintain the policy environment within which other organisations act. This section focuses on discussions of agency, where the aim is to unpack the claim that NGOs have agency in the HIV/AIDS policy field. The institutionalisation perspective provides a theoretical context for looking at agency as a process within a certain power environment rather than as an abstract attribution (Guzzini 2005). Therefore, the section is a response to the question: what does it mean to have agency?

Anthony Giddens suggests that actions and agency are not simply aggregates of disparate actions, but involve 'reflexive monitoring, rationalization and motivation as embedded sets of processes' that are located in 'a discursive moment' (Giddens 1984: 3). Here, the relationship between the actor and its social context is set through a reflexive process which leads to action. According to Norman Long, agency 'is embodied in social relations and can only be effective through them' (Long 2001: 17). He also argues that agency cannot merely be the having of the power of persuasion but also that it needs to rely on 'the emergence of a network of actors who become partially, though hardly ever completely, enrolled in the "project" of some other person or persons' (Long 2001: 17).[14] This distinction between mere persuasion, which can be related to open coercion, and the idea of enrolling into some project within a network is an important analytical tool. Furthermore, the latter can be seen from the perspective of what Rose calls 'to govern at a distance'. This is about a process of institutionalisation in which an authority 'acts to structure the field of decisions rather than directly imposing rules or mandates' (Cooper 1998: 93; Jepperson 1991: 145). In this sense, the idea of governmentality is important, as it suggests that by establishing guidance for action, through channels of expert knowledge and production of tools so that subjects can govern themselves within a set of social relations, a certain normative outlook is employed and managed and thus maintained (Foucault 2000).

This perspective also allows the analysis to look at the process of socialisation, which involves being encultured in a common value and meaning within a network. While an actor is encultured through everyday practices within a particular world of values and meanings, he is also in 'a constitutive relationship' with the institutions of this world (Giddens 1984: 17). Following Lynne Zucker we can say that 'to arrive at shared definitions' actors will have to negotiate 'what defines real for these actors' (Zucker 1991: 84; also see Acharya 2004). Here the earlier discussion on institutionalisation mechanisms within a certain power context becomes central, as it endows actors with differentiated persuasive abilities. These relations are mediated through discursive means which are implicit in the idea of enrolling for a project. The project can be expressed in the forms of setting common aims, goals and missions. Then negotiating a relationship between two actors that are at different levels of the organisational environment can be seen in terms of processes of 'authorisation' (Scott 1991: 175; Finnemore and Sikkink 1998). According to Meyer and Jepperson, 'in negotiating the definitions and rules of [a] system, agents negotiate the basis of their existence and authority' (Meyer and Jepperson 2000: 115). In this, local organisations or NGOs are authorised, legitimated or brought in to participate in the *project*. It is at this stage of the process, that of bringing various NGOs into the policy environment, that their agency is attributed. The isomorphism of their abilities and capabilities to the concept of agency appears as they adopt and become more *professional* in order to deal with the procedural and relational requirements of their position within the system.[15]

This process not only locates the notion of NGO agency within a social process from the perspective of institutionalisation, but it also locates the possibility of an action in relation to HIV/AIDS as determined by it. Donald Davidson suggests a relevant analogy in his discussions of agency. He argues that:

> a man might have the power to destroy the world, in the sense that if he were simply to push a button before him, the world would be destroyed. Yet he would not be free to destroy the world unless he were free to push the button.[16]
>
> (Davidson 1980a)

The distinction of having potential freedom to do something as a physical or psychological attribute and the conditions under which an action can be taken is important. It moves from discussing action as a possibility based on some naturalistic (or individualistic) endowment to the discussion of action under certain *intentionality*. This is linked to meanings and values (or missions) as a condition of that action within a certain social environment. It is this environment that will, in the end, direct the action with both intended and unintended consequences. Davidson's discussion allows one to step outside the common assumption of attributing agency, an ability to act, to NGOs on the basis of a set of abstract and generalised organisational characteristics linked with effectiveness and efficiency independent of social context, as a sort of free agent.[17] His argument suggests, for our purposes, that the actions of NGOs, considered as intentional activities, are much more related to their social environment, which provides the description for their actions, than a natural propensity for certain ways of acting based on their organisational characteristics.

The ongoing discussion underlines a particular understanding of agency that is related to, as Davidson suggests, intentional action which a social environment makes available. Although Giddens disagrees with the link between agency and intentionality, his definition of agency nevertheless seems to follow a similar logic: 'agency refers not to the intentions people have in doing things but to their capability of doing those things in the first place' (Giddens 1984: 9). It seems that Giddens's usage of intentionality is more in line with one that considers intentions as 'freedom to act' on the basis of some context-independent propensity, whereas Davidson's usage indicates a capability within a social context. Giddens seems to prioritise the individual's independent action by suggesting that 'agency concerns events of which an individual is the perpetrator, in the sense that the individual could, at any phase in a given sequence conduct, have acted differently' (Giddens 1984: 9). In this mood he clarifies his position in terms of action and intention by stating that by intention he means 'characterizing an act which its perpetrator knows, or believes, will have a particular quality or outcome and where such knowledge is utilized by the author of the act to achieve this quality of outcome' (Giddens 1984: 10). However, considering his insistence on 'reflexive monitoring' as central for an individual's actions, questions about the sources of an actor's knowledge and beliefs in actions must be raised. Although he insists on differentiating intending and doing in order to be able to talk about intended and unintended outcomes, it is clear that there has to be an explanation as to where the source of the doing is, or in other words why an actor believes in a certain way or knows about *this* way of doing. It is problematic to respond that both intended or unintended outcomes are the result of an actor's doing based on a decision to act that is independent of environment. Otherwise an actor's doing would require an individual decision in the abstract. This approach takes freedom to choose a way of acting as a strong freedom, which suggests that an actor's actions are 'uncaused' (Hampshire 2005: 118–23). This understanding in turn limits the analysis of agency in general, and agency of NGOs in particular, because what they do is articulated independently of the policy environment and based instead on reified beliefs about the nature of NGOs. It seems that Giddens's insistence on this issue misses the point developed by Davidson and others[18] that, in deciding to act, an actor's decision is intentional in so far as it is underpinned by beliefs and knowledge provided by the social environment. Therefore, intentionality is not solely related to the outcomes but also related to the framework for decisions as expressed in values and meaning within a social environment.

Giddens's suggestion of looking at agency as a capability would make more sense as the idea of a capability which is influenced by the values and meanings in a social environment, with a resulting impact on an actor's actions. This also supplements Norman Long's action-oriented approach. He points out that 'actors always face some alternative ways of formulating their objectives, deploying specific modes of action and giving reasons for their behaviour' (Long 2001: 18). Although Long is following Giddens in developing his perspective on actor/agency, he is also aware of the constraint on agency imposed by both the socio-political and cultural environment and the multiple repertoires available to actors in deciding to act.

Central to the view defended above is that actions of actors can be considered under different descriptions provided by different social relations (worlds). In other words, actors can be located in various social environments with different, multiple intentionalities attributed to them. Contra Giddens, whether NGOs choose to act this way or not, this does not mean that they are acting free from an environmental condition. Therefore, in assessing an agency it is central to locate such analysis within the particular social environment that is providing the values and meanings for an actor. Put differently, this perspective discourages an analysis of NGO agency in the abstract, based on a general understanding of organisational forms independent of their environment. It suggests that, if the agency of NGOs is related to a capability of doing something, then it needs to be analysed within a social environment that constructs this capability. Furthermore, this articulation locates NGOs into a set of social relations within which they are constantly relating to a set of actors, creating their identity and constructing their responses to events. Thus, following Meyer and Jepperson, the possibility of NGOs' agency to take part in the HIV/AIDS policy environment to help people is related to their ability to participate in the 'standardized and stylized' ways of acting within the international policy environment (Meyer and Jepperson 2000: 107).

Nevertheless, the organisational emphasis immanent in the NGO literature is difficult to overcome (Holzscheiter 2005). Even Dorothea Hilhorst's innovative research is not immune from this NGO-centric orientation. Hilhorst critically adopts an actor orientation in looking at a number of NGOs in the Cordillera region of the Philippines. She analyses their everyday life and how this influences what they are and what they do within socio-political networks. She considers these NGOs as interface points within social networks where values and meanings are negotiated. In this, she seems to follow Giddens in his articulation of agency and action. Therefore, she considers NGOs as spaces, or interfaces, providing a capability for such negotiation among various actors participating in NGO activity whereby, in turn, NGOs themselves are able to influence various actors. For instance, in elaborating a point about the limited role played by culture in mediating relations among staff of various levels of seniority, she notes that:

> some staff members subject to management criticism were openly defended, some issues evoked heavy discussion without regard for smooth relations, and diversity among staff members, alternative possibilities for response. Organisation practices were therefore not *invaded* by Philippine culture, but NGO actors *drew on* [the dominant Philippine] culture.
>
> (Hilhorst 2003: 168, emphasis in original)

She then goes on to show how the NGO allows this space to be differentiated from the local culture. Her analysis implies a distinction between social context and what the NGO does that, in her view, both provides capability to people and makes it capable itself for action independent of any discourse providing such ability (Hilhorst 2003: 11; Foucault 1990). Moreover, the emphasis given to the agency, which is observed in the NGO and differentiated from the socio-political and cultural context, appears to be given an implicit acontextual quality. Of course, there is a tension in this when Hilhorst suggests that 'the tendency towards hierarchy was counterbalanced by ideas prevailing in the office that were drawn from feminist, participatory and indigenous discourses, as well as discourses on management' (Hillhorst 2003: 169). Thus, the interface which opens up the space was not the result of a particular organisational form but due to various intentionality sets that are described from various discourses/worlds.

Considering NGOs as interfaces is a more productive move than those usually found in the literature. However, it still does not say much about what the framework is for the assumed capability of NGOs and what they are capable of in that framework. It is silent about how the perception of agency is institutionalised under particular social-political contexts, These problems show the importance of Davidson's contribution.

The agency discussion developed by Giddens in relation to the idea of capability needs to be supplemented with Davidson's position that agency is a capability to act where that capability is meaningful or available to the actor under a certain description. 'Description' here can be taken to mean discourse legitimating certain ways of acting and being, based on a set of values and meanings embedded in knowledge claims (in Hilhorst's case a feminist one, a managerial one or a participatory one). Thus, Hilhorst's tools can be seen as techniques for governing from a distance to maintain a particular NGO outlook. Therefore, the particular conflict resolution processes based on various discourses become a function of a set of values and norms that have been set down as the relevant knowledge domains. While this is progress, it can be taken yet further by looking at this as a process of institutionalisation of social capability.

If we consider NGOs as an interface then it follows that the actors related in the interface represent different social contexts. Thus, it provides various sets of differentiated identities for actors, and that is values and meanings for the process of institutionalisation by which a perception about the capability/ agency is formed for NGOs. Rather than assuming that the NGO form *per se* provides a generic space within which people can utilise various forms of action unavailable to them in a particular culture, it is more productive to think what values and meanings allow this space to be created in particular social settings. In this way, the capability attributed to NGOs, or agency, will be related to what they are expected to do within a process of institutionalisation rather than analysing them by what they are assumed to do, independent of any social context, be it local, national or international.

In summary, in this section I discussed a theoretical framework that considers the important relationship between the environmental processes informing the emergence of claims of agency. It also underwrites the analysis of agency in terms of NGO capabilities. It argues that these need to be located within social processes implicit in multiple institutionalised settings which frame their identity and agency in a differentiated manner. In this sense the agency attributed to NGOs within the international policy environment in general, and within the HIV/AIDS field in particular, should be analysed at least from two domains: from the domain of international policy as one institutional framework and from within the target community perspective. The former institutionalises NGOs on the basis of their assumed connections with people on the ground. This attribution, which informs NGO activities, is about the values and knowledge base of the former rather than those that arise from 'the demands of their work activities' (Meyer and Rowan 1991:

41). In order to evaluate NGO agency on its relevance for what it aims to achieve for people's lives, the social environment of the people who are targeted and the way this environment locates NGOs must be discussed. This approach views NGOs' activity as being a part of various institutionalisation processes at the same time, each involving dissimilar capability assumptions on the basis of differentiated cultures and value systems underpinned by dissimilar rationalities. The question that naturally follows is: what does this framework tell us about the role of NGOs within the HIV/AIDS field? This is looked at briefly in the next section. It requires us to look at whether the international institutionalisation of NGOs in the HIV/AIDS policy field is relevant for people's everyday lives.

NGOs and HIV/AIDS: a question of agency

The international policy processes create particular capability sets for NGOs within the international policy field which can be seen as agency. According to UNAIDS, in order to engage with comprehensive prevention at a larger scale a multi-sectoral approach is central in which 'key collaborators include faith based organisations, NGOs, organizations of people living with HIV and private industry and workers' organizations' (UNAIDS 2004c: 91). The role of civil society organisations is also recognised in delivering treatment and in finding innovative approaches in the area (UNAIDS 2004c: 106). The UNAIDS report goes on to argue that 'civil society organizations often innovate approaches to the epidemic, and can channel funds to communities, augment state service delivery, and monitor national government policies' (UNAIDS 2004c: 157). Through these definitional arguments, UNAIDS indicates areas of capability for NGOs. In other words, the acknowledgement of NGOs' work in the field is also a way of articulating their agency in relation to the international policy priorities, where recognition is based on the existing priorities that are implicit in general policy frameworks. In this way a clear agency is attributed to NGOs in the field of service delivery which is focused on care, prevention activities and treatment. The approach considers these organisational forms in generic terms with an agency that can be capitalised on independent of socio-political contexts. A good example of this can be seen in the extrapolation of an abstract agency from the innovative work of a few organisations engaged with treatment, such as Partners in Health and Médecins Sans Frontières, to suggest a generalised NGO agency for these kinds of interventions in general (UNAIDS 2004c: 106).

Institutional values I

The report also provides insights about the ideal relationship between governments and these actors by stating that governments 'need to provide a positive environment' by establishing mechanisms such as 'legal recognition' and 'tax incentives' and also that their administrations 'need to be flexible enough to include local NGOs' (UNAIDS 2004c: 158). Here, the above-articulated generalised capability framework is strengthened by locating it within a generalised relationship with governments.

The relationship established in this manner between governments and NGOs, which creates an important capability for NGOs, is a familiar one from the World Bank's intervention strategies too. As one of the largest donors in this field, the Bank has developed a Multi-Country HIV/AIDS Program for Africa (MAP) (World Bank 2004). Since its inception 28 African countries and three regional programmes have received US$1,088 million (World Bank 2004). One of the five principal reasons for developing this facility, the Bank argues, is that both national and international support have been too slow in scaling up programmes developed by NGOs. The key characteristic of MAP is its direct funding of 'the community organisations, NGOs, and the private sector for local HIV/AIDS initiatives'. In this process two related governance issues are central: (a) 'the creation of a high level HIV/AIDS coordination body' (in the shape of a National Aids Council with broad membership) and (b) getting governments to agree on channelling funding directly to 'the community and civil society sector' and to 'use and fund multiple implementation agencies, especially community-based and non-governmental organisations' (World Bank 2004). These aims are also used as the eligibility criteria for MAP participation. Recognition of civil society organisations or NGOs in this framework shares the reference points for their capability articulated by UNAIDS. The convergence between UNAIDS and the World Bank is not a coincidence but a reflection of the common perception of NGOs within the international policy circles.[19]

The implicit relationship between these perspectives and the capability attributed is more explicit with respect to the recognised role of NGOs in innovative treatment delivery in the 2004 report. It illustrates a relationship between international frameworks and the agency of NGOs. With the changing focus in international fora in terms of treatment, the abilities attributed to the NGOs were gradually, and more firmly, articulated in UNAIDS reports. For instance, while in the 2002 report the difficulty of delivering drugs under a stressed developmental context was considered to be important, few attempts in this respect were recognised as working examples (UNAIDS 2002b). In contrast the 2004 report recognises the ability of NGOs on treatment as one of the characteristics of NGOs in this field: 'NGOs have been treatment pioneers' (UNAIDS 2004c: 106). Given that the organisations used for illustration of this point have been involved in treatment for a long time, this suggests that the shift between two reports can be attributed to a changing perspective at the international level. According to the UNAIDS report 2004, in the field of treatment NGOs have a double role of delivery and innovation for the methods of delivery (UNAIDS 2004c: 106). It is in this context that NGOs are constructed as pioneers in treatment. Thus a new capability, an agency, is added to their arsenal in addition to the already-recognised capabilities in care and prevention, capabilities which are linked with the traditional advocacy and service delivery roles, set out by the World Bank and others.

The combination of the Bank's insistence on the inclusion of NGOs in general and the UNAIDS recognition of new areas for NGOs to be involved in provides new spaces for NGO activities, with implicit capabilities attributed to them for those areas. The agency considered from this angle makes NGOs capable of delivering international policies based on an assumption of their closeness to people and communities, and based on generalised organisational assumptions about flexibility that permit them immediate response.

In these articulations one sees a direct link to a particular institutional thinking on the role of various sectors dominant in the literature on third-sector organisations, a neo-Tocquevillian civil society (Seckinelgin 2002). In thinking about direct funding to civil society organisations and NGOs, the international policy actors, such as the World Bank and UNAIDS, have a specific understanding of the role of this sector in relation to governments. Furthermore, this thinking is also a function of the earlier discussions on the role of civil society in the development sector, where governments were seen as corrupt and very bureaucratic, while NGOs were seen as more flexible and directly connected to the people. In addition, in this framework to aid democratic institutions, NGOs were considered as the right agencies by creating pressure on governments for change. Therefore, HIV/AIDS and related NGO activity are now brought under this value and norm system which is also changing to reconsider the role of states as policy enablers rather than public service providers. In other words, NGOs are institutionalised within the international policy processes, and their role reflects changes in the perceptions of international actors. Following James Ferguson, this can also be attributed to the particular construction of African problems as an object of development within the world view of these international organisations which are engaging with the HIV/AIDS crisis (Ferguson 1994, 1999; Mitchell 1995).

Institutional values II

This perspective on HIV/AIDS is a variant of a general institutional world view which dominates policy frameworks. It has been developed on the basis of Poverty Reduction Strategy Papers (PRSPs) on the limited government and state involvement in social services and controls on public spending. The PRSP process is evidence of one of Barnett and Finnemore's organisational pathologies, 'Insulation' (Barnett and Finnemore 1999: 722–3). However, contra Barnett and Finnemore I argue that even if there is a feedback loop at the international level (Barnett and Finnemore 1999: 723) the outcome is normalised within the existing world view held within the international organisation. For instance, according to the World Bank's *Local Government Responses to HIV/AIDS: Handbook* (World Bank 2003):

> while it is not appropriate to expect all LGAs [local government author-
> ities] to roll out extensive HIV/AIDS programmes, in general they can
> play an important role in identifying local needs mainstreaming HIV/
> AIDS activities within LGA departments and coordinating responses
> (i.e. facilitating partnerships).
>
> (World Bank 2003: vii)

The importance of partnering with civil society organisations, community
groups and people living with HIV is emphasised throughout the book. The
book suggests that development and implementation of HIV/AIDS is not the
core business of local government; its main role is to identify and prioritise
areas of problems 'to create [an] enabling environment for the participation'
of other stakeholders in these areas (World Bank 2003: 13). Considered from
this angle, the question of NGO agency becomes more closely related to the
developmental frameworks that are relevant in the international policy context.[20] Therefore, the role of NGOs in this area becomes more meaningful by
the sectoral positioning of civil society organisations into a set of activities
where they replace the governments.

The maintenance mechanism of this institutionalisation, or the mechanism
for governing from a distance in this system, can be seen in two processes
leading to isomorphism (both coercive and mimetic)[21] in the HIV/AIDS policy field. One is the way funding relations are developed and the second is the
organisational mechanisms required by the international actors for intervention. Both of these processes construct NGOs as agents. The MAP requirements for coordination and accountability from its participants provide a
good example of this. Similarly, the LGA handbook also has clear indica-
tions along these lines since it provides tools for developing an enabling
environment and well-defined categories of actors and specifies the area of
intervention. In developing their HIV/AIDS strategies for funding, LGs are
told that they will need a strategy and good management. In this, to receive
funding a strategy should be considered as 'shaped by clear priorities and
outlining activities, inputs, outputs and outcomes' (World Bank 2003: 21).
These priorities are also substantiated by suggesting that 'the main objective
of the LG HIV/AIDS Response Strategy and its implementation is to support ongoing local responses to HIV/AIDS, leverage funding, build partnerships to fill unmet needs in the locality (i.e. VCT services, adolescent outreach
programs etc.)' (World Bank 2003: 22). And this is just one illustration of
how categories of what can be done are transmitted.

The categories that are established according to the social relations in, and
perceived according to, the international systems are also transmitted by creating new policy frameworks for action. For instance, one such process can be
observed in the creation of National AIDS Councils as required by MAP and
the UNAIDS Three Ones policy that has developed to be the guiding
principles for national authorities and their partners (UNAIDS 2004b). It
contains three organisational principles: an agreed HIV/AIDS Action

Framework to coordinate all partners' work; a National AIDS Coordinating Authority with a broad multi-sectoral mandate; and one agreed country-level monitoring and evaluation strategy. These are said to be totally in line 'with OECD/ DAC criteria' and they 'seek to accommodate different aid modalities, while striving to ensure effective aid management procedures and to reduce transaction cost for countries' (UNAIDS 2004a). By translating the concerns of the donors to fit the institutionalisation process shaping the national sectoral relations, NGOs are further located within the interests and values of the international system.

These are the institutional boundaries within which NGOs exercise their agency. As Davina Cooper notes, this is not a 'zero-sum game. Governing institutions can give resources to and empower individuals and groups' (Cooper 1998: 181). The process channels what can be done by NGOs and controls how it should be done, and it is clear that a certain developmental logic is maintained in these relations.

Of course, this interpretation might be criticised by claiming that the above-discussed institutionalisation in fact allows NGOs to engage with policy makers and they can exercise their agency in influencing policy frameworks. At a superficial level this may sound right, but I agree with Mary Douglas when she suggests that institutions 'fix processes that are essentially dynamic, they hide their influence, and they rouse our emotions to a standardized pitch on standardized issues' (Douglas 1986: 92). By devising a coherence strategy based on three national levels, the influence of the international policy environment in providing guidance is rhetorically distantiated. In this manner a critical link between the international decision makers and local actors is broken while maintaining the influence of the former on the latter. The policy management is located at the national level in such a way that donors interact with a limited number of actors and yet still govern the nature of interventions, that is decide what are the appropriate means for policy implementations in the priority areas.

Institutional values III

This process fits closely with the prevailing thinking about the nature of actors who are the main participants in policy and decision-making processes at the international level. Although many international organisations grant observer or participant status to non-governmental actors, the decision-making process and negotiations leading to the final policy are by and large still under the mandate of the state actors and governed by their foreign policy interests (Chabbott 1999; Wendt 1999). Daphné Josselin and William Wallace observe that, although in the last 40 years the influence of non-state actors on the international policy-making process has increased through knowledge and advocacy networks,[22] the state remains central to international politics. They argue that 'global campaigning is unlikely to bring positive results unless at least some state actors (and preferably those in the

LIVERPOOL JOHN MOORES UNIVERSITY
LEARNING SERVICES

West) endorse the agenda of private organisations' (Josselin and Wallace 2001: 257). They also point to a dependency relationship of these actors on states in terms of funding and note that they 'are willing to serve as conduits for foreign policy of their government' (Josselin and Wallace 2001: 258). This understanding highlights a peculiarity of international relations. International relations discourse only considers non-state actors as having some influence in so far as they are taking part in the discussions related to the systemic level.[23] Therefore, as a natural default, this system would not see local NGOs as directly relevant actors to the social relations in the international social space (Josselin and Wallace 2001; Wendt 1999; Boli and Thomas 1999). In general this view frames the process and locations of NGOs within international politics at large.[24]

From this perspective then it is possible to consider, for example, Three Ones, in line with Douglas, as a process that maintains itself, in this case, in relation to the values and norms of the international system by controlling the categories and classifications of priorities, tools and knowledge within an information system in the institutional arrangements. In this way, the agency of NGOs is actually removed from direct engagement with the international policy decision-making process.[25] In the context of the system discussed, this is also done through the mechanism of management and accountability procedures (the process of normative isomorphism)[26] that are supplemented by Western knowledge claims within the international policies. Douglas articulates the outcome of this process for those who are participating in the system as 'a narcissistic self-contemplation' which implies 'any problems we try to think about are automatically transformed into their own organisational problems. The problems they proffer only come from the limited range of their experiences' (Douglas 1986: 92). These points resonate with the present discussion, since they speak of a loss of an important critical distance for those actors taking part in the institutionalisation process. They lose a critical engagement with the overall value and norm system they are engaged with. As a result, the international process goes on reproducing the system without questioning its fundamental values. Finnemore and Sikkink argue that NGOs in this process are constructed, implicitly, as platforms for norm promotion by the international actors (Finnemore and Sikkink 1998: 899).

From the point of view of new intervention methods discussed in the HIV/ AIDS field, it can be argued that while most gesture towards achieving certain aims most actors, in particular NGOs, are mediated and regulated by identified organisational problems. In order to achieve these aims the application of proven management tools is delivered in many capacity-building exercises by international donors. This also reflects a general tendency in the literature to focus on management problems of NGOs as the route to achieve their aims. Arguably these tools and methods are established to form NGOs and their functions in such a way that international actors can recognise and access their work. While clearly good management is important, it does not provide the independence and agency required to influence long-term sustainable behaviour change for dealing with HIV/AIDS in its many diverse socio-cultural contexts.

Why does this matter?

Thus far I have argued that agency considered as a capability to do is a function of institutional processes within which actors are located. The agency attributed to NGOs in the HIV/AIDS field follows this pattern. They are considered to do things according to certain values on social relations and according to certain policy priorities on the disease. In this sense there is no doubt that NGOs are capable *to do* within the framework provided by the international processes, in other words to deliver services and provide agency for interventions to supplement areas where governments are not *supposed* to intervene or are too bureaucratic to initiate fast and flexible strategies.

While NGOs are attributed capabilities following this instrumental rationality in this field, the implicit aspirational links between NGOs and people underpinning the sectoral perspectives in the international sphere should not be ignored, because NGOs use these categories and classifications to manage their relations with people. There needs to be consideration on whether the link between people and attributed agency actually holds in order to evaluate NGOs as capable organisations in relation to people. Then the question that should be asked is how the institutionalisation of NGOs rearticulates the links between NGOs and people from the perspective of local institutionalisation processes. The following insights from the research in Sub-Saharan Africa are used to focus on those areas where NGOs are supposed to have capability in engaging with people.

One area to be assessed in this situation is one of the most common intervention areas by NGOs in the field: sensitisation and condom distribution. A veteran NGO worker in Botswana argued that *NGOs got it all wrong for years by talking about condoms and distributing them without really knowing how they are used. The information provided*, according to her, *has created a stigma and a fatigue from being told unless condoms are used people will die*. She suggested that *this was a wrong way of engaging with the issue, as creating a strategy based on a threat was not effective but was merely going to add to the moralisation of sex and exacerbate the stigma*. She also argued that *this flawed approach was applied by most organisations and supported by international donors and policy makers who provided the methods of implementation and the messages used*. According to an international NGO working in Rwanda, as a result of PEPFAR (US President's Emergency Plan for AIDS Relief) policies they were not getting funding for condoms but I was told that of course *we have to diversify our resource base with these interventions and get German GTZ for funding to support our condom initiative while doing other service delivery interventions under PEPFAR*.

The example which was used in Chapter 1 from Zambia also provides an interesting case. There it was argued that there were a few problems with condom promotion by NGOs. A senior NGO worker said that, *in an attempt to get people to use condoms, a lot of NGOs initiated not very socially or economically appropriate interventions, some of which as a result added to the stigma or devaluation of condom use in general . . . another issue was the problem of frequency of use. Some people felt that after using condoms three times they were covered and could stop using condoms.* Overall he was suggesting that *NGOs had a huge credibility problem with people on the basis of their past experience.*

In these typical examples from the region there is a pattern which appears to falsify the assumed relationship between people and NGOs as people's organisations. While NGOs remain flexible organisations staffed by local people, their link to influence behaviour change in their own communities is questioned. In becoming actors for service delivery NGOs are locating themselves in a set of social relations institutionalised at the international level. In this they are articulating their needs on the basis of international frameworks. This process frustrates their ability to respond to the needs articulated within local institutional processes and relations. The instrumental question of how to develop a poster, or deliver a particular condom message, is taking over and is leaving the issue of whether the message itself is relevant, or the articulated target group is relevant, critically unquestioned. In other words, the critical insights which NGOs may have as a result of their links with communities are bypassed. It is also true that NGOs use the idea of their closeness to people as a policy trope to have access to resources and negotiate their relations within the international system. In this process, however, the NGOs' closeness to local communities is becoming a function of having local staff rather than having a localised agency.

This issue has been raised by a number of people who have worked in the field in Botswana, Lesotho, Rwanda and Zambia in various capacities such as HIV positive activists, NGO workers, communication analysts and participants in international policy environments. The common problem observed was that the assumptions behind the interventions reflect policy interest and what is seen as important within international policy frameworks that are based on international policy targets decided on the basis of generalised target and risk groups. This takes place more and more through capacity-building exercises, whereby local groups are trained in the ways of international actors and in substantive content about how to engage with the designated target groups or patients as the beneficiaries of implementations. From the perspective of a major donor in one of these countries it was clear that the appropriate intervention actors were civil society and NGOs. However, since they lack capacity, the donor has to do a lot of organisational capacity building around how to manage money, how to maintain their project focus and build specific expertise and how to access funding. The same view was also expressed by an international NGO that was given funding to work on VCTs through local civil society. They found no capacity available for such work and therefore they had to build capacity for local NGOs and community groups to be able to work together. In the view of a local expert in Maseru, Lesotho, there was a lot of activity but *workshops are designed and nothing is done in a real sense as no follow-up or anything else is done. Mostly as some of these organisations have to spend the money within a given time they would have a workshop in an expensive venue and invite all the usual suspects. Workshops, training sessions are about paying people to attend. Training in what? Capacity building for whom?* In terms of the work done, another counsellor suggested that there was *no real sense of groups working on the ground; they are mostly international and there is no real sense of coordination.*

Particularly in the processes following the US President's Emergency Plan for AIDS Relief (PEPFAR) in 2004, which is to provide around US$15 billion funding for 15 countries, the institutionalisation of NGOs can be seen more clearly. The funding from this framework is channelled through the US-based large INGOs to directly help the communities via their own organisations and groups. However, it is soon realised that in many countries these organisations do not exist in the way the funding framework requires. Therefore, intermediary contractors are brought in to build capacity. For instance, the weakness of existing NGOs and community groups in Lesotho led to Pact-Building Capacity Worldwide[27] being brought in. According to their documentation Pact, Inc. (Pact) in Lesotho is working 'under an associate award issued by the United States Agency for International Development's (USAID) Regional HIV/AIDS Program for Southern Africa (USAID/RHAP)'. Its main aim is to provide funding for assistance to registered 'Basotho non-governmental organisations (NGOs), faith-based organisations (FBOs) and community-based organisations (CBOs) currently providing support or with the capacity to quickly and efficiently provide support in response to the HIV/AIDS crisis in Lesotho'.[28] This need for capacity building is linked with PEPFAR's focus on service delivery-based interventions as well as its strong emphasis on abstinence.[29] The inclusion of local groups has been justified as a mechanism to 'ensure flexibility to target resources to address areas of greatest need; and ensuring results'[30] by the president. This case is a clear example of how the international policy perspective is shaping NGO activities.

According to a large US-based INGO working under the PEPFAR framework, while they were rolling out voluntary counselling and testing (VCT) and treatment facilities across Rwanda, *there was no way local organisations could maintain or sustain this level of intervention without international funding and capacity building for the immediate operational functions. However, so long as local organisations participating in the projects are able to achieve to involve a certain number of patients set by the donors in the VCT process, we would be considered as successful according to the funding regime.* In terms of the government's ability to take over, it was argued that, *particularly in the ARV area, this is a problem. There is a problem of training and lack of capable physicians. It is not clear how the takeover can be sustained. Coordination and overtaking is a long jump (particularly considering that the government is decentralising its health services). We are playing the role of welfare state. Services are needed so we are delivering but the question of sustainability does not even come into this debate.* Thus, while technically achieving good numbers in delivering services, the long-term process is not even discussed. In another organisation working under similar conditions it was also suggested that maybe international NGOs have too much involvement with national policies owing to a lack of local expertise. Yet some NGOs sit on national committees and participate in discussions about what needs to happen. Given the link between international NGOs and the international policy actors, it appears that this INGO participation is another way of institutionalising governments into the international policy frameworks. In Lesotho, a similar view was expressed in a more direct manner: *government is very much in donor agenda as they want to see them happy.* This is clearly linked with the donor commitment to provide large sums of aid over five years, which sometimes can be larger than individual countries' individual budget lines.

Most of these cases demonstrate a pattern where NGOs' assumed location within communities is used as a policy trope, while their links with people, that would have allowed different ways of thinking about interventions, are not valorised. Therefore, while NGOs become partners and gain access to resources and negotiate within the given frameworks of the international system, the assumed benefits of these institutionalisation processes are not realised by people who are in need and supposed to be linked with NGOs. By attributing agency to NGOs, the international system constructs the organisational form as a resource category, within its own world view, to be utilised as an efficient and effective way of engaging with the disease at community level on the basis of categories and classifications provided by them to NGOs for intervention. Some of these are very clear when looking at people on the basis of particular risk groups and target groups, or under the generalised category of patients. This last category makes sense in international policy circles since the idea of being a patient, from medical models being used, indicates a certain agency and capability (Parker 2001; Campbell 2003). However, by being categorised into one of these slots people usually become disempowered within their own socio-cultural and economic contexts. In this process of recategorisation, people's critical perspectives in relation to social institutions they live in are ignored. Also, as the implementers using these categories, NGOs gradually become dissociated from their social spaces. In the eyes of the people they become actors of international interventions rather than long-term partners for change.

Conclusion

Following Douglas, I argue that to attempt an analysis of NGOs as value-free organisational forms is a reflection of, or a technology for, governmentality within a particular Western thinking,[31] and thus such attempts are not value-free. In other words, the conventional focus on organisational form and getting management technologies right in order to be able to participate in the international policy environment neutralises our understanding of what these NGOs can actually do. In this way NGO agency is constructed within the institutionalisation context of international policy.

The perspective developed here considers agency as a capability of doing something. Therefore, it links any claim of agency with what an organisation is actually able to do and achieve, rather than considering agency as an aspirational potentiality, as is done in NGO-related claims. Following from this understanding of agency, a capability of doing is located within a set of institutional processes that direct who can do something in an issue area and what this doing can be. In other words, the institutional framework for agency is considered as central to actors and their capability sets.

This idea considers the capability set as a function of the environment within which an organisation is located. It also argues that international organisations construct and maintain behaviour types and means of action for particular aims guided by accepted norms and rules of acting in their particular field. This general starting point is deepened by Douglas's articulations of how social institutions function. Using these allowed the discussion of the mechanisms within which actors are incorporated into such institutions and how this process influences their actions and their impact in the field. The conceptualisation also views NGOs as institutionalised in various socio-political contexts at the same time. Therefore, the agency claim needs to be understood as a function of what an organisation is capable of doing and for whom this represents an agency. Overall this constructivist framework points out a major problem in considering a generalised agency based on certain aspirational qualities of NGOs. It points out a need to look at whether a claim for agency is founded on particular socio-political contexts within which NGOs are *capable* of doing certain things. In order to attribute agency, such analysis needs to look at what they are able to do and why they are able to do *that* within a particular context. Furthermore, such analysis should be supplemented with an understanding of the institutional relations relevant to these questions. In other words, a response to the question of *who considers what is done as a success* is central.

The HIV/AIDS field is an important policy area within which NGOs have become very important actors. The analysis here suggests that NGOs do have agency from the perspective of the international system, which considers them as good service delivery actors to be utilised to overcome bureaucratic government structures. In this process there is a convergence of identity of NGOs and an understanding about what they can do and how they can do it. In this isomorphism one of the main assumptions is the closeness of NGOs to people; it assumes that their interventions will have an important impact on the ground. In the context of HIV/AIDS it assumes that they are able to achieve or support long-term sustainable behaviour change. However, the assessment of such agency needs to be looked at from the perspective of local institutional processes and how they relate to these so-called people's organisations. On that score, the claimed agency leaves a lot to be desired. The result is a paradoxical situation: while NGOs are able to participate as actors in the international system because of their claimed links with people, this same participation leads into an institutionalisation process which breaks their links within local institutions, thus creating the need to question their agency.

In this discussion the aim is not to suggest that NGOs have no agency. It is very clear that there are successful and innovative organisations.[32] However, it is misguided to extrapolate a generalised agency for the NGO organisational form from such important work. The success and the achievements of these organisations need to be analysed within the socio-political and cultural contexts of their work and the way different groups have engaged with their chosen intervention areas.

3   Medicalisation

We need social drugs. New drugs will help the disease but they will not solve the social problems and stigma.

(S. in Uganda, 2002)

While spending the day in an HIV/AIDS clinic, I had a long interview with S. He was very open about his status and had been so publicly. He was acting as an HIV positive activist to put a face to the anonymity of the disease. He told me that his wife had died from an AIDS-related disease and now he was looking after their young daughter on his own in the city. Gradually our conversation touched on the question of treatment. He commented that this was *a very important change as I would be able to look after my daughter and try to support her while growing up*. But *nothing will change the social stigma*, he said. This was a surprise to me as at the time in Uganda HIV/AIDS campaigns were highly visible and everyone seemed to know about the disease. Elaborating, he said that *everyone knows about it but it does not change people's attitudes. Still when I go back to the village no one wants to talk to me about my condition. But if the elders realise there is another person with potential HIV, they ask this person to come to the city and talk to me*. He said *none of these pills will overcome the stigma; we need social pills*.

From this one can observe the delineation of two processes which have become more pronounced today. People with the disease have become gradually more subject to medical interventions as treatment has been made more available. This, however, has not changed the context much within which people experience the disease. They are still exposed to some variant of stigma. Clearly, this is not to argue that medical interventions or treatment in particular have exacerbated the stigma problems, but rather to point out that treatment has not led to change in the attitudes that occur within social contexts towards those who are infected or affected by HIV/AIDS. This latter process of stigmatisation becomes more significant as more and more investment on treatment is prioritised without any corresponding increase in the focus on how to deal with the stigma and its associated social and economic consequences.

Since its emergence in the 1980s HIV/AIDS has been seen as creating ill-health conditions that highlight social, economic and cultural fault lines in societies and as exposing processes of marginalisation and exclusion. Despite this, attempts to deal with the disease and its consequences have been addressed more and more through medical concerns and methods. Decisions on policy interventions have been based more and more on HIV/AIDS as a medical condition without similarly serious attention being paid to its social, economic and cultural aspects. In particular the emergence of treatment as a feasible option in developing countries has pushed the interventions this way. Here, in the way S. uses 'social pills better' as a metaphor is indicative of the existing approach of dealing with problems by using the logic of medical interventions. Here, the process that has been highlighted is called 'medicalisation'. It not only represents an encounter between Western science and its attempt to deal with what is designated as the subject matter of medical interventions, but it also indicates an encounter that changes people's everyday lives. Furthermore, it works through an already-existing colonial substructure of medical expansion, within particular power relations discussed in the Introduction as the location to develop HIV/AIDS interventions. In the following section I briefly look at the concept of medicalisation to highlight why it is relevant for our understanding of HIV/AIDS interventions.

Medicalisation

In his literature review on the topic of medicalisation Peter Conrad provides a number of basic definitions. He describes the concept as 'a process by which nonmedical problems become defined and treated as medical problems, usually in terms of illness or disorder' (1992: 209). By doing this he combines two earlier definitions, one by I.K. Zola, who coined the concept, and his own earlier definition. I.K. Zola used it to indicate the expanding scope of medical rationality 'as a process whereby more and more everyday life has come under medical domination, influence and supervision' (1983: 295). The other concept is Conrad's, who saw the process as 'defining behaviour as a medical problem or illness and mandating or licensing the medical profession to provide some type of treatment for it' (1975: 12). Both definitions are useful for providing a way of looking at the relationship between medicalisation as a social process and the people who are coming into contact with this process. According to Zola, the process of bringing more aspects of daily life under a medical rationale eventually leads to more social control (Zola 1972: 487–504; also see Bilton *et al.* 1996).[1] According to Lock and Scheper-Hughes, medicalisation 'entails a missed identification between the individual and the social bodies and a tendency to transform the social into the biological' (Lock and Scheper-Hughes 1996). The issue Zola is addressing is how problems that are faced in various aspects of life are now addressed with solutions based on medical treatment and considerations. Marcel Verweij points out that medicalisation is foremost a conceptual process, 'a change in discourse and a concurrent change of the way people see and understand certain things in their lives' (1999: 92). Conrad's position supports this view since he argues that it 'consists of defining a problem in medical terms, using medical language to describe a problem, adopting a medical framework to understand a problem, or using a medical intervention to "treat" it' (1992: 211). This also indicates that medicalisation can be initiated at various levels with varied scope. Conrad suggests that the process can occur at the conceptual, the institutional and the interactional level (1992: 211). One of the most important aspects of this is the link between the processes at various levels and the medical profession. Conrad notes that, while the process is one of definition and conceptual rethinking of people's conditions and subsequent provision of *treatment*, 'this is a sociocultural process that may or may not involve the medical profession, or be the result of intentional expansion by the medical profession' (1992: 211). In other words, the medical profession's contribution to this process is conditioned by other institutionalisation processes that are promoting or creating the conditions for medicalisation. This also links to the expansion of colonial medicine that was discussed in the Introduction. In her *A Colonial Lexicon of Birth Ritual, Medicalization and Mobility in the Congo* Nancy Rose Hunt provides an important example of how the medicalisation process was conjoined with colonial politics on resource extraction, religion and the particular concern of racial purity (1999). Thus, while medicalisation can be observed as an expansion in the scope of the medical in people's lives, the process is also critically underpinned by changing political relations in the social contexts where it occurs.

Paul Chodoff's perspective provides another way of looking at the issue. He sees medicalisation as the application of:

> a diagnostic label to various unpleasant or undesirable feelings or behaviors that are not distinctly abnormal but that fall within a gray area not readily distinguishable from the range of experiences that are often inescapable aspects of the fate of being human.
>
> (2002: 1)

This fits with Hunt's study where it was clear that medicalisation was a process by the colonial powers transforming the everyday experiences of people that were seen as undesirable in the Congolese context. There are a number of ways in which the transformation occurs (Bilton *et al.* 1996: 430–2): (a) the incorporation and redefinition of local and common approaches to health, (b) the efficacy of scientific medicine is prioritised and (c) alternative medical approaches are marginalised. Furthermore, as pointed out by Conrad, this process also involves a process whereby a right way for dealing with undesirable behaviours is articulated through medical treatment and control (1992: 213). According to Henry Ivarature these represent in developing countries 'the medicalization of public policy objectives', that is 'a rationalization and a bureaucratization of what is perceived as a "health problem"' (2000: 47). He also agrees with the general view that this involves a degree of social control in which 'medicine marks the social limits of gender behavior and specifies what is considered normal and what is deviant' (2000: 49). He argues further that this process provides a source of domination, in which, for instance, a gender group becomes the focus of public policy. This position was further supported by Phillippa Levine's work *Prostitution, Race and Politics: Policing Venereal Disease in the British Empire* (2003). In this, she argues, for instance, that in their approach to venereal diseases medical professionals through their 'concern about particular behavior, responsibility and culpability were associating VD with sexual promiscuity'. In this way concern for propriety merged the medical and the moral in colonial medicine (2003: 65). These categories perceived as 'aberrant sexualities and of oversexedness' had become 'medical conditions' (Levine 2003: 65).

In addition, Verweij argues that the medicalisation process is relevant for preventative medicine. He argues that in this case medicalisation refers to 'the phenomenon that people tend to consider even normal situations or activities from a medical perspective' (1999: 91). Of course another important aspect of this occurs with the individual who becomes the basis of interventions, albeit as a part of a particular target population. As noted by Lock and Scheper-Hughes (1996) the individual within a certain social context is typically transformed into a patient.[2] In this the patient is related to the medical profession within a particular power relationship which is underpinned by scientific knowledge claims. It is at this point that the social control aspect of medicalisation becomes important since the imbalanced relationship between the medical professional and patient results in a loss of control over everyday life. Furthermore, according to Verweij, personal responsibility in relation to illness and the risky behaviour leading to it come into the picture as a part of this control mechanism whereby risky behaviour is construed in moral terms (also see Becker 1993). As individuals are targeted more in terms of prevention, it is assumed that 'they become more responsible for their own health and illness', as they are more exposed to information about risks and how to avoid them (Verweij 1999: 92, 99). Conrad differentiates three forms of social control in this context: medical ideology, which 'imposes a medical model primarily because of accrued social and ideological benefits'; collaboration, in which 'doctors assist as information providers, gatekeepers, institutional agents and technicians'; and technology, where 'medical technologies such as drugs, surgery or types of screening become means for social control' (1992: 216).

The consequences of medicalisation have important implications for HIV/AIDS interventions in Sub-Saharan Africa. Conrad argues that 'the social consequences of this process occur regardless of [the] medical efficacy' with which medical interventions are evaluated (1992: 223). He argues that this is due to the social delinking of people as patients from their socio-economic and cultural contexts whereby the process 'individualizes what might be otherwise seen as a collective social problem' (Conrad 1992: 224). Here

Verweij's concerns in relation to the impact of preventative medicine are also relevant. Considering the way it is used as a public policy[3] tool, preventative medicine is an important pathway for medicalisation. Verweij argues this is partly linked to the creation of uncertainty and the risk for patients which in turn creates lack of 'confidence in the solidity of their health' (1999: 97). He insists that, when the medicalisation process creates problems of confidence, people are made vulnerable in the long term and their well-being is compromised (see also Barsky 1988). He also reiterates that, once preventative medicine makes information about illness and avoidable risks available, the responsibility for illness shifts to the individual. This, he argues, can lead to a position where individuals are expected to deal with the illness on their own if they do not follow the guidance provided (1999: 99). This expectation is based on an assumption that individuals are free to choose, though of course people have more than one source of information and more than one reason, apart from health, when they choose to act in one way or another. Verweij claims that:

> the practice of preventative medicine stimulates the idea that persons have a moral obligation to guard their own health and consequently that persons ought to participate in prevention programmes and that they may be morally blamed if they do not.
>
> (1999: 107)

Verweij considers medicalisation in terms of the impact that the content of preventative interventions has, but of course the process also works at a deeper level. Following Conrad, in the logic of preventative approaches an ideological bind can be observed which assumes a link between model behaviour and how that behaviour can address the targeted ill-state within targeted individuals. Given the prevalence of preventative approaches in HIV/AIDS interventions and the increasing preponderance of treatment-based approaches, these concerns have important implications in the context of policies in Sub-Saharan Africa.

Yet caution is required here. As demonstrated in Hunt's work, in John M. Janzen's (1978) *The Quest for Therapy in Lower Zaire* and in D.C. Dorward's (1974) 'Ethnography and administration: a study of Anglo-Tiv "working misunderstanding"', the medicalisation process at the level of implementation is not complete. On the one hand the medicalisation process is in competition with the existing traditional definitions and previous medical practices. They intermingle with the public policy-based expansion of Western medical practices. On the other hand, as Levine documents, the expansion is also about the delegitimisation of the local medical practices that are considered to be 'barbarous and filthy' compared to modern and civilised Western medicine (2003: 80–4). Independent of all of this, the spatial differentiation between the practices and the processes creating medicalisation according to Western knowledge, as located within hospitals and clinics,

LIVERPOOL JOHN MOORES UNIVERSITY
Aldham Roberts L.R.C.
TEL. 0151 231 3701/3634

and the existing local practices, located within traditional everyday spaces, allows people to switch between multiple worlds of experience.

However, Conrad argues that, 'when competing definitions are represented by strong interest groups, it is less likely for problems to be fully medicalized' (1992: 220). The institutionalisation processes (religious, colonial and international) within which expanding medical knowledge and practices are lodged in Africa create different circumstances. Within this context, interest groups, even if some user groups such as people living with HIV/AIDS are considered as interest groups, may have little impact to compete with the ongoing medicalisation processes other than just functioning according to the different rationalities available to them. As a result, the expansion of certain preventative methods and the growing availability of treatment create an image of successful medicalisation in the public arena whilst the existing local practices and understandings are located and utilised outside the public medical spaces. The problems expressed about medicalisation become exacerbated in this cross-country transference of medical logic, whereby people are not only absorbed into the bio-medical sphere but are also abstracted from their own social contexts.

Also relevant to this is the way in which the doctor–patient model of Western medicine is based on 'deeply rooted patriarchy' (Zola 1991: 8) and how this relates to the people in the context of HIV/AIDS in Sub-Saharan contexts. Interestingly Verweij contests this by pointing out that there has been a growing understanding of patient rights (1999: 102), which complements Conrad's suggestion about user groups. However, this falls rather short of addressing the complicated situation of HIV/AIDS in Africa, given that the medical model was instrumental in expanding the scope of colonial power into people's everyday lives. In this process medicine was a marker both for progress and for Western values (Levine 2003). Therefore, it is not clear now how the doctor–patient model relates to, and what its implications are for, the experience of people who, in an early episode, were infantilised by a combination of politico-evangelical medicine which was supposed to put them on the road of progress and civilisation.

With all that said, there is, of course, no doubt that HIV/AIDS is a medical condition. Introducing the concept of medicalisation is not intended to suggest otherwise. However, what it does is indicate that the disease being a medical condition does not itself change the social causes of its spread nor its consequences. The concept sets out a process that works at two levels: at one level social concerns are gradually subsumed under the medico-scientific frame of reference. More and more aspects of social relations by which people make sense of their lives are considered under the categories of medicine, in relation to ill health, risk groups and their associated medical solutions. At another level, the process is also implicitly about the creation of generic patients with particular problems as categorised by the experts. Here, people are not only repositioned as patients, but they are also gradually abstracted from their social contexts and the local knowledge systems. This double move is evident in the existing HIV/AIDS interventions. In the process of delivering prevention messages or discussing treatment-related issues, the assumed superiority of the Western knowledge on medicine reasserts itself as a justification for initiating the programmes which need to be implemented and for which compliance is expected from the patients in order for the disease to be dealt with. It is not hard to see how this attitude follows from what Levine identifies as the link between the prevalent understanding among the medical profession and the growing scientific approach to medicine of the nineteenth century: 'the increasingly scientific veneer of medical research and practice marked medicine out as a modern discipline unencumbered by prejudice, passion or superstition' (2003: 60). Therefore, the process of medicalisation is not only about expanding the scope of medicine, but it is also about how that process is linked to implicit power relations and central assumptions about the position of medical experts and patients.

Signs of medicalisation

Tony Barnett and Alan Whiteside, looking at the history of HIV/AIDS interventions from the 1980s onwards, argue that both the Global Programme on AIDS (GPA) and WHO's response were 'medically and epidemiologically driven and adopted short term and conceptually limited fire-fighting perspective based on experience of other' outbreaks of diseases (2002: 74).[4] They also claim that most of these interventions were based on a priori thinking about infectious diseases as an emergency combined with concerns on economies of scale (Barnett and Whiteside 2002: 74). I agree with Barnett and Whiteside in their assessment of this situation, that the approach represents an important attempt by international actors to contain the disease.[5] However, it has also had important long-term implications. While this approach might have been the only one available institutionally to deal with the disease, there has also been little change in the international approach since the 1980s. Barnett and Whiteside correctly point out that, for those like Jonathan Mann, it was clear from their field experience that there was more to the disease than clinical interventions. However, they also claim that policy change was difficult since 'institutional inertia was hard to resist and directed policy and action firmly into the clinical–medical framework' (2002: 76). Thus, even non-clinical socio-economic and cultural aspects of people's lives are referenced to the medical frameworks, which are based on establishing medical professionals as the source of expert knowledge. Once this position articulates policies, it guides people and their behaviour in their everyday lives for dealing with the disease. Here the process also follows the doctor–patient model, highlighted before. In short, medicalisation is permeating through at least two processes. One is the way its general logic becomes influential in the policy process independent of policy content, that is, for policies that may not be directly related with medicine. The other is by expanding the scope of medical interventions to rearticulate what can be done from within medical sciences.

In this section I look at the issue at these two levels. I analyse the reason why this policy has become adopted and how it is supposed to work. In doing this, the ambiguous relationship between medicalisation, politics and perceptions about the target groups will be analysed.

A magic bullet: treatment?[6]

At this stage I look at the issue of treatment in general. Then I look at the case of the policy on co-trimoxazole provision to highlight a number of factors that are general to the treatment thinking.

The treatment policies that have developed for the rolling out of antiretro-viral drugs (ARVs) during the early 2000s in multiple country contexts have been mostly based on medical research demonstrating their efficacy. The possibility of using highly active antiretroviral therapy (HAART) in resource-poor settings has added a new possibility to the policy toolbox. In turning the research into policy, the crisis logic immanent in the international policy circles is the determining factor in the way treatment is presented. There is a priority list for interventions in this kind of medical emergency. At the top of the list are vaccine-based interventions, then there are those interventions which allow people to live longer, and in the absence of these there are the prophylactic interventions that deal with opportunistic diseases. In this vein, one of the arguments for rolling out ARVs has been to keep people alive until there is a vaccine to deal with HIV. This logic focuses policies directly to the logic of medicine, and what needs to be done is articulated on those bases. Policies then focus on the technicalities of delivering the treatment, and concerns as to the long-term implications of having millions of people on medication remain marginal.

There are a number of vaccine initiatives both in Africa and in industrial-ised countries. The largest of these is the Global Alliance for Vaccines and Immunisation (GAVI), which is funded by the Bill and Melinda Gates Foundation, that brings together the WHO, UNAIDS and the World Bank. However, given the complexities involved with the virus and its interaction with human biology, it is argued that a vaccine will remain elusive for the foreseeable future.[7] Thus, the role played by ARVs will be very important indeed. As ARV treatment has become a reality in Africa, the policy debate has become more overtly medicalised. There are a number of ways to provide evidence of this. The increased funding for treatment, the creation of the Global Fund in part to support the rolling out of treatment in Africa, and the international 3×5 campaign initiated by the WHO in 2002, aiming to provide ARV treatment to 3 million people by 2005, have expanded the scope of medicalisation. The justification for this general ARV campaign is clear if one considers that at the time of the 2000 International Aids Conference in Durban, 'an estimated 7000 people in Africa had access to effective combination antiretroviral regimens' (Wainberg 2005: 747). Although the WHO campaign did not manage to achieve its target by 1 December 2005, it focused attention and funding towards ARVs.[8] Once the research established that ARV provision in resource-poor settings was a technically feasible possibility based on directly observable therapies (DOTs) in 2002, a number of international policy actors revised their intervention strategies to shift their focus on to the provision of treatment. Given this possibility within resource-poor settings, access to drugs has since become a human rights issue within the broader issues on people's right to health and thus people's right to access to treatment.[9] As a result, the moral obligation of those who can provide treatment has become part of the discussion, particularly in the debate between pharmaceutical companies and civil society groups such as the Treatment Action Campaign in South Africa. While this is an important discourse for advocacy in the international policy environment, it still remains to a degree within the emergency logic of the response to HIV/AIDS. It emphasises that there is a need now and the drugs have to be delivered now. While this is imperative, there nevertheless remains a gap between the delivery of ARVs and the establishment of sustainable health systems which can cope with the resulting demands of the millions of people who will be on medication over the long term.

It is important to understand what ARVs do.[10] By using multiple drugs,[11] ARV therapy aims to control the replication process of the virus within the human body, thus reducing the detectable viral load (of HIV RNA) as much as possible.[12] This suppression can boost the immune system and thus allow people to return to a healthier state whereby they can function in their everyday lives. The therapy aims also at maintaining the level of suppression for as long as possible. In this way the occurrence of opportunistic diseases is also prevented. Since 1996 this treatment has revolutionised the way the disease has been considered in industrialised countries. It is not uncommon to hear HIV talked about as a chronic disease which can be managed with clinical interventions over a long time. By reducing the HIV viral load ARV therapy has also increased the number of people surviving in industrialised countries (Gulick *et al.* 1997; Hammer *et al.* 1997; Palella *et al.* 1998). This has allowed people with HIV to maintain their lives and to participate in the society. Therefore, the aim of the international policy has been to replicate these same results in resource-poor settings, that is, to provide drugs which will keep people functioning in the society and help them to maintain their lives. However, there is growing evidence within the industrialised countries of resistance developing to some of the drugs used in combination (Little *et al.* 1999; Balotta *et al.* 2000; Yerly *et al.* 2001). It is noted, for instance, that 'in the United States, as many as 50% of patients receiving antiretroviral therapy are infected with viruses that express resistance to at least one of the available antiretroviral drugs' (Clavel and Hance 2004: 1023). Furthermore, it is pointed out that 'increases in the prevalence of drug-resistant virus among patients with established HIV infection may be associated with more frequent transmission of drug resistant virus to newly infected persons in their community' (Little *et al.* 2002: 392; Grant *et al.* 2002). Another complication is related to the long-term drug use, which creates a complex set of other health problems (D'Adesky 2004: 351–4). There are a number of reasons for the development of resistance: the suppression of HIV with ARV therapy is not complete owing to 'poor penetration into protected sites containing a reservoir of HIV, drug toxicity, interaction between drugs and lack of adherence to complex treatment regimens' (Lalezari *et al.* 2003: 2176). Thus, HIV continues to replicate in the presence of drugs and develops gradually into drug-resistant virus variants. Under these circumstances new drugs will have to be developed as second, third and probably fourth line to keep people on drugs until there is a vaccine to deal with the disease. Some of these developments highlight the central role played by existing health systems in terms of monitoring the reaction of people who are on ARVs, providing new drugs when necessary and the provision of palliative care when the circumstances of people on drugs change. It makes clear that the provision of ARVs is only one part of the overall health needs of people living with the disease if they are to fully benefit from access to the treatment.

There are a number of ways in which medicalisation is manifested in discussions of treatment. One of the most important is the emphasis on the technical availability of ARVs and the assumption of outcomes from this provision that is independent of any other change in the systems within which people are given these drugs. In Uganda, in early 2002, the main focus was on prevention since there was no real possibility of rolling out ARVs at the time. Although prevention messages were aggressively presented across the country,[13] the possible availability of treatment was seen as very important for dealing with HIV/AIDS. This was the common view not only among those civil society groups working in the prevention field, but also among clinical professionals in the health services. They claimed that those who were rich enough to pay for themselves were already benefiting from the treatment. As I was told, *the rich can just get their treatment either from outside the country or from the private clinics in Kampala. They come out during the day and get treatment. It also means that they don't have to tell anyone about their condition. It is the problem for the poor.* Of course, within a few years of these conversations the situation has changed with the increasing funding and the reduction in the cost of drugs. Therefore, it could be argued that the divide between the poor and the rich is no longer central to the treatment issue as more and more countries roll out treatment as a priority for everyone who is in need. Indeed, the international perspective on this suggests that by making treatment widely available the problem can be addressed. While I was meeting a group of HIV positive people in 2004 in Lusaka, Zambia, the conversation moved on to the funding the Zambian government was being given at the time by the Global Fund to deliver ARVs. Although it was clear that this was received very well within the community and people were hopeful that ARVs were going to change their circumstances, a number of important questions were raised. F. was happy that drugs were *arriving* into the country but he said *How will they decide who is going to get the treatment? There is not enough for everyone. Will they give it to those who can already access them?* N. agreed with him on this, but added that *it is good to have them. Maybe we can be among the people who will receive treatment! But who can guarantee that we can have them for life? Who will pay for them?* Such comments reflect a set of new questions. It is clear that availability of treatment is a positive change, but the comments make clear that problems still associated with poverty and a general sense of deprivation will influence the outcomes of the treatment process. Further-more, the last question highlights two important issues in people's minds: long-term sustainability of treatment (they too are aware of the limits of international policy pledges and provision from their past experience within the development context) and the conditions of their own economic system which cannot support the treatment of large numbers given its associated clinical requirements.[14]

In Maseru, Lesotho, in the spring of 2005, I was talking to a number of HIV positive people, who argued that treatment was really important as it had allowed them to feel positive about themselves and had allowed them to maintain participation in their communities. Lesotho has been one of the target countries of PEPFAR and other international funding sources such as the Clinton Foundation and thus has been receiving large funds for HIV/AIDS interventions. Given the small size of the country, there seems to have been a strong push by international actors to influence the HIV/AIDS situation.[15] As a result, a number of initiatives were launched including a policy for rolling out treatment for everyone who is in need through the health system. Also, there has been an important campaign for a global country-wide HIV testing. All of these moves and policies are in the right direction. However, the everyday experience of people differs from the praiseworthy goals. A., who was on ARVs at the time of our meeting, talked about the uncertainty attached to their condition. She said *Are we all going to die?* When asked what she meant, she replied, *We are on treatment now but this provision will end. Most of us are receiving treatment within clinical trials. Who will support us once the trial ends? We are told that government will help us but . . . how? They don't have anything . . .* She added, *We cannot really do much about it. We used to get food when we went to the clinic for the treatment but now it has stopped. They told us that there is not enough money to provide food. But without food it is not easy to have the treatment. I am poor. I can only eat, sometimes, once a day, and I have to work for it. Then I get tired.* She described her line of work as sex work. She said, *I don't want to do it . . . but sometimes there is nothing else to do.* Her comments indicate a certain precariousness of the treatment that was made available. Her comments also show how as patients they were not really in charge of what was happening to them. Though treatment was delivered, nothing else seems to have changed in her life, including the work she was doing out of desperation. In the same group, E. was also very sceptical about the way treatment was made available. He argued that they were part of a drug-testing exercise and *What will happen to us when tests finish and they go back to their own countries to produce drugs? Will we get them free?* Similar views were also expressed in Butare, Rwanda, in a meeting with a group of HIV positive people, which occurred in the meeting room of a clinic where they were meeting once a month as a PLWHA support group. There, the question of not having enough to eat and how to look after oneself was the main concern for many who were on ARV treatment. For a number of people in this group ARVs were fine, but in no way sufficient to deal with their problems. Although they were healthier than they were without ARVs, there still were no means to overcome the poverty which was aggravating their health condition.

These views highlight a set of problems which are not going to be addressed by treatment roll-out. They highlight structural problems associated with the way people experience the disease. The most central problem appears to be with poverty, in relation both to individuals and to systems such as health and social protection that are central for sustainable interventions. In fact poverty at both levels influences whether people can benefit from the availability of treatment or not. On the one hand, what is meant by poverty here is related to whether people have enough food to sustain themselves while they are on treatment, whether they have enough resources to commute to where treatment is available, whether they have resources for them to be able to take a break from their work to rest and whether, if they have any of these resources, they can rely on them in the future if their condition deteriorates in due course, while on the other hand poverty is linked to health systems and problems of access to these. The most central problems are the lack of infrastructural capacity, the lack of qualified clinical staff, doctors and nurses, and the lack of comprehensive human and material capacity for maintaining existing health interventions alongside new HIV/ AIDS-related interventions. In some countries the entire clinical primary health care needs to be revived. For example, in Cyangugu, Rwanda, I spoke to three local doctors who have been involved with HIV/AIDS for a long time. They strongly emphasised that the country was facing an absorption problem owing to the lack of infrastructure and human resources required to distribute the available drugs and also to address the health needs of the people related to the disease (this was not limited to just the ARV treatment). They argued that *decentralisation is a good process as resources are coming to regions, but hospitals etc. are still very much in urban centres and require long-distance commutes for what is a largely rural population.* What they were describing is a long-term problem in relation to treatment-related policy interventions. Of course, their concerns question the general move to provide ARVs by those who have limited training in the delivery procedures and DOTs.[16] They point out that, even if a village nurse can actually deliver treatment to people, the larger context of health in relation to the disease cannot be addressed in this manner. Their questioning highlights the problem in this move by demonstrating a linear monocausal medical thinking associated with the medicalisation I have been talking about. It is clear that just delivering treatment drugs will not solve the problem beyond a limited short-term period. Given the associated side effects of the drugs, the potential for developing resistance to drugs within the multiple therapy, and the psychological effects of being on a treatment for a long time, it is clear that there is a need for comprehensive health support beyond the mere delivery of a treatment. Furthermore, some of these health issues require that people are not only trained in the procedures of delivery but also trained in the monitoring and evaluation of the health of patients in order to assess whether or not resistance is developing and whether a resistant strain of HIV is spreading among the newly infected. This kind of capacity requires an extensive clinical infrastructure and continued investment.

The impact of treatment on people has created an impetus for making it available to everyone in need. However, given that the technology is relatively new, there are uncertainties about possible negative impacts of being on drugs in the ARV cocktail. There are various views on drug resistance and its relevance to the treatment policy. It is agreed that there has been increased one-drug or multi-drug resistance in groups that have been on protease inhibitors. According to D'Adesky, there is a consensus about the benefits of ARVs for individuals, as they reduce suffering and as viral load is lowered by decreasing the risk of HIV transmission. However, she points out that at a population level the consensus is less clear, as the 'global introduction of therapy is likely to lead to a gradual increase in MDR [multi-drug resistant]-HIV and there will be consequences' (2004: 353–4). The possible implications of treatment for individuals in the short term and population in the long term present further difficulties for policy makers. The different strands of thinking on this issue are well exemplified by two comments by Susan Little and Sally Blower as reported by D'Adesky:

> It is old risk–benefit analysis. The short-term risk of drug resistance when treating people is very small compared to the huge personal benefit for the patient, but long-term consequences for the population are significant if you don't intervene with more potent drugs or a vaccine before resistance gets out of hand.
>
> (Little, as cited in D'Adesky 2004: 354)

> People in Africa are infected and dying. We need to be clear: Are we trying to treat people? If we are treating, then let's treat as many as possible as well as possible – that's the only strategy. But if we want to have an epidemic control strategy, then what is it? Is it to have as little drug resistance as possible? Or to decrease transmission rates? Or decrease AIDS death rates? We can decide a treatment strategy, but at this point, it's so vague and wooly that nobody articulates what they want.
>
> (Blower, as cited in D'Adesky 2004: 354)

Both comments present major challenges for treatment policy within resource-poor settings. Little's view not only suggests the need for a comprehensive clinical system to be able to monitor and support treatment, but also shows up the requirement to develop new drugs to replace those to which patients have developed resistance. This requires new research and development investment by pharmaceutical companies. Although the first-line ARV costs have gone down, this has been partially due to generic drug production and also the international drive which was discussed earlier. Therefore, it is not clear whether the same pricing patterns will hold for new lines of drugs. Furthermore, with more countries, such as India, coming under the WTO TRIPS regulations, generic drug production for the next generation of ARVs might not be feasible, as was the case for the first-line drugs that have been used so far (Shadlen 2007, forthcoming). Under such circumstances, the burden of the problem once more is on the shoulders of Africans: Will they receive these drugs if they develop resistance? Who will be able to afford the next generations of drugs? Can they be rolled out too? Given that the vaccine option remains unfeasible in the near future, international actors should be asking themselves whether or not they are prepared to provide treatment at all costs when MDR-HIV or one-drug resistant strains emerge in the population. This requires long-term thinking and a rethinking of the way medicine is produced and globally distributed in general. And, of course, there is the moral imperative to rethink all these structural relations given that, as Blower states, people are dying.

Blower's comments are indicative of what has been driving the policy in this area so far. Since people are dying she does not want to be hostage to concerns over drug resistance (D'Adesky 2004: 354). The comments are clear that we need to treat people as best we can under the circumstances. In this, there is an implicit emergency concern within which treatment appears once again as a fire-fighting tool. Her questions highlighting the lack of clear reasons behind treatment policy are also indicative of this. However, while the treatment is necessary to address the people's needs at present, provision of drugs alone can respond neither to the moral imperative nor to the needs of people in the medium to long term. If the evidence from the US and the UK in demonstrating substantive increase in drug resistance among the chronic ARV users is to be believed, drug provision can only be the first step for dealing with people's needs. Therefore, the necessity of treatment will have to be connected to the issues raised by Little in her statement on a long-term policy package. Otherwise the implications of today's treatment may have a devastating impact in the future. In the next section I will look at this tension in a particular context of a drug policy.

Research in Zambia

On 19 November 2004 the media carried an important news item: an anti-biotic hope for children with AIDS. As reported in the *Guardian* on that day, 'deaths among children infected with HIV in Africa could be almost halved if all those with symptoms were put on a simple, cheap and readily available antibiotic' (Boseley 2004). The article noted that the antibiotic, co-trimoxazole, would not stop the children developing AIDS, but that it would allow them to live longer before they require 'powerful and toxic antiretrovi-ral drugs' (Boseley 2004). This article and the media interest in general were based on a journal article published in the *Lancet* reporting the outcomes of a study conducted in Zambia by the Medical Research Council and funded by the Department for International Development, UK (Chintu *et al.* 2004).

Before I outline the research it is important to look at the way this work has influenced the 2006 *Report on the Global AIDS Epidemic*, presented to the UN General Assembly meeting on AIDS in May 2006. It reports: 'In 2005, UNAIDS and UNICEF issued a global call to action that challenges the world to ensure that antiretroviral therapy and prophylaxis with the anti-biotic cotrimoxazole reach 80% of children in need by 2010' (UNAIDS 2006: 165). The report also argues that access to this antibiotic is 'critical where antiretrovirals are not yet accessible' (UNAIDS 2006: 166). The justification for this policy is grounded in the study that was published in the *Lancet* in 2004: 'the antibiotic has been shown to reduce risk of death in children living with HIV by more than 40% (Chintu *et al.* 2004)' (UNAIDS 2006: 166). Given the policy impact of this particular research it presents a highly rele-vant case study for understanding the link between policy and medical research, in addition to highlighting how medicalisation works. Therefore, I first provide a summary of the way this research was reported before analysing how this is relevant for the ongoing discussion in this chapter.

On 20 November 2004 the *Lancet* published the results of a drug trial in a paper entitled 'Co-trimoxazole as prophylaxis against opportunistic infec-tions in HIV-infected Zambian children (CHAP)'. The aim of the trial was to assess the efficacy of the daily use of this antibiotic in areas where there is a high level of bacterial resistance to the antibiotic (Chintu *et al.* 2004: 1865). The researchers indicate that there exists a body of evidence for the positive efficacy of this antibiotic for dealing with opportunistic diseases, both in children and in adult populations (Chintu *et al.* 2004: 1865). However, they also point out that most of this evidence comes from low-bacterial-resistant areas. Therefore, they suggest that there is a need to assess efficacy in areas where there is high resistance to the antibiotic. The trial was a double-blind randomised placebo-controlled one. It looked at HIV-infected children between the ages of 6 months and 5 years at University Hospital, Lusaka, Zambia (ibid.). However, in reviewing the procedures of inclusion 12 months into the trial the theme modified the criteria and included 'children up to their 15th birthday' as it had become evident that 'an increasing number of children over 5 years were being diagnosed with HIV' (Chintu *et al.* 2004: 1866). Recruitment was based on the paediatric outpatient clinic in the hospital, and the consent of the patients' guardians or parents was obtained. The authors also indicate a major difficulty in the recruitment of asymptomatic children from 'primary care clinics in Lusaka to increase generalisability of results' (ibid.). They indicate that this attempt was largely unsuccessful since parents were not happy to have their healthy children tested for HIV (Chintu *et al.* 2004: 1870). They also excluded those children who already had opportunistic infections or whose life expectancy was four weeks or less.

The trial followed procedures of randomisation based on giving sequential study numbers to children and randomly allocating the trial drug. Then they stratified the randomisation by age. Children were assessed when they were enrolled for the trial, once they were given the trial drug and again every four weeks for 16 weeks and every eight weeks after that (ibid.). At regular intervals, full blood tests, white blood cell differentials and malaria parasites were measured. Here the role of carers must be emphasised, since they had the role of bringing children back to the clinic at regular intervals for checks and also delivering trial drugs to their children and bringing empty bottles back to the clinic. In order to enrol for the trial:

> 1185 children were assessed for eligibility and 851 of them were tested for HIV antibody. Consent was given for 541 of the 699 HIV positive children to be enrolled and they were randomly allocated for the trial between March 14, 2001 and January 8, 2003.
>
> (Chintu *et al.* 2004: 1868)

However, 'in October 2002 the data and safety monitoring committee advised that because of the higher event rate and lower loss follow up than expected' recruitment should be reduced to 540 (Chintu *et al.* 2004: 1867). Furthermore, the same committee in October 2003 recommended that the 'trial should be stopped prematurely because of a substantial and sustained benefit in the co-trimoxazole group' (Chintu *et al.* 2004: 1867).[17]

The authors start their discussion by claiming that:

> our results show that HIV-infected children living in Zambia, an area with high levels of in-vitro resistance of common bacteria to co-trimoxazole (69–80% Mwansa, J. personal communication), this drug reduced mortality by 43% and Hospital admission rates by 23% compared with match placebo. Follow-up in the trial was excellent and few children stopped taking their medication.
>
> (Chintu *et al.* 2004: 1870)

They also acknowledge that 'the mechanism of action of co-trimoxazole prophylaxis in this trial is not entirely clear' (Chintu *et al.* 2004: 1870). Yet they note why it might be working following what is known about some opportunistic diseases, such as *P carnii* pneumonia and nasopharyngeal aspirants, and suggest that there needs to be more research on molecular resistance studies to understand the interaction between the trial drug and various conditions. Towards the end of their analysis they tentatively suggest that, although over a third of children in the trial had CD4 counts higher than the threshold at which antiretroviral therapy is recommended by the guidelines, given the possible lower values among the HIV negative cases the 'threshold for clinical care in industrialised countries might not necessarily be appropriate for children in resource-poor settings' (Chintu *et al.* 2004: 1870).

Following from this, the report ends by concluding that 'we believe, therefore, that our results can be generalised to a policy that could be applied universally to children with clinical features of HIV infection in Africa: all should receive co-trimoxazole prophylaxis irrespective of age and CD4 count' (Chintu *et al.* 2004: 1870). This recommendation is also included in the summary at the beginning of the report's interpretation section. They go on to recommend that 'the results of this trial should provide an impetus to provide clinical care with co-trimoxazole prophylaxis and nutritional support, irrespective of levels of resistance to this drug' (ibid.). Then they end the report by noting that the relationship between the benefits of this drug for children using antiretroviral therapy remains to be seen.

The study was quickly followed up by a joint statement from WHO, UNAIDS and UNICEF (2004), which stated that 'WHO, UNAIDS and UNICEF, guided by recent evidence, have agreed to modify as interim the current recommendations for cotrimoxazole prophylaxis in children. This is based upon recent trial data from Zambia' (2004). The statement follows the trial report and endorses the drug: 'for HIV infected children with any sign and symptoms suggestive of HIV [it] is a key intervention that should be offered as a part of a basic package'. It also requires the drug to be used for 'all HIV exposed children born to HIV infected mothers, in settings where HIV infection status cannot be reliably confirmed in the first 18 months of life' (2004: 1). The document then provides details of who should be getting this drug and the duration of treatment in some detail. In this it also clarifies the above statements. For instance, any child with HIV is clarified as being one with 'any clinical signs or symptoms suggestive of HIV, regardless of age or CD4 count' (2004: 2). In the following section the guidelines for duration of the treatment are provided. Again here the statement fits very closely with the trial report. It is stated that children with HIV should get the drug indefinitely 'where ARV treatment is not available' and then once ARV treatment is available it should be given six months or more after there is evidence of immune restoration. The statement also added that 'with current evidence it is not yet clear if cotrimoxazole continues to provide protection after immune restoration is achieved' (2004: 2). Another important part of the document is the operational guidelines that set out requirements for a 'regular sustained supply of high quality drugs' and the availability of enough supplies for children. Furthermore, this is made the governments' responsibility whereby they have to make extra budgetary allocations for this intervention. The statement also provides guidelines for the monitoring and evaluation of the drug use and its impact. At the end of the statement are two references, one of which is the *Lancet* article that had prompted the organisations to review their earlier guidelines on this issue.

Implications and questions

These guidelines and the report leading to them have been formulated into a policy that can be measured against the target set in the UNAIDS 2006 report described above. The case study indicates an institutionalisation process for medical research which has become part of the international intervention strategy. This process of institutionalisation is also the pathway leading to medicalisation. Here the process is linked with the justification behind the research and the way it has been considered as evidence for policy making. This has also wider implications in terms of mass medicalisation which is based on the provision of co-trimoxazole across Africa.

The reported research invites two types of analysis: (a) the internal validity of the research, that is, 'How warranted is the causal conclusion in the model?' and (b) the external validity of the research, that is, 'How does the model conclusion provide warrant for causal claims outside the model?' (Cartwright 2007: 36). The first question is responded to in the research in the discussion of the detailed procedures for a double-blind random control trial (RCT). The RCT procedure is used by researchers to control for all but one cause, that is related with the intervention in the treatment group.[18] The added blindness procedure aims at controlling for causes that can be missed by the randomisation, for instance in the co-trimoxazole trial the consideration given for siblings being in two different groups (Chintu *et al.* 2004).[19] Nancy Cartwright argues that, as a deductive method, the conclusions of an RCT 'can only be as certain as the premises' (2007: 31). In the case of the trial drug, there is a reason to believe in the hypothesis that it works against opportunistic disease associated with HIV/AIDS. This is established by Chintu *et al.* on the basis of a set of earlier research, albeit in areas where there is less bacterial resistance (2004: 1865). The Zambian trial builds on this to test whether it would also work in an area where there is a high rate of bacterial resistance. Under these circumstances, the trial demonstrates a clinically significant result within the context of the RCT. In this setting the drug deals effectively with the *Pneumocystis carnii* which is a common opportunistic disease among HIV positive African children,[20] though, as mentioned before, the trial does not seem to yield much information about HIV negative children's condition in this respect. Here we have a sub-population of children with HIV who are selected according to the criteria presented earlier in Lusaka. In other words, what the RCT tells us about is the causal link between the treatment and the outcome within a particular sub-population under the particular circumstances of the research. It is not necessarily the case that what is observed as a clinically significant result will apply outside the particular sub-population. The upshot of this is how the claims that can be derived from an RCT procedure can be used for generalised policy claims (Cartwright 2007). It is clear that to do this requires meta-assumptions which frame, but are outside, the RCT procedure.

This issue of scope of RCT conclusions takes us to the second area of analysis, that is the question of external validity and policy implementation, since ultimately what makes research relevant for policy is its applicability to a population beyond the research sub-population. Clearly external validity is implicitly assumed from an established causal link between co-trimoxazole and the reduction in pneumonia in the tested group to the claim of a generalisable policy as made in the report we have been analysing. Yet a further step is taken when international organisations established a measurable target to be delivered by 2010 (UNAIDS 2006). The question is what warrants these steps.

One answer to this is about the method. RCTs are seen as providing justification for generalisability. Another view is that the method does not provide such justification. Cartwright's view on RCTs is that they 'provide information about an overall effect of a cause, averaged across subpopulations in which it may behave differently' (2007: 38). This position raises some complications for the generalisation step taken in the report. She argues that 'the method itself tells us nothing about what the cause does elsewhere' (2007: 39). In other words, what is observed does not say anything about what happens when there are other causes, which there are in the context in normal uncontrolled everyday life. To this extent, establishing one causal link in an experimental context raises questions of this sort when its results are generalised.

If we relook at the policy recommendation in the report, it states that 'children of all ages with clinical features of HIV should receive co-trimoxazole prophylaxis in resource-poor settings, irrespective of resistance to this drug' (Chintu *et al.* 2004: 1865). Given the research design discussed in an earlier section, the sample on which this statement is based seems to be very small indeed. It appears that researchers are generalising their outcomes to a population which is not covered by their sample. The sample can be seen as a representative of children with HIV within a certain age group in Lusaka (or maybe even those children coming to University Teaching Hospital in Lusaka). Thus, the conclusion can be reasonably generalised to all children with clinical HIV features in that location. Also, it is foreseeable that, if the sample group is representative of children with HIV in Zambia in general (though this is not clear without considering possible differences), a policy covering Zambia might be developed. But, rather than taking these steps, the report generalises, to the extreme, to 'resource-poor settings' throughout Africa. The assumed generalisability of a sample group of 540 (initially 700) to millions raises important questions.

Looked at carefully, the situation captures a number of issues which have important implications for external validity assumption that is implicitly justifying the policy. These issues are interlinked and are related to conditions of expanding medicine use and socio-economic and cultural concerns. While a certain efficacy of the trial drug is evident, it is not clear how this drug would react in complex medical circumstances. For instance, it is not known how it works with ARVs, yet the guidelines state that it should be used with ARVs for at least six months or more. According to the baseline characteristics, 175 children were admitted to hospital before the trial for tuberculosis (32 per cent treatment, 33 per cent control group), a higher rate than for acceptance for pneumonia of 147 children (28 per cent treatment, 28 per cent control groups) (Chintu *et al.* 2004: 1866). However, what is not clear is whether there is an overlap between patients in both groups and, if so, how this might impact interventions in relation to TB, both in the short and in the long term, when the trial drug is provided to the general population. This is particularly important given that it is already acknowledged that Zambia has high levels of bacterial resistance to co-trimoxazole. Another area which is not clarified is the way the trial drug might interact with malaria. It was noted that 'prevalence of malaria in children in hospital was low' (Chintu *et al.* 2004: 1870). One explanation given for this situation is linked with the provision of open access hospital care to those participating in the trial. In this it is assumed that patients could have been treated for malaria. Of course, this is a good procedure, but it does not yield information on how the trial drug would be responded to in an area of high malaria prevalence. Here the research is also opaque about where resistant bacteria are most prevalent: in the general population children or children with HIV? Though the research is not clear on how this drug would react when it is in the context of other drugs or diseases (or in general, as acknowledged by the researchers – Chintu *et al.* 2004: 1870), it nevertheless claims that a generalised policy was seen as appropriate.

As I have already noted, the trial was conducted under particular conditions in a clinical setting where strict observance of the trial drug use, attendance at the clinic and other conditions were monitored and managed. Although there is no discussion of whether there were any incentives used to obtain clinic attendance, it is suggested that participant children at least had open access to the clinic 'where they could receive free medical treatment' (ibid.). It is not clear how far the impact of these conditions is systematically taken into account for the observed beneficial outcome or for the beneficial outcome in general. Either it is assumed that similar environmental conditions can be maintained once the policy is applied across Africa or it is simply assumed that these conditions have no impact. Here the issue is the relationship between the efficacy of a drug under particular conditions whereby children were provided with a comprehensive medical intervention (which at times also provided anti-malarials) and the everyday context where such provision is either lacking or difficult to reach. This raises another question related to the location of the trial in Lusaka. All participants were able to visit the hospital at regular intervals and were able to do it under the supervision of their parents or guardians and clinical members of the research group. It is not clear whether this is a replicable scenario when one moves out of cities that have appropriate health systems. Of course a retort might be that this is a very cheap and easy-to-deliver drug and thus that it can be made available widely. However, it still needs to be delivered and monitored at certain intervals by clinical professionals.[21] In other words, there is a question about whether the clinical experimental conditions of delivery can be replicated across a country and across an entire region for the delivery of treatment and the monitoring of drug use. This then takes us to another issue which needs to be addressed for external validity to hold, that is, the supply and availability of the treatment.

The revised WHO, UNAIDS and UNICEF guidelines clearly state, under the category of 'Operational issues', that the supply and availability of co-trimoxazole for treatment and prophylaxis are to be maintained by governments. The drugs should be delivered through existing drug distribution systems. In this the providers are to make sure that there are always enough supplies for children 'until after their next appointment for regular monitoring. This should ensure doses are not missed' (WHO *et al.* 2004). Combined with the monitoring requirements to make sure that children are assessed for tolerance and adherence in regular clinical checks, the requirement for rolling out co-trimoxazole requires a well-established and well-funded system of delivery and monitoring. Furthermore, it also assumes that this kind of clinical expertise and capacity exists widely within the reach of most communities. This assumption is at best optimistic and at worse unfounded. Even if cities act as clinical health centres too, it is not always possible for people to have access to them with the required regularity, and from the perspective of children this can even be much more difficult.

To see the difficulties that can arise, when visiting a health clinic which is dealing with sexually transmitted diseases and HIV/AIDS among other things in Butare, Rwanda, I met a self-help group of people living with HIV. They were using one of the rooms in the clinic for their regular meetings. On that day they were watching a documentary made about HIV/AIDS and how people are developing various coping mechanisms. The group consisted of 25 people. It was an equal mix of men and women. Their group leader was a female AIDS patient, N. She told me that they meet once a month to help each other. She said, *There is no one else to help. It is not much but at least we can talk to each other.* I asked why they meet only once a month. She said, *People coming from outside the town cannot afford to come more than once and sometimes they cannot come at all. Not everyone comes all the time.* When asked what the main problems are that they face, she said, *We are poor. Sometimes we have nothing to eat. We help each other but it is not enough. Drugs are fine but without food it is not easy.* Then she talked about how if you are poor it is not possible to leave your village to seek help. She said, *The real problem is with children who are left to look after their siblings, and they have*

HIV themselves and might be looking after other siblings with the disease. She talked about a member of their group *who is a young girl looking after her five brothers and sisters. She has the disease and one of the youngest ones has too. They are poor and she cannot leave them alone to come here. She stays at home alone all the time to look after them. Sometimes we can go and help her but it is not enough because I cannot go most of the time because I am tired.*

The situation N. was describing is not unique. A lot of people are not able to have access to health systems because of their distance from facilities and their living conditions, which may force them to make choices to look after their siblings or parents rather than use their resources to go to places where they may have access to help. The problem was also highlighted in Cyangugu, Rwanda. Talking to a number of health specialists who are working with people with HIV/AIDS, I was told that, although the country is decentralising its health system to increase its coverage, the existing infrastructure does not allow it to be very decentralised, particularly in relation to specialised HIV/AIDS-related interventions. For these services people still have to commute to more urban centres. Given that Rwanda has a large rural community, they considered this a major problem. Similar issues were raised by a group of women in a village 45 minutes outside Maseru, Lesotho. In the discussion they raised problems they face in dealing with HIV/AIDS-related problems in their village. They talked about how people were trying to help each other on an everyday basis. One of them, F., said, *But no one has much. We are trying to help each other by giving from what little we have. It is for every day. There is a limit. We cannot help each other for more serious problems. We will need drugs.* Then H. followed this by saying, *Of course, people want to help each other but there is a limit. People get tired emotionally and physically. It is hard to go all the time.*[22]

In the village the only available local health clinic was a small two-room space attached to a church. Outside the building there were 50 people waiting to be seen for various reasons. There was only one nurse to respond to all their health needs and also reach out to the village to deal with those who could not have walked to the clinic.

These views are exemplars of the problem of provision of sustainable health interventions where infrastructural problems on the one hand and poverty on the other hand are determinants of how people benefit or not from interventions. It is also clear that the decentralisation of health systems or the provision of country-wide systems is not permeating to all levels owing to the lack of human resources and clinical settings to manage sustained interventions for HIV/AIDS. Furthermore, the ongoing availability of drug provision is an important issue, especially in countries where the particular drug is not produced in the country. Given these conditions of supply and haphazard monitoring, it is particularly important to consider what might be the side effects of generalised co-trimoxazole use. These circumstances clearly raise doubts over the external validity of the claims which are taken out of the experimental setting in the research to make general policy claims. For the authors, the question is how it is possible to provide this general policy advice independently of these other relevant issues being considered.

Magic bullet revisited

Overall the research and the policy prescription it has produced do not take into account the socio-economic context of children and how they live, in the implementation context of the policy. One can ask in what ways this is an indication of medicalisation. The logic in the drug trial report seems to be that children are children everywhere. In other words, it makes a distinction between the biology of children, which seems to have responded to the drug in the trial, and the social, economic and cultural conditions of children under which the drug will be made available and which will influence its use. The policy recommendation appears to be an inference from the former position. The case presented builds its argument on an a priori assumption about the nature of children on which the drug needs to work. Therefore, while the RCT provides evidence for the link between using co-trimoxazole and the reduction in the incidence of *Pneumocystis carnii*, it does not necessarily provide evidence for its generalised implementation. Thus, it appears that the determinants of the use of evidence for policy are based on medical assumptions rather than the issues I have highlighted in discussing external validity. This is one aspect of the medicalisation process whereby socio-economic and cultural determinants of policy implementation are sidelined in favour of medical analysis whose validity is claimed on the basis of medical research. Richard Horton links this inference to the assumed superiority of knowledge claims in medicine that are based on the assumed accuracy and independence of scientific method from human error in producing unbiased results (2003: 47–50). The model he has in mind is that of the RCT procedures like those used in the treatment trial I have been discussing. He raises a number of questions to suggest that this method is far from reflecting what happens in everyday practice: 'here one cannot plan a consultation in advance, the doctor must deal with a unique patient, not the average of several thousands, the doctor must help determine the patient's care, not randomly allocate it to one of multiple possibilities' (2003: 49). His concerns are similar to the issues I raised about external validity. The interesting aspect of Horton's comments is the way he also locates doctors within this context of implementation where what they can do is referenced to the everyday conditions.[23] This suggests that there is a fissure between the medicalisation process and what medical professionals can actually do. Medical professionals are also located within a 'policy' context, whereby they become part of the implementation, rather than being in the experimental RCT context. Therefore, we can see that medicalisation as a process is not limited to the way solutions to social problems are proposed by the medical profession but that it is related to a deeper and more diffused process where a meta-assumption on the nature of human beings and certain claims about scientific method and knowledge determine the way policies are formulated. Cartwright suggests that, while the evidence based on results under experimental conditions can be stable, the same is not *ipso facto* arguable for the same evidence in a policy context (2007: 37–43). The policy environment is unstable by its nature. Moreover, the policy could change the environment of policy implementation; in other words, the policy environment can become unstable owing to our own interventions. This general question of how far the results of the research can be stable under intervention within the context of everyday life is central to policy thinking. Yet it seems to have been ignored in ongoing policy discussions.

Horton identifies another central problem. He argues that the over-reliance on experimental knowledge turns people into patients.[24] This process abstracts them from their everyday lives, as experience of a disease in its context is not considered to be good evidence for medical purposes. Horton points out that:

> the fact that we privilege desituated evidence over situated experience means that messy social issues of family, income, occupation, class, gender and leisure and how they influence the interpretation or application of that evidence receive little attention from today's professors of medicine.
>
> (2003: 55)

Considered from the perspective of the policy context, once the policy process is medicalised, whereby policy tools are described according to achieving certain clinical outcomes as demonstrated in the RCTs, people's experiences within particular contexts becomes irrelevant for policy implementation. Policy becomes focused on achieving the outcomes identified within the experimental context. Subsequently policy considers a possible delivery mechanism for the drug as the relevant socio-economic cultural aspect of the problem, without engaging with the larger conditions of drug use in a given context.

It is at this point that the institutionalisation, discussed in earlier chapters, and medicalisation are intertwined. International policy actors also assume an a priori justification based on medical evidence for clinical possibility as the feasible tool for policy design. This can be observed for instance in the policy on treatment in general. It is demonstrated in the case of co-trimoxazole, with an instance of this general attitude in the UNAIDS report 2006. In the institutionalisation of a medical attitude, concerns about the environmental conditions of the implementation become secondary. In looking at the guidelines on the use of co-trimoxazole one can observe that the environmental considerations, or operational issues, are discussed in a desituated manner too. Thus, the logic of medicalisation articulates a generic set of political and economic conditions appropriate for the delivery of treatment which is independent of the ground realities, the capacities of individual countries and governments. The guidelines are symbolic of an institutionalised medical perspective within the international policy environment. While one reason for this is based on the scientific claims of medicine to provide 'hard' evidence, it is also based on the logic of fire-fighting or, as suggested by UNAIDS, crisis management in a context of *emergency*. Both processes reinforce a view which attempts to isolate a possible intervention target that is well defined and limited, and then develop policy within that targeted field to overcome the identified problem. Thus, international policy makers appear to give priority to medical evidence over anything else. However, from the experiences of people it is clear that this targeting is far too narrow and does not sufficiently incorporate the complexities of everyday life.

4   What do we need to know for HIV/AIDS interventions in Africa?

We know what works.[1]

(Peter Piot, UNAIDS)

We know what works.[2]

(Julian Lob-Levyt, DfID)

The reversal of the AIDS epidemic can happen if proven prevention interventions are used in combination and brought to scale.

(Global HIV Prevention Working Group – GPWG)

Recently, statements like these have been circulating within international policy circles. They have been expressed publicly and argued for in authoritative documents such as the UNAIDS annual reports. They denote that we know what works in terms of the best technologies for dealing with HIV/AIDS. These technologies typically involve condoms, voluntary counselling and testing (VCTs), availability of drugs, peer education for sensitisation and information transmission and the associated best practices for implementing these tools. These are taken as the generally accepted content of our knowledge for dealing with the disease and the widely used tools for implementation. Most of these tools target prevention-related activities. However, the evident negative state of affairs in relation to HIV/AIDS around the world (UNAIDS 2006) cautions against such strong knowledge claims. It raises a doubt that perhaps *we don't actually know*. It shows that looking at knowledge claims is imperative, since more and more is claimed under the banner of *we know*, and more and more people are receiving what *we know works*. Yet despair, misery and poverty are faced by increasing millions in Sub-Saharan Africa. Maybe what we know is not the most important part of what needs to be known for intervening in people's lives. But why is this knowledge claim important?

Marcel Verweij's concerns about preventative medicine are relevant in understanding the implications of this knowledge claim. Considering the way it is used as a public policy[3] tool, preventative medicine is an important pathway for medicalisation that is immanent in the claim 'We know what works.' Verweij errs on the side of caution in considering the possible harm preventative medicine can have rather than its role in providing protection. He argues that some of this potential harm is linked with the creation of uncertainty and risk for patients, which in turn creates lack of 'confidence in the solidity of their health' (1999: 97). He insists that, if the medicalisation process is creating problems of confidence, people are made vulnerable in the long term and their well-being is compromised (also see Barsky 1988). He also points out another important implication which is linked with the policies that are justified using the knowledge claims of the policy makers. Once preventative medicine policies make information about illness and avoidable risks available, the responsibility for illness seems to shift to the individual. This, he argues, can lead to a position where individuals are expected to deal with the illness on their own by following the guidance provided (1999: 99). Then a problem of confidence is created by the policies and the health behaviour required for these. This is the tension between policies and the way people think about their own health in their everyday lives. It is constantly reproduced within the policy implementation process. Arguably, while this institutionalises the policy actors' role as the providers of generic policy tools which are technically proven to be useful, they pass the responsibility for the outcomes of policies to the people. In other words if policies are not producing the expected outcomes it is often seen as a problem of poor patient adherence rather than as a problem of policy formulation.[4]

Here, another important aspect of the issue is the assumption that individuals are free to choose or comply with the requirements of policies. This is an abstracted assumption whereby the context of implementation is assumed away. People have more than one source of information and more than one reason when they choose to act in one way or another. Verweij suggests that:

> the practice of preventative medicine stimulates the idea that persons have a moral obligation to guard their own health and consequently that persons ought to participate in prevention programmes and that they may be morally blamed if they do not.
>
> (1999: 107)

By looking at these issues Verweij considers medicalisation in terms of the impact of the content of preventative interventions, but the process also works at a deeper level. Following Conrad, in the logic of preventative approaches one can observe an ideological bind which assumes a link between model behaviour and how that behaviour can address the targeted ill-state within targeted individuals. Robert Crawford in his considerations of health promotion as ritual argues that 'the creation of a "reflexive subject" conscious of her own health and willing to undertake rational self-surveillance and self-reform is an essential part of a ritual act that serves as a disciplinary social order' (2000: 220). Here the medical ideology becomes evident since it assumes a distinction between an assumed and targeted natural behaviour of a body and the actual social behaviour of a person in context (Preda 2005: 188–91). In this sense, policies are creating populations that can be supervised according to policy parameters. These are:

> focused on the species body, the body imbued with the mechanics of life and serving the basis of biological process: propagation, births, mortality, the level of health . . . their supervision was effected through an entire series of interventions and regulatory controls.
>
> (Foucault 1978: 139)

The distinction between model and actual behaviour allows international actors to constitute policies that are trying to develop, monitor and evaluate this self-reflexivity in the target populations that have been transformed into patients or target groups.[5] In this sense *what we know* is instrumental in justifying policies that then act as social control mechanisms in people's everyday lives. The process between the transmission of prevention messages and the compliance with them becomes a control mechanism for people's everyday lives, one which can be evaluated according to the substance of these prevention messages. According to Crawford, 'rituals work to imprint and legitimate prevailing arrangements, roles and agenda; they are a means for extending power through incorporating individuals within institutional projects' (2000: 220). In this vein the claim that *we know what works* acts as a trope which both indicates the location of the power within the international policy domain and initiates the process of incorporation by justifying the implementation of the policies covered by that statement. Given the prevalence of preventative approaches in HIV/AIDS interventions, and the increasing preponderance of treatment-based approaches, these concerns have important implications in the context of Sub-Saharan Africa.

In this chapter I question the claim of *knowing what works* in the HIV/AIDS policy area, a claim which suggests that we know how policy or policy tools work and how they impact on people's lives. I am interested in the link between the claim to know and the field to which the claimed knowledge is to be applied. In the last chapter I argued that the medicalisation process acts as an organising principle for international actors and their policies. The method of voluntary counselling and testing (VCT), for instance, was initially used to target behaviour change in the absence of ARVs; then gradually it became directly attached to ARV provision.[6] In this move one can observe a priority change in the international policy. The knowledge claim in all of these policies acts as an anchor for two processes: institutionalisation, where international actors are endowed with the power owing to their knowledge, and a medicalisation process that constitutes the substance of this knowledge and in which a realm of intervention, actors and the objects of the policies are established for policy interventions. Here, by using *we know what works* as a trope, international actors designate the limits of their intervention as well as the nature of the interventions. Knowing gives direction to what is to be done, that is, to action in a particular realm that is also known. In turn, the resulting action impacts on people independently of whether they know (or agree with) what we know. I suggest that this disjuncture between the policy makers' knowledge claims, which are used as justification for policies, and the people's everyday knowledge creates an important obstacle for dealing with HIV/AIDS in the long term.

I argue, by looking at the two main policy tools that are promoted, that we don't know much about things that are essential for effective interventions. Furthermore, I argue that the knowledge underwriting these tools makes it difficult to know what can work on the ground. The pronoun 'we' is used throughout this chapter to indicate the assumed delineation of 'us' who know and 'them' as patients who are waiting for our help. This presents not a belief on my part but a perspective that is common in the international policy circles, as well as in those actors who have become policy implementers, such as various organisational forms in civil society (NGOs, community groups and faith-based groups). In this sense, the investigation is located within the general discourse of international policy within which policy makers and planners have articulated policies and tools for interventions in what is usually seen as underdeveloped, third world countries or more generally as the South. The relationship between knowledge production and the international development discourse has been treated as an important area of study (see Chambers 1993; Crush 1995; Escobar 1995; Farmer 1999; Geertz 1983; Harriss 2001; Hilhorst 2003; Hobart 1993; and Pottier *et al.* 2003). A number of scholars in development studies have argued that there is an important link between the knowledge base and the subsequent action in the development discourse (Escobar 1995; Ferguson 1990; Geertz 1983; Long and Long 1992; Quarles van Ufford 1993; Richards 1993), and that Western knowledge claims over-determine the characteristics of actions and actors that can participate in the development process. Nevertheless, the mechanism of this institutionalisation process creating our knowledge is not elaborated. HIV/AIDS policies are frustrated by the disparity between knowledge claims in international policy and the everyday knowledge of people about their own conditions. There is a need to understand how this international knowledge domain constructs its own actors and then constructs pathways for their interaction with the target groups.

The questioning of knowledge claims presented here takes HIV/AIDS interventions in Sub-Saharan Africa as an instance of a particular logic. Following Mark Hobart, the logic concerns the general international developmental discourse driving policy discussions. He argues that 'the relationship of developers and those to-be-developed is constituted by the developers' knowledge and categories, be it the nation-state, the market or the institutions which are designed to give a semblance of control over these confections . . .' (Hobart 1993: 2). Looking at this also requires an understanding of the basis of this knowledge claim in terms of 'the part played by western scientific knowledge' in development that grounds the HIV/AIDS interventions (Hobart 1993: 1).

In other words, the grounding of *what we know* based on particular categories and classifications makes sense of people's lives according to a certain knowledge that international policy makers have (Karnik 2001; Booth 2004; Preda 2005). This, however, may not have any resemblance to the way people categorise themselves, according to their own knowing of themselves. As a result, the way people know their own circumstances implicitly questions what we know. This highlights an important cleavage between the prescribed policies and their implementation field. Both the international developmental frameworks and the deeper claim of knowledge about the scientific (ostensibly medical) nature of HIV/AIDS create a set of knowledge claims in terms of actors and actions informing the policy. Therefore, in order to unpack the impact of the statement that *we know*, a theoretical discussion of this knowledge production is required.

How do we think about this?

The fundamental concern expressed here relates to international policy actors and their claims. Therefore, as a way to analyse the impact of *what we know*, this investigation switches from the general idea that to deal with HIV/AIDS we have to inform and teach people how to apply our knowledge and transmit what is to be known; it switches to how we need to evaluate and know what we are doing on the basis of people's everyday experiences of our knowledge. This needs to be an active engagement at all levels of policy thinking with people, rather than simply designating recalcitrant behaviour *from the outside* as non-adherence. Put more bluntly, it is not about why people in Sub-Saharan Africa are not engaging with what we are telling them on HIV/AIDS, but why *we* don't understand what they are telling *us* on HIV/AIDS. Talking to such people about their experiences raises doubt about the claim that *we know*. The argument here is not about whether we should help or not; it is about what the knowledge base is for this help.

This switch of ideas requires a theoretical framework for two reasons: first, to unpack the structure of the knowledge claims immanent in policy implementations; second, to allow a move that would permit a more dynamic understanding of the disease as it is experienced by people within certain social and cultural knowledge contexts beyond their attributed beneficiary or *patient* status. This move valorises people's own experiences and recognises a dynamic agency within their socio-cultural contexts. By understanding these processes, some of which are constructed as *non-adherence* in the language of international policies, one can understand the sites and forms of resistance to the institutionalisation process that has been discussed. The problems raised in the claims of knowledge of HIV/AIDS for policy implementations require a multidisciplinary social science approach, since holding to any *one* discipline's boundaries limits the possibility of engaging with both our perspective qua policy makers and knowledge claimants and their perspective on the ground. As a method it is closer to what is described as an 'epistemological critique' by George E. Marcus and M.J. Fischer. It aims at the critique of 'modes of thought in social action and institutional life' and to expose 'both habitual ways of thought attributed to social actors as well as the conventional social-science ways of representing them' (Marcus and Fischer 1999: 152–3; see also Douglas 1986).

I present two domains of knowledge on the HIV/AIDS intervention in two steps. The first section investigates what we are saying when we claim we know in the context of HIV/AIDS policies. In this section it is shown that the grounds of the knowledge claim are legitimated very much on the medical research grounds that I have discussed in the last chapter. The second section looks at the location of everyday knowledge by presenting its particular relationship with the disease within the context of policy interventions. Then I discuss a theoretical framework. This section argues that knowledge needs to be considered from two perspectives depending on its domain of production. The discussion sets out the possibility of looking at the issues from the position of the people living in the context of the disease in order to inform overall policy frameworks. Lastly, the conclusion argues that we cannot claim to know in this area for policy interventions unless the policies are informed and developed through the perspectives of people living with the disease.

We know what works!

The section looks at the claim of knowing what works. This is done by looking at two widely promoted policy tools and their justifications. The aim is to elaborate that what is implicitly assumed in the knowledge claim is the assertion that *what we know works*. In particular the tools that are taken as working are located within a knowledge framework for interventions established through particular categories and classifications.[7] I look at how they are introduced and then comment on how the use of these tools has changed.

Tools

To be clear, the discussion starts with the report *Access to HIV Prevention: Closing the Gap*. It was published in May 2003 and produced by the Global HIV Prevention Working Group. It suggests that scaling up the proven prevention interventions in combination would reverse the scale of the epidemic. It provides a list of interventions: 'combination prevention uses a range of science-based strategies, from encouraging delayed sexual activity to condom promotion, from voluntary HIV counselling and testing to programs for injecting drug users' (GHPWG 2003: 1). These interventions aim to reduce infection rates by initiating a behaviour change in the target populations over the long term. The report deals with several interventions as a part of the combination strategy; among these methods are: behaviour change programmes, sexually transmitted disease (STD) control, voluntary counselling and testing (VCT), harm reduction programmes for injecting drug users, and prevention of mother-to-child transmission (PMTCT). These methods are also seen as 'highly effective' (GHPWG 2003: 36).

In this chapter, I focus on two central behaviour change tools used in prevention programmes, condom use and VCTs. Condom promotion has been, for a long time, at the forefront of the prevention of sexually transmitted diseases in general and HIV/AIDS in particular, whereas VCT is a new way of looking at prevention and has been rolled out in most of Sub-Saharan Africa in recent years. It has been considered an important development as a general intervention tool for dealing with HIV/AIDS. In this sense it is seen as a good way of initiating a possible behaviour change whereby people start using condoms. As its title suggests, the report recognises gaps in the implementation and availability of these proven interventions around the world, both generally and in Sub-Saharan Africa in particular. In the area of condom distribution, the report states that, in 2002, 358 million condoms were distributed and that governments would like to scale up in this area: it forecasts that some 1.9 billion condoms will be required for Sub-Saharan Africa.[8] In terms of VCTs, they state that 'only 6 per cent of people who want counselling and testing in Africa have access to it' (GHPWG 2003: 10). At the end of their analysis, they urge all parties supporting policies in the affected areas to increase their input in order to scale up the provision of condoms and accessible VCT programmes.

The UNAIDS annual report on the global HIV/AIDS epidemic 2002 also claims that 'today we know what works'. However, as is suggested in 'knowledge is not enough', it is clear in the report that socio-political and cultural variables are taken to be important in interventions and that these have to be taken into account when interventions are designed (UNAIDS 2002b: 81). Nevertheless, this awareness is not generally reflected in the main discussions of prevention methods, which constitute that which we know works, reasoning for which is usually given to the reader in a broadly scientific form. The link between the tools of intervention and potential behaviour change is assumed throughout without clear evidence.

Here, too, condoms are seen as 'key to preventing the spread of HIV/AIDS and sexually transmitted infections together' with other methods such as sexual abstinence and the postponement of sexual debut (UNAIDS 2002b: 86). This is also the case according to the US Centers for Disease Control and Prevention (CDC), provided condoms are used correctly. The UNAIDS report suggests that condom-based prevention faces two main problems: availability and the absence of correct knowledge, in particular among the youth. Although societal disapproval on the basis of social and cultural norms is seen as a significant barrier to the effective impact of the condom-based interventions, such interventions nevertheless rely on and expect individuals to take control of their lives and decide to use condoms. Also, what is not discussed much, if at all, is the fact that such behaviour change needs to be consistent throughout a lifetime to be effective.

In addition to general information campaigns, VCT interventions are seen as 'key components of prevention and care programmes' (UNAIDS 2002b: 122). It is claimed that VCT provides people with options: once they know their status, behaviour change becomes possible. As it requires post-testing counselling, people can be helped and directed towards the relevant care services. With the aid of a diagram, UNAIDS (2002b: 123) locates VCT at the centre of HIV-related services ranging across PMTCT, coping, acceptance, behavioural change, STI prevention, normalisation and stigmatisation, and peer and social support. In this way VCT is demonstrably located at the centre of the interventions.

The above information elaborating the knowledge of tools can be analysed at two levels. On the one hand, the above-mentioned policy move can be looked at in relation to the utilisation of these tools. In relation to VCTs, this shift is related to its association with ARVs in particular under recent funding arrangements that have been focusing on ARVs. Talking to a European NGO working extensively on VCTs in rural Rwanda in 2002, it was clear that they were very keen to get people tested and they assumed that this would influence people's behaviour independently of the contextual constraints on people's choices. Therefore they went around the country in their mobile unit trying to convince people to test (without capacity for support in the long term). Since then, this has changed; in 2005 more and more organisations encouraged VCTs for the purpose of rolling out ARVs. According to another large international NGO, this has to do with the international policies that incorporated VCTs with treatment under the prevention into treatment policy: *more and more aid has targeted treatment and not prevention.* It was also pointed out that the take-up rate was high, but that they did not exactly know why and what the impact was.

In terms of condoms, there has been a more interesting shift owing to the largest donor's attitude towards condoms and sex within the PEPFAR framework. In 2005 for instance according to a US-based NGO working under this framework there was nothing *in the country* [Rwanda] *other than abstinence and condoms for high-risk groups.* There were no campaigns for the public distribution of condoms in the country. It was only possible to target condoms to those groups specified within the PEPFAR framework, such as prisoners, the military and the police.[9] *If you are not married and not having sex with a non-regular partner you don't get to be considered. There are no gradients. Young people are left alone, no pressure to engage with 20–45* [age group] *unless they are one of these groups: police/military. You don't get exposed to condoms or other prevention techniques.* However, another organisation working under the same framework suggested that at least it allows them to target these groups, and for other condom-based interventions they get funding from European donors. Here it was said that the problem is *acknowledgement; publicly people are not talking about condoms. The problem is with the public policy.* The free availability of condoms, as opposed to some social marketing mechanism, combined with an educational drive on the issue of condoms and other prevention methods, seems to be lacking. In both cases it is important to realise that the shift in the way the tools are implemented results from a shift at the international policy level. Even if we assume that the content of what we know is sensible it does not seem to have much impact on the way what we know is implemented in a framework. Thus, it seems that the policy shifts reflect the interests and aims of the international actors. It is also important to point out that PEPFAR is highly criticised, even within the donor community, but given the amount of financial input it provides in an *emergency* these criticisms have limited impact within the international governance of the disease, by compartmentalising what various funders do. Of course, this accommodation ignores its possible negative impact across communities where the abstinence message has been rolled out independently of whether the people targeted are sexually active or not.

On the other hand it is possible to consider the relevance of the research establishing these tools as ideal. For example, the research related to condom use and VCT is largely monocausal in that it treats VCT as the only related single variable at the expense of many others which might provide richer and more accurate explanations for behaviours observed in the study groups. This line of critique questions the epistemological licence provided by research that is utilised as justification for various policies in the reports. Furthermore the knowledge claim fails to provide what has been discussed in the last chapter as external validity conditions. Although the research informing the policies around condoms and VCTs discussed in this chapter did not happen in a laboratory, it still aimed at constructing experimental conditions. Therefore, the question of external validity still applies. In this, the knowledge claims should be analysed in terms of their understanding of the people they are targeting and the implicit expectations placed on these people. Such analysis would, as indicated in the last chapter, suggest that knowledge based on scientific/speculative models uses categories that are not appropriate for the targeted people.

Assumptions on VCTs and condoms

Both the referenced and the non-referenced research papers used in the reports can be seen as speculative knowledge.[10] In this model, observations are made from an accumulated understanding that creates an a priori framework for interpreting observed facts and issues. G.E.M. Anscombe argues that, once something happens for which an observational account is available, this knowledge of what happened then constitutes how the same (or similar) actions are observed and interpreted. In this, 'observation is merely an aid, as the eyes are an aid in writing'.[11] In this way, actions become comprehended on the basis of categories of the knowledge that was refined through earlier research. These knowledge claims then provide descriptions for action. Thus, the HIV/AIDS policy reports embody a certain understanding of human action in relation to health and health information based on speculative knowledge available to the researcher on the field of condoms and VCTs (see Morrison *et al.* 2000; Agnew 2000; Efficacy Testing Group (ETG) 2000). The descriptions in the various research studies are mediated through particular categorisations and classifications implicit in the assumptions underpinning the research. These assumptions are relied upon to justify the policy tools discussed.

One of the central categories of this kind is the idea of 'individual'. It is taken as the basic unit of analysis for understanding health behaviour based on social cognition theories (see Gochman 1988). According to Barnett and Whiteside, 'programmes that were rooted in this perspective retained a restricted view of sexuality, reflecting the rather simple perspective of experimental psychology rather than taking account of the complex realities of human sexuality and its social and cultural nature' (2002: 75). The focus on individual intentions and choices for using condoms and the will to be tested are by and large informed by theories of behaviours such as the theory of reasoned action (TRA). While these theories acknowledge the importance of cultural context in assessing beliefs in relation to health, this is considered from some intellectual distance (Agnew 2000). TRA, for example, looks at the behaviour of an individual by analysing the sources of action; it 'makes no provision for the effects of factors outside of the actor's control' (Morrison *et al.* 2000: 29). According to Catherine Campbell, they 'conceptualise the individual as a rational information-processor, whose behaviour is determined by combination of factors', including psychological and perceived norms (Campbell 2003). Here, the emphasis is placed on the individual, whereby behaviour change is related to the cognitive faculties of the individual. No concern for socio-cultural context to sustain such change is articulated. It is assumed that once the information is given the individual will make choices in the right direction.

Another central category of this thinking derives from its general approach. It relates to the understanding of cultural interpretations and the expressions of action in terms of HIV. While cultural expressions are referred to as beliefs informing decisions to act in certain ways, the research is taken to have uncovered how individuals really act, independent of their cultural contexts. For instance, in VCT research it is acknowledged that the socio-cultural and economic context is central for the effective implementation (ETG 2000: 111). Nevertheless this is still based on an understanding of how abstract individuals behave. For example, some findings of the research claim to have demonstrated that:

> individual HIV-1 infected men were more likely than uninfected men to reduce unprotected intercourse with primary and non-primary partners, whereas HIV-1 infected women were more likely than uninfected women to reduce unprotected intercourse with primary partners ... Couples assigned VCT reduced unprotected intercourse with their enrolment partners significantly more than couples assigned health information,

but no differences were found in unprotected intercourse with non-enrolment partners.

(ETG 2000: 103)

Claims such as these are abstract and do not relate to context. In addition, although most theories acknowledge cultural context as important and as having an impact on health behaviour, the expression of cultural reasons for not complying with policies is questioned or at times taken to be invalidated by the scientific research. According to a research study in Ghana, many strategies of intervention into youth behaviour in relation to condoms 'should address ways to overcome barriers to condom use' (Adih and Alexander 1999: 71). It then suggests that:

to correct the misconceptions about condoms, promotion strategies should include information on how to use condoms correctly, including not using expired condoms so as to prevent breaks or tears. It must be also emphasised that with practice, condoms become easier and more fun to use.

(Adih and Alexander 1999: 71)

In this way cultural expressions are taken to be contextual obstacles to be eliminated to help individuals engage with what is assumed in the proposed policies. So the claim that behaviour can be changed is validated by a scientific knowledge claim that under certain conditions individuals have changed behaviour after being through VCT[12] and an assumption that young people would like to be tested and would change their behaviour once tested. In short, the view is that if we overcome the cultural problems people will use condoms. Note that in these discussions the main assumption focuses on the individual behaviour of the potential condom user and the VCT participant. Socio-cultural context is reduced to an externality which needs to be eliminated to release individuals to act in the way that has been assumed in research. This thinking permeates the documents, where nearly all interventions target individual behaviour change.

Another important aspect of the thinking in the research is that individuals at the receiving end of the policies are looked at according to categories established in the research such as: couples, enrolment partners, women of 15–49 or young people. For example, in the afore-mentioned VCT research, people (3,120 individuals and 586 couples) from four countries from various continents and regions were divided into groups of young, unmarried and those who have primary or secondary education. They were further divided by 'assigning a partner type on the basis of the participants' relationship status and living arrangements: primary partner, non-primary partner or enrolment partner' (ETG 2000: 105). Furthermore, the behaviour of people in these categories is then observed and analysed according to the implicit assumptions of how an individual would act given the right information. For example, if women or men find out about their status, say as positive, they will prefer safe sex, particularly if they are part of a couple; or, if their status is negative, this will reduce the possibility of unprotected sex with casual partners (see ETG 2000: 103–7). In a similar vein, if young people are given the right information that condoms prevent HIV infection and have access to condoms they will use them (Adih and Alexander 1999: 69, 71). Clearly, these forecasted actions are ascribed according to the research conducted and, in a feedback loop, the same descriptions constitute the way the actions of the beneficiaries are evaluated to inform us about what to do next.

Interventions, considered from this perspective, assume and expect that individuals want to know their status and then act on it once it is known. Thus, they not only provide descriptions for expected intentional action from people, but they also interpret any action according to these descriptions. In this way certain actions, such as not using a condom, are seen as non-action. The absence of such action is interpreted mostly in terms of lack of information (that is not knowing) or lack of availability of services (that is an access problem) rather than as a different intentionality from the one assumed in the policies. Once it is established that a generic individual within a certain category makes a positive choice on the basis of available information, this directly leads to the expectation that, if information and the tools are provided, people in general can overcome cultural issues and implement the tools independently of the knowledge they normally use to function within their socio-cultural context.

In practice, though, people's actions take place independently of the speculative knowledge that we have as the basis for developing policies in this area. In the end, what we know is related to the general, to universalisable ideas. The next section looks at examples of people's action that appear to us, thinking with the speculative knowledge, as non-acting. The section demonstrates that what is revealed in such action should lead to a rethinking of what we know.[13]

People's experiences of 'our knowledge'

In line with the general purpose of this investigation the following cases are used to question the claim *we know* implicit in HIV/AIDS policy interventions. This is done with the intention of defamiliarising our understanding of the role of particular tools, condoms and VCTs, in the HIV/AIDS context (Marcus and Fischer 1999: 137). These illustrations present a knowledge base distinct from what we know. In these examples the tension created by our knowledge, used as the basis of HIV/AIDS policy interventions within people's everyday lives, is revealed. This aims at disrupting the accepted common sense about these tools within policy circles, by introducing the way these tools are perceived within their domain of application. Also, it presents a distinct domain consisting of a different kind of knowledge and repertoire for engaging with HIV/AIDS from the everyday perspective of infected and affected people. Therefore, these experiences question the implicit external validity claims, that is the assumptions by which research results can be generalised outside the particular research context where they are established. In this way the external validity claims that are used to justify the policy formulations within this knowledge domain are questioned.

The following snapshots are employed to highlight and exemplify, following Mary Douglas, the sources of seeming non-action, by looking at some relevant socio-cultural and economic mechanisms that inform people's everyday actions in various contexts (Douglas 1992: 252; Ferguson 1999). They question the way in which behaviour change is discussed on the basis of particular models. Specifically, the case studies show that the relationship between the available information and the conditions of behaviour change appear to be much more complicated than is assumed in many of the behavioural models. The general assumptions about the available information and the subsequent behaviour change also appear to be over-simplistic. Thus, the general idea that once people know they are in danger they will behave differently, use condoms and start to abstain is challenged.

I now present cases in three areas within which people's actions are shaped.[14]

Social-cultural issues

In a suburban hospital in Gaborone, a group (three male and five female) of young HIV positive people were trying to establish themselves as a community group. We gradually talked about how things could be changed and how it might be possible to have an impact. One of the participants, K., said,[15] *Mostly women are in danger. We have to change men. (What do you mean?) Men don't participate. It is difficult to talk. There is a tradition of promiscuity. Men's sleeping around is accepted and not discussed. Men also don't talk about their problems with people, let alone problems with sex. (Even among themselves?) Yes.* In this instance two men are smiling with a certain unease. The older one says, *We might be the guilty group on this. (Is this a cross-generational issue?) It is, but denial of the disease is a major issue among the youth. (Why?) Potential embarrassment of talking about it. Attitudes of men are the same when they are teachers, police, doctors. So, you will feel embarrassed to talk to them about sexual issues.* In order to elaborate the question, I asked the young men, *Is this the case, and what can be done?* He smiled and shook his head; this was his only response.

The social norms about men's behaviour in the society are clearly providing the grounds for action: *not to talk or not to test.* The gender relations and the social status of men in the society in this context are sustaining a particular image for men. The cultural boundaries of what men can talk about are clearly limiting what can be done in Botswana. According to David Chizao Ngele of the Botswana Network of People Living with HIV and AIDS

(BONEPWA), men are very difficult to capture because they don't come to meetings and, even if they do come and listen to the information, they 'consider themselves beyond the information; also they don't immediately relate info to themselves until such time that there is something wrong with them'. Even in this situation, such a person would not talk to his fellow men and would act as if there was nothing wrong with him. The general understanding of silence around certain areas, such as sex, clearly sets limits on what can be discussed and acted on. Talking about condoms by outsiders will be listened to, but in the end it is excluded by the listeners as it does not provide a feasible action under the descriptions available to the listeners from their everyday experience.

This was also clear in the reaction of the young participant in the group discussion. Even though the group are very open and clear about their HIV status, this young man preferred to smile rather than participate in the debate by talking. Bawani Mutshewa, a peer educator in the HIV/AIDS field for ten years in Botswana, suggested that *talking and behaviour change are not the same. If they can justify their actions, they don't change behaviour.* She has observed this issue in her training sessions with young male trainers talking to groups. They try to inform their peer groups and talk to them about HIV and behaviour change. However, *once the session ends those young men immediately switch back to their habitual behaviour and pursue young women who are responding as if they have not been told about the disease.* Clearly while the messages provided are direct, they do not go far enough to engage with the socio-cultural descriptions that frame, for example, the flirting conventions in the group. In this context, for example, an abstaining young man might be stigmatised. In this sense what Mutshewa describes as justification appears to be much more than mere excuses, and more like socio-cultural categories of behaviour that are observed by people. Furthermore, the socio-cultural norms and communication forms influence whether people are perceptive to the generalised messages or not. This then results in the above-observed discordant behaviour. A similar issue was mentioned by another peer educator, F., who himself was a young man in Butare, Rwanda. F said that first *we do peer education in various steps, but condoms are not talked about. We try to get girls to say no to sex. This is important as sometimes among the young people around here no means yes.*

In 2005 in Bujumbura, Burundi, at a group discussion about prevention methods and the way they are promoted, J., who has been involved with HIV activism, argued that there is a stigma and talked about the logic behind it. (His comments are also important for VCT-related interventions as this is related to ascertaining a person's HIV status.) He said, *It is a disease because you have done something wrong so it is your sin. There are not many people in the public declaring their status. It is particularly difficult for politicians as revealing might position them in contrast to their constituents that judge him as a sinful individual.* In relation to prevention he said, *Since HIV is related with what you are doing* [a wrong] *once you reveal yourself and say you are HIV positive you then cannot go about sensitising people. Condoms are difficult to distribute as people do not like to take them.* Then he explained, *In Kirundi, sex-related words or language is related with swearing and other bad behaviour. It makes it difficult to talk about anything about sex in public. People would not listen to these as they try to make sense of why they are talked in this manner. Sex is big taboo. Only people in same age group and sex group might talk about it. It is not done publicly.* The language issue was also highlighted by U., a senior communication specialist who worked on HIV campaigns. She said that *it is very difficult to get agreement about sex-related words when we are designing posters as people are very reluctant to go with the general prevention messages that explicitly talk about prevention methods.* She also said that *it is difficult under these circumstances to get people even trained as they are reluctant to talk or show to others how for instance to use condoms. They get frustrated.*

Gender issues

M., who lives on the outskirts of Kampala, is in the central hospital's ante-natal clinic for the third time in the last three years. She is usually not working but selling fruit on the roadside while her husband is the main income earner. He is usually in the city or travelling between towns, leaving M. alone in their community. She is Dr L.'s patient. According to the doctor, two of M.'s babies have died. She has HIV positive status. The babies died as the disease passed from mother to child. The doctor has never seen M.'s husband. The hospital has been working on testing new methods to stop this transmission process in such cases by using new drugs developed in industrialised countries. The hospital is also the location for a research experiment administered to many pregnant women. The doctor in charge is frustrated, *as she knows M. very well from previous years.* She thinks that, *although M. has been informed many times about her condition and its consequences for her babies, she keeps coming back pregnant. But also she sometimes misses her crucial appointments, as she cannot leave her home as she wants.*

Here one can see that the intentional action assumed and expected by policy and the research underpinning policies on condoms and VCTs is challenged: why is she not reacting appropriately given that she is in a stable relationship? Surely she should be getting appropriate drugs at the right stages of her pregnancy and, as she knows contraception is better for her health, why is she not doing anything about it? Although clearly she knows her status and she is given all the available information about the disease and knows how it passes, she still shows up pregnant and at times she does not attend the follow-up clinics to get her pills. All of this suggests that it is better to consider this situation on the basis of what motivates *her* rather than using *our* categories, to construct her seemingly contrary actions to her own *benefit*. In other words, rather than considering her situation according to the implicitly assumed behaviour type in the description provided for certain actions in the policies, it is better to do the analysis based on the actions that are available to her in her context.[16]

Similar patterns appear in other cases. In Maseru, Lesotho, while discussing the impact of the disease and prevention with a number of HIV positive people who were in their 20s and were coming together in the offices of a small local organisation in 2005, Z. argued that *When people are poor there is nothing but to sell themselves . . . this is also true once you are on drugs; it* [poverty] *is still a problem. Bosotho men they don't want to use condoms. Even if you say well I am HIV positive they still want to have sex without condoms. Women are not able to say anything about it. Also when they push their husbands or boyfriends to go to testing they are becoming violent; they don't want to be tested.* T. agreed with her and added, *You know, condoms we have are not good for pleasure so people are not using them. Stigma is there, outside the cities. People want to talk to us but whether they change anything is a different question . . .*

People clearly know what the disease is and what it does to them, but when they act as if they are not very concerned the outside observer assumes that they don't know. M. is acting as a woman, a wife, and a wife with a child. Such roles provide meaningful categories in her social context for action. For example, her role as a wife does not allow her to discuss her state with her husband. In addition, changing her treatment of her baby or attempting to use contraceptives might indicate that she has failings as a woman and wife. Even going to the hospital regularly might create suspicion. In the context of the disease, the community might assume that she has HIV, thus making her vulnerable. In the case of Z., the context of poverty is influencing how she can act or not. The position of women in relation to the choices of men to use condoms also constrains what they can do. In addition, T.'s response brings up another issue which is not usually discussed in condom-based prevention policies: pleasure and the way it is viewed within a certain socio-cultural framework.[17] Most of the interventions on condom use or VCTs have tried to create self-reflexive individuals, particularly within the context of sexual behaviour. And, of course, part of this self-reflexivity is also about a responsibility to a community and that community's health (this is where we add morality to the medical interventions). However, neither policies nor their implementation have paid enough attention, or understood, the fact that sex is not merely a health issue; it involves pleasure too. Furthermore, sexual behaviour also plays a role in how people negotiate gender-based social relations.

Thus, the categories setting out pathways for action should be related to cultural and/or economic rationales. In other words, they should reflect agency in context. Clearly, for a child-bearing woman to talk to her husband about condom use might result in a divorce and bodily harm, neither of which is desirable. An insistence on contraception, including those tools such as microbicides that are being developed, which appear positive in abstract general terms, might also have adverse cultural implications in terms of child-bearing capacity, which is viewed as a desirable in the community. Such gender-based issues are also observable among different age groups. They are not particular to adults nor to relations within marriage.

The reaction of a group of mixed young people in Maseru, who were involved with discussing prevention methods in their schools as peer volunteers, was very interesting in highlighting the impact of gender norms and the way they influence people's behaviour independently of known prevention messages. When they were asked 'Can you talk about HIV with your friends?', N. pointed out, *You know, I had a school assembly where they talked about sex. Everyone was laughing. No one was listening . . . After that we had guys defending their status.* Most of them argued that *No, you can't talk to your friends about serious stuff. They will take the piss for a month. Others you can talk to but friends, no, no . . .* When asked 'Can partners – girl-/boyfriends – talk to each other?', they said, *Not really, at least girls can't. They are dumped if they get too sensitive . . .* Girls in the group agreed with this and added, *Girls don't have much to say if they want to be with someone.* S. said, *Men want to do what they want to do . . . They want to get laid not to be lectured.* N. also suggested that there are people who get raped but said, *Who are you going to tell? If you go to the police they think you are a prostitute. A lot of rape is not reported.*

Socio-economic issues

The question of poverty is also central. In Rwanda many pointed out that the inability of people to get out of poverty influences what they can do in relation to the disease independently of whether they are tested or not. For a senior director of an international NGO, involved with VCT provision, poverty was linked with nutrition. He said, *VCT does not work without nutrition and that is not possible to do. Our donors are not allowing us to engage with it. There is hunger in the country.* He added, *But we just have to keep testing with the hope that maybe we will make a difference.* A field worker in one clinic gave a possible reason for the seemingly high uptake of this VCT service. His view was also shared by a number of others that *the Rwandese community was vertically structured and oriented and people would generally follow vertical interventions.* The link between poverty and HIV, in terms of both nutrition and access to other resources such as care and treatment, was consistently made. One donor representative strongly emphasised the importance of food security for communities and that it should be underpinned by the introduction of new crops.[18]

Sometimes access to these resources is constrained by the concerns about remaining in a family. Gender dynamics create other implications too. An HIV positive person in Kigali argued that this was not always very easy: *Men are sending women to test but once it is clear that women are HIV positive then they separate and tell them that it is not their business.* This was also argued by another field worker in the HIV positive people's group who stated that there is a problem with mothers disclosing their status, which might lead to a divorce. In another VCT project, the field worker noted that *while most couples stay together they also see if they are discordant they split or one of the partners comes back with another partner in a few months.*[19] According to another specialist, *There is more and more poverty as the affected are unable to work for the family. It is a vicious circle.* In a rural clinic, an HIV positive person said, *I have the illness. I have not got the money for the hospital. I cannot work because of the illness.*

One of the important mechanisms for the spreading of the prevention message in Rwanda is the church and church-related charity organisations. The head of one of these charities said, *Food is important. They need to have food regularly beyond, as they do, once a day when there are these interventions* [VCTs and ARVs]. He also highlighted another process which clearly has implications for poverty within communities. He said, *In order to get married, couples will have to be tested. Most districts require it now. But we also hear that there are illegal marriages* [outside the church] *to avoid this requirement. We have introduced this requirement into the tradition by saying that 'Knowing the person is also knowing their health.' (How about the widows and discordant couples? Are these groups becoming much more vulnerable?) Given that they have not been tested with their discordant state it will be really impossible to get married. However, there does not seem to be any other obvious way.* In terms of widows, while acknowledging that remarrying was a serious problem for infected people or widows of deceased infected people, he said, *Widowhood is becoming accepted. Women with children are better off than men who are widowed, as children are becoming caretakers. Men are more interested in remarrying.*

In Zambia, another effect of poverty was pointed out by K. and J., who are members of a network organisation for people living with HIV in Lusaka. Both have been diagnosed and have decided to go public about their status so that they can manage their lives better.

(Do most people reveal their status?) No, they don't, can't. (Do they test for the disease?) Not always. Employment is important. (What do you mean?) If you reveal your status you would lose your job. It is not legal but employers find a way to stop you working. (How does this influence people?) They don't want to go to test. If they are tested they hide the result, from everyone. Mostly they act as if everything is normal. They need money to look after themselves and the family. You know, if you are tested positive and get sick you need your job for the money. They also keep infecting. (What happens if they lose their employment?) They become desperate: no money, no food, a lot of stress and the disease moves faster. Some go back to their villages but do not talk about the disease. Some get married, as they need someone to look after them.

According to them, decisions on whether to test or not are framed within concerns of employment and obligations to the family, and within socio-cultural perceptions, legal procedures and economic conditions. The impact of the larger economic environment and, in particular, decisions based on ongoing developmental interventions that are influencing people's opportunities must also be considered as relevant to these issues. Consider, for instance, Zambia's copper industry, one of the biggest industries in the country, which has become smaller and smaller. Its related job market has shrunk and this has influenced whether people can afford to change jobs or not.

It is also clear from K. and J.'s comments that the stigma attached to the disease leads employers to find other reasons to stop people with HIV from working. For the unemployed, this creates a problem, as the next potential employer becomes suspicious of their reasons for seeking new employment. Clearly, while HIV patients are trying to remain in employment, their status as patients in a particular culture is interfering with their rights under labour law. This creates a paradoxical dilemma for people with the disease. They need resources to be able to initiate a change in their lifestyle, as asserted by the research on the impact of VCTs, to look after themselves and try to establish a future for their family. Yet the disease makes it nearly impossible to remain in employment. Therefore, people either refuse to test or, even if they are tested, the test results are ignored in order to keep employment.

The people whose views are presented here as examples are acting in the way socio-cultural contexts expect them to act. In turn the socio-cultural expectations expressed in the local categorisations and types are shaped and influenced by historical and economic changes. The impact of colonialism and the changes experienced in the family and community structures as a result of decades of development interventions have undoubtedly influenced the way people engage with each other and their cultural practices (see Boyer 1990). Therefore, non-compliance with the expectations of policy frameworks or international policies at large reveals a dynamic process within which people make sense of their lives in each context. Furthermore, race, gender and class relations influenced by these processes are central to understanding what non-action means and what leads to it. In other words, non-action or non-adherence as observed by outside experts has an important meaning and describes socio-cultural relations within which the particular individual is located. However, it is central to understand that cultural and socio-economic aspects are mutually constitutive. No culture remains the same; it changes and responds to changing times. As a result, the reactions to international interventions recounted above manifest actions that are based on descriptions produced by some combination of these aspects: the local cultural, social and economic context, the past history of development interventions and so on.

Colliding knowledge domains

What we know provides a tool for action, for example by categorising people according to regular couples, singles and people in multiple relations for VCT purposes. But this misses the point, in that it does not engage with the fact that in many contexts people have multiple regular relations across various spaces within which they conduct relations. For example, presenting a relationship as a couple in an urban VCT clinic does not necessarily imply that these persons are not in other relations in their rural connections or while travelling in other urban areas (see Sikwibele *et al.* 2000; Baylies *et al.* 2000). From the perspective of regular settled relations, all of these might present themselves as regular household-based relations, albeit in differentiated spaces. The clear statements in research towards couples shape interventions more towards couples, which then creates a general barrier in various contexts based on the selection bias that has been carried from the research to the implementation. In a similar vein we know that condoms are very effective when used properly and constantly, or that counselling couples is very useful when they are talking to each other. However, how these things are performed as activities with others actors influencing them from a given context, as highlighted earlier, seems to be something we don't really know. How and whether these methods fit the socio-cultural functionings of a community are not articulated. One of the areas where this collision of knowledge can be observed is in the education and training of local medical staff to deliver what we know works to their communities. In order to be able to deliver our message these people have to change their behaviour too.

According to a senior nursing staff worker in Maseru, Lesotho, *It is difficult to get them* [nurses] *training in VCTs as issues are not easy to talk about. You cannot talk about some of these issues openly with people. Sometimes it is all about issues such as 'Eat food, do this, do that' or if the person is switched on they can say 'Don't do it again.' The question of how you counsel is a big problem. It is difficult to talk about condoms, particularly in Catholic institutions such as the hospitals. People give them behind the scenes but they would not like to house posters about them.* And, presumably, this tension is also observable in many other areas of interventions that involve peer educators: NGO workers, pharmacists and other local people who are trying to deliver pre-formulated international messages to their communities.

What, for example, does it mean for a young man, a counsellor, to get hold of a condom in Botswana or in Lesotho without feeling that he is being watched and judged by his peers or by a pharmacist or a nurse? Furthermore, what is the impact on his actions of this clash of expectations, on the one hand from the information distributed on condoms and on the other hand from his social-cultural context as a young man both as a person who needs condoms and as a counsellor? We might infer from this that we do know that in this situation the young man as a person would prefer to ignore the information and not do anything. In this way the young man's action becomes inaction in correlation with what we know. Moreover, we then argue that his inaction is related to the cultural parameters which are influencing behaviour change negatively. Yet when we do this, what is reflected in his perceived non-action is ignored and also constructed into an idea of culture which is stagnant. The best example of this approach to culture is seen in the debates on stigmatisation. Considering that sick people in general are not a source of such strong stigmatisation in most contexts, one needs to consider stigmatisation as a complex response rather than a crass cultural position. One needs to think what is being stigmatised: behaviour leading to the disease, the person, the relations. Then we might be able to engage with what is seen as a problem in HIV/AIDS from a particular context rather than considering such expressions of stigmatisation as direct opposition to our position. Yet stigmatisation, within the existing policy frameworks, typically leads to a response which is to provide more information and to distribute more condoms. This is done while still not knowing much about the stigma/non-action, which is actually a manifestation of complex relationships among social, cultural, economic and historical conditions and their response to a new happening (HIV/AIDS, international policy responses and actors) in a given context. The problem here is not simply a technical implementation issue which can be remedied if we change the delivery mechanism of the tools that are discussed. It is about the dominance of one domain of knowledge informing the policies. This needs to be challenged in order to be able to influence policies from the targeted people's own perspectives.

The tension evident in most of the examples above can be seen as what Verweij describes as prevention policies' potential negative impact when they create grounds for lack of confidence, hopelessness and indirect vulnerability for people. Before I move on to the next section, I would like to add that this collision of knowledge is the source of the disconnect between policy implementers and their target groups, as implementers are not usually able to ignore their own knowledge base. Volunteers, for instance, who are thrown into the world of NGOs in an attempt to help out at the time of this emergency are a good example of this. Their knowledge base does not fit with what they observe. And there is also a big question of whether they have the right skills to understand what is going on, on the ground. In Lusaka, Zambia, in a local NGO, which was supported by a bilateral donor to work on HIV/AIDS sensitisation in a community outside the city within an industrial area, the programme director was a bright, very well-educated, Western volunteer. After building a community centre where they were hoping to attract women to meet for discussions on HIV, they got some people to come. It became clear that the local community had emerged around a particular industry and through migrant labourers coming to the area from other parts of the country. Thus, it has a particular outlook as a community. In the discussions, sex work, which had developed over time, was pointed out as one of the important issues on HIV. However, when I asked the programme coordinator what was the sexual profile of the community, what were the patterns of sexual relations and what people themselves thought about sex, the programme director had no answers. I was told that there had been a research document produced on some of these issues a year ago or so but since the director was very involved with the project she had not had the time to read this document in the nine months since she had arrived here. There was no doubt that this person was doing her best. She had her target group/

population and her policy tools to get to them. According to her knowledge base, everything was in order to be able to implement the project. It seemed what people thought about their own sex lives and relations was not central to the intervention. This, of course, is not a unique problem to NGOs. Many international civil servants mentioned this problem: *When you are working on a project you really focus and after a while you don't look beyond the project.* But of course this is a peculiar problem since it is associated with the way we know and how we apply this under the logic of the projects that do not give space and time to engage with the people as they function in practice. The next section outlines a theoretical framework that would allow us to understand how this disjuncture in knowledge is produced and also how people might rethink the claim that we know within the existing policy tools.

How do we rethink what we know?

Arturo Escobar suggests that 'development has relied exclusively on one knowledge system, namely, the modern Western one. The dominance of this knowledge system has dictated the marginalisation and disqualification of non-Western knowledge systems' (1995: 13). The discourse on HIV is conjoined with that of development. Both are located within the Western tradition of analytical reasoning. This tradition provides the awareness for what is to be known for HIV and the conditions of knowing subject, from within a particular social framework (Sahlins 1976: 166). The behaviour change models underpinning VCT and condom-based interventions, for instance, assume a model individual behaviour located in a Western context. Therefore, there is a need to look at the knowledge that produces policy frameworks by relying on a particular Western epistemological system in the field of HIV, since in its application it produces the marginalisation and disqualifications of people's own knowledge of what works. Policies on condom use and VCTs are based on Western behavioural models (the health belief model and the theory of reasoned action) and on how they can be used to change people's behaviour (see Parker 2001; Campbell 2003). The examples above show that there is a gap between these behavioural models and what determines people's behaviour in a context. This gap has important implications for the way policy tools are articulated. The problematic impact of this discourse presents us with a renewed urgency to fuse philosophical analysis directly with the developmental concerns in order to unpack the manner in which policies are produced. In this way the hope is to be able to think about 'new practices of seeing, knowing and being' (Escobar 1995: 223), as well as help to construct policies which are sensitive to local people's views and contexts. Thus, in what follows I propose a philosophical framework to understand the source of the claim 'we know what works' and its potential impact on people. It looks at how knowledge is constructed in our claims.

The central concern of this chapter relates to the knowledge claims in HIV/AIDS policy implementations: what it is, how it works and what it produces.

The two sets of knowledge, Western knowledge and people's own everyday knowledge, that are discussed above can be seen in terms of speculative and practical knowledge. The relationship between these is articulated by G.E.M. Anscombe in her seminal work on intention and action (Anscombe 1957). Her theory of *action under description*, and the basis of this in her thinking about knowledge, has direct relevance for this study since it unpacks the mechanism of knowledge about people (see also Davidson 1980a, 1980b). It allows us to understand people's behaviours and our reaction to them, as discussed in the examples, in relation to a process that is influenced by the two domains of knowledge. Anscombe's work allows one to ground the process of how people become objects of attention, as patients and beneficiaries of HIV/AIDS policies, and also points towards an uneasy relationship in the process whereby one mechanism of knowing is privileged over another (or, in Hobart's terms, ignored and dismissed or, in Escobar's perspective, marginalised and delegitimated). It is this relationship which is central for understanding what the claim *we know* produces.

Anscombe's idea of action under description can be summarised as follows: an action can be described in many ways by attributing different intentions to the actor in relation to it; then when we describe an action as it takes place (ours or others') we attribute an implicit intention to it. This description depends on the describing person knowing a form of this action. In the case of HIV/AIDS, and in the particular cases discussed, our perspective on the disease provides the set of descriptions for the actions of targeted people. For instance, our descriptions construct M.'s resistance, for example not using contraceptives, as discussed above, as a non-action due to ignorance or lack of information. In the case of Botswana, the same set of descriptions are used to interpret the young man's resistance to condom use and his reticence to talk about the issue as non-action. However, M., or the young man in Botswana, might and probably would, given the discussion above, describe their actions in a form that is different from the one which is available to us. M. cannot talk to her husband about her situation as his reaction might be violent and might result in M. being pushed out of her community. In this way M. cannot, for example, stop breastfeeding or suggest contraceptive use to her husband. The intentions of the young man in Botswana may relate to his difficulty in asking for condoms since the providers, including some medical providers, consider such demands to be related to inappropriate sexual activity and thus, while providing condoms, they disapprove. As a result, what is a non-action for us can be seen as valid actions under the descriptions available to M. or the young man in their contexts. These contextual descriptions provide intentions that are different from the ones assumed in the behaviour models underpinning the policy tools.

According to Ian Hacking, if 'the field of descriptions changes . . . so the actions that I can perform' (Hacking 1995). This limitation to intentional action was articulated earlier by Anscombe when she argued that intentions need to respond to a 'why' question (Anscombe 1957: 6). In this way, an action takes place dependent on a particular descriptive context or, in simple terms, the context in which 'why' is asked. A description is an act of describing and implicitly ascribing the intent of the actor in relation to a knowledge base. In this sense, a certain act of doing X cannot take place unless X is available in the knowledge base as a description for such an act (Anscombe 1957: 23–4). Therefore, description is a function of the knowledge base that provides a cognitive map for attributing intent. Depending on the available knowledge on X, there may be different categories of doing various things, dependent on descriptions from various perspectives, from which an intention to do X can be evaluated. But the intention of doing X can only be evaluated by us using descriptions that use categories of doing available to us.

In the cases discussed, there are different sets of knowledge on HIV/AIDS available to different people. People engage according to the different categories or roles that provide them with cognitive maps about what can be done in their particular contexts. While K. and J. in Zambia appear as patients according to our behavioural descriptions, which provides an intention for their particular actions under that perspective, the behaviours and responses to the policy tools are based on, in M.'s case, her being a wife and a mother in a particular community. If M. talks to her husband in line with our expectations about contraception, she will be confronted by her husband's reaction, which may well lead to destitution since he is highly likely to leave her. In contrast to our expectation, that knowing his status leads to healthy behaviour change, in J.'s case revealing that he has been to testing could jeopardise his employment. Acting on the basis of our expectations and tools in this situation, he would face job loss combined with a decline in his ability to maintain a family, which is likely to lead in turn to a state of serious depression and further health problems. In short, his economic ability to look after himself and the economically depressed context are the descriptive contexts that inform his intentions and actions in terms of our policy tools.

These cases reveal that some of these local categories framing intentions for these people's lives are not compatible with our assumptions about why and how people choose to change their behaviours. Furthermore, the disjuncture between people's actions and policy makers' expectations demonstrates that these local descriptions directing action are not accessible to us in developing the policy tools. This presents a challenge to us for making sense of people's actions. What if doing X is described by the actor in such a way that it provides an intention which is not covered by the knowledge of X that we have? In other words, if the action appears to be based on an unlikely intention according to us or if we don't have a description for this action, is it, therefore, a non-action? Anscombe attempts to overcome this problem by suggesting that 'roughly speaking, a man intends to do what he does' (Anscombe 1957: 25). So, in what is done there is a description.[20] Here the link, between what is claimed by an actor and us evaluating what is done/said, is an interesting one. Wittgenstein suggests that in talking about intention, in doing this or that, 'I want to tell him something about *myself*, which goes

LIVERPOOL JOHN MOORES UNIVERSITY
LEARNING SERVICES

beyond what happened at that time' (Wittgenstein 1997: 659, emphasis in original). Then my description of my action would be based on something about me, the knowledge I have which may or may not be the same as your knowledge, albeit articulated as a response to your question: why? So when one describes (say) an HIV/AIDS patient's intention in Africa we say something about *ourselves* by ascribing something of ours on to her action, whereas her response, verbally or behaviourally, is telling us something about herself and her context, albeit in response to our question. In other words this response is a link between our speculative and her practical knowledge. And the response can be used as a way of evaluating what is being assumed in the speculative knowledge from the practical perspective.

Implicit in these arguments is the status of knowledge and the way the two domains of knowledge interact, denoted here as a distinction between intuitive knowing in a context and knowing through external observation. The second one, which relies on the speculative model in most of its engagements, has been misunderstood in the Western philosophy according to Anscombe. As a result, description in our thinking relies mostly on speculative knowledge (see also Richards 1993). When this is considered in combination with the fact that observation takes place on the basis of certain categorical knowledge or description of what is being observed (see Vitebsky 1993), a description tends to be given for an action which is independent of what the actor might express intuitively. Furthermore, Anscombe argues that speculative knowledge would still know what happens even if an action fails to occur. She asks: 'if . . . my knowledge is independent of what actually happens, how can it be knowledge of what does happen?' (Anscombe 1957: 45).

Implications of this approach

Using Anscombe's questioning it is possible to consider practical knowledge as related to the actor exercising a certain knowledge to act. Thus, this knowledge base for description would make action, on this basis, intentional. According to her, this indicates a certain '"knowing one's way about" the matters described in the description under which an action can be called intentional' (Anscombe 1957: 48). Considering action as the execution of intentions, this knowing becomes part of the knowledge base that provides descriptions for action. If one assumes that speculative knowledge describes an action following certain rules based on its categories and classifications, then practical knowledge in this sense is much more about an execution of intentions within a given context dependent on the actor's knowledge of her location in that place independent of the speculative categories.[21] This shows that action is 'socially constructed and fundamentally collective in nature' (Parker 2001: 168). The speculative knowledge is inferred from already known objects while the practical knowledge relies on a certain situational understanding (also see Vitebsky 1993). Here by 'situational' one does not suggest a realm of abstracted understanding but an understanding inferred from being in a situation that is familiar to one and responding to the situation within an available repertoire of meanings.

This discussion raises several issues in relation to HIV/AIDS policies. With it one can view the claim *we know what works* as indicating a set of descriptions embodied in particular policy frameworks and one can juxtapose these with their implementations, implementations in which people, asked to act in a certain way, execute certain intentions. In this, people are made in what we know and how we know. As a result we ascribe certain characteristics to people. Then we assume that the actors should follow a certain behaviour. Therefore, the discussion presented above can help provide a response to the question of this chapter by pointing out a disjunction between the needs expressed by people and the 'what we know' which directs policy implementation.

Of course, this approach relies on a particular viewpoint on knowledge. According to this perspective, knowledge is related to categories, codes, processes and people's attempts to give meaning to the experiences in their lives (Long 2001: 189). This attempt to make sense of lives' accumulation of what is codified, categorised and classified as particular knowledge gives impetus to further action by informing what is to be done on that basis (see Hacking 1995, 1998). This process can be seen as embedded in the concepts that we use for articulating people's experiences. Categories allow behaviour or experience to be generalised to indicate a pattern or a certain kind which is then used to analyse individual occurrences. The question is related to the fact that the categorisation, around condoms and VCTs, describes possibilities of action in general whereby it also starts to make up people, as suggested by Hacking, independent of the context in which they live (Hacking 2003: 40; see also Mudimbe 1988: 72–3). Thus, rather than empowering and providing spaces for action, it removes people's existing agency within the context. These categories allow us to talk about groups of people as sex workers, orphans, pregnant women, youth and so on. Furthermore, we are also talking about the elaboration and structuring of these categories around clear, identifiable behaviour types. There is no doubt that these groups are discernible, but the people in them are more than what typifies them or their behaviour or allows them to be slotted into one of these categories, such as their perceived sexual habits, age or marital status. Yet interventions are mostly based on knowledge of these limited categorisations.

Within the scientific categories that have directed research in the HIV/AIDS field, this process can be observed by focusing on 'surveys of risk-related sexual behaviour and on knowledge, attitudes, and beliefs about sexuality that might be associated with the risk of HIV infection. Most of these studies have aimed to collect quantifiable data' (Parker 2001: 164). As Wittgenstein notes, 'concepts lead us to make investigations; are the expression of our interest, direct our interests' (Wittgenstein 1997: 570).[22] Thus, concepts, such as the behaviour models used in HIV/AIDS interventions, should be considered as having particular histories and as implicitly expressing a certain constellation of relations and interests.[23] Thus, this perspective highlights the gap between the categories informing the policy tools and the categories through which people react to those tools, as exemplified in the previous section.

This problem with HIV/AIDS is general to international development and has been discussed in the literature. For instance, Hobart observes that 'the problem of underdevelopment and its solutions' are based on such reference points within Western scientific knowledge. He calls it 'world-ordering knowledge' that 'ignores and dismisses indigenousness knowledges' (Hobart 1993: 1). Hobart's world-ordering view links to Nelson Goodman's more philosophical arguments about worldmaking that were discussed in Chapter 2. Goodman argues that 'worldmaking as we know it always starts from worlds already on hand – the making is remaking' (Goodman 1978: 6). In this sense, categorisation carries in itself a certain continuity with its domain of articulation. Thus, development discourse from its location within the Western categories shapes what it observes and on the way dismisses people's own understanding of themselves (see Mudimbe 1988, 1994; Said 1978). A change in categories also implies a change in the grounds for action and a parallel change in the kinds of person that could take action as a result (see also Douglas 1986: 100; Hacking 2003: 107). Goodman's contribution supplements this argument here, as it suggests that this changing space is mostly influenced by whoever is considered to be the world-maker. Here the world-maker can be observed in the form of the international policy experts, or the HIV/AIDS adviser, who constructs and decides about the target groups and groups at risk by recategorising people according to an expert knowledge claim.[24] The change initiated will be located within this maker's socio-cognitive world, therefore categorising what is out there according to a particular social map. While the process is enabling for the world-maker as an agent, its impact on the agency of what is categorised as patients or as risk groups, in the present context of people in the middle of HIV/AIDS, is less straightforward. As Parker comments, 'new knowledge and information about perceived sexual risk will always be interpreted within the context of pre-existing systems of meaning' (Parker 2001: 167). The relationship between the world-maker's or policy maker's meaning and the available pre-existing meanings can create a potentially counterproductive policy environment.

Since policy in general, and the HIV-related policies discussed in this work, can be seen as an intentional action towards a domain with an expectation of intentional response (action) from that domain, this mismatch in the knowledge worlds produces ineffective policies. In the present investigation, the policy interventions, actions are justified on the basis of the implicit claim *we know what works*. The justification here links itself on to one side of the knowledge debate by attributing a certain nature to what is considered to be infected and affected, taken to be what we know through particular categories and classifications of HIV/AIDS. In this, people are constituted as kinds of people in relation to a particular HIV/AIDS knowledge. The problem here is the relationship between such emergent thinking, which informs policy interventions, and the already-existing knowledge in social contexts.

By considering action under description in this framework, one can look at the relationship between the claim 'we know' which prescribes certain action and its knowledge base. This would look at codes, categories and classifications that are used in making descriptions for expected actions as the outcome of HIV/AIDS interventions, *best practices*, meaningful. The distinction between the two domains of knowledge then questions whether this knowledge, that informing the particular policy prescriptions, is relevant to the everyday lives of people. This requires understanding that the claim we know not only prescribes action, but also constitutes the subject that is addressed in these prescriptions as a particular target or risk group. Most critically, Anscombe's thinking on practical knowledge enables the reinterpretation of non-adherence to policy implementations, observed among many people categorised as target groups in HIV/AIDS interventions, as an intentional act. This in turn suggests that there is a particular description (knowledge) which is not available to the policy prescriptions, rather than some lack of motivation or initiative. In this way, the present knowledge base underpinning the policy is seen as insufficient for claiming *we know*.

Conclusion

I have argued that perceived non-action should be considered and analysed as an indication of a certain knowledge base and a source of categorisation that provides a description for action accessible to people whom we perceive only as patients, infected and vulnerable. In this way, the claim that *we know* is questioned. I have argued that this claim is not only unstable but also becomes unsustainable as the source of policy interventions. There is a disjuncture between what we know on the basis of speculative knowledge and the reality of what people know in terms of the context of the disease. This has demonstrated the limits of what we can know and also the problems with thinking that we know. I argue that our knowing is mostly based on medical knowledge and behaviour change hypotheses that are inferred from this knowledge domain. It is about the disease in the abstract to which an abstract set of responses is developed. This creates an immanent flaw in engaging with the disease. As it is commonly used, the perspective is far from giving, empowering or utilising the already-existing agency of the people in order to be able to deal with the problems of HIV/AIDS.

This conclusion highlights the impact of the claim *we know* in three central areas for dealing with HIV/AIDS: the context of the disease, the assumptions about behaviour, and the culture as the context of people's everyday lives. Knowledge claims about these areas must be opened up for discussion and contestation by people from the domain of interventions.

Although we know about the disease, we don't know much about the disease in context (see Farmer 1993, 1999). The trust in the procedures and logical outcomes of methods of intervention reduces the engagement between the policy makers and the people who are in need to an instrumental relationship in which the former communicate only what they know works. In this, people emerge as a population that is subdivided into target groups or a designated set of vulnerable groups, differentiated according to the categories available to the policy makers. While the person with the disease becomes an agent within these categorisations, the policies do not reflect much about a person's functionings and her abilities within her own context. Some of these socio-cultural issues are seen as externalities influencing her health choices, externalities relative to our knowledge claims based on models of individual behaviour. Thus, the policy framework remains in a differentiated, and to a degree dissociated, space from a person's everyday life. In this way, many interventions can be seen as removing a particular agency from its context in an attempt to empower a generalised agency.

We keep assuming that these interventions will work because we know that people choose actions according to their *obvious* (*sic*) health benefits. However, we are ignoring that it is the person who needs to choose between what we are promoting and what is available in her context. She will make such a choice *if* (and how) this offer makes sense to her in a particular socio-cultural context. Unless such linking is made possible within the policy and its implementation, as a certain continuity between what is on offer and the context, what we are trying to communicate and get people to act for will remain 'a completely radical expression of agency that achieves no continuities', thus making itself irrelevant for that particular context. In short, this is connected with Goodman's suggestion about the world-maker, and our interventions are based on our socio-cognitive world rather than the cognitive maps provided by those we are trying to help.

Since we are still insisting that *we know* and hence are not really trying to understand what people know, a set of major weaknesses, which are internal to the way policies are created, have become institutionalised as technologies of interventions. In this, the idea of culture is reduced to seeming behaviour types taken to represent a static culture, without thinking about what is manifested in such behaviours or about what the conditions are of particular 'cultural actions'. Most of the policies refer to culture as a reified category which is important, but which acts as a barrier to our efforts. In this way, people's agency for change in a particular context is removed and replaced by our categories, which are presented as the only way for change.

In summary, by looking at a theoretical framework, this chapter has highlighted the centrality of the categories or types used in our policies, reflecting a particular orientation to knowledge, in engaging with HIV/AIDS. It also has highlighted that these categories target vulnerable people or groups of vulnerable people and in that, by juxtaposing speculative knowledge against practical knowledge, they reduce dynamic processes of social-cultural, economic and historical conditions to a manifestation of something much

simpler like a single act of sexual intercourse or sexual relation. While, arguably, we do this for our own understanding, for us to make sense of things, the
implications of this process within the policy implementation context are
severe, as it reduces people's self-knowledge to a cultural externality that is
considered to have marginal value for dealing with HIV/AIDS. Unless our
knowledge (speculative knowledge, directing us to claim *we know*) is directly
connected and rethought on the basis of people's knowledge of their lives
(practical knowledge), the claim *we know* remains spurious: *we don't know
what we think we do.*

5 Language as a transformative mechanism

In the context of UNAIDS work [and for the purpose of this chapter] civil society refers to people living with and affected by HIV/AIDS, and the organisations of these people; NGOs currently or potentially working on HIV/AIDS issues; religious organisations; and international NGOs in fields such as development, human rights, education and health, that are contributing – or could contribute – to preventing HIV infection and reducing the impact of the epidemic on individuals, families and communities.

(UNAIDS 1999)

Civil society is the arena of associational life located between the state and the family or household, where society debates and negotiates matters of common concern and organises to regulate public affairs. It embraces highly institutionalised groups such as religious organisations, trade unions, business associations, cooperatives, local organisations such as community associations, farmers' associations, local sports, cultural, business groups, international, national and local NGOs, credit societies, professional associations, and looser forms of association such as social movements, networks and virtual groups. These forms of associations are distinct from the state and the market in that they are non-authoritative and non-profit-distributing.

(DfID 2002, and see 2003)

In this chapter I look at this issue of language: why should language be an issue or even a problem? To answer this requires analysing the role of international actors. Typically, the main research on HIV/AIDS and international policies focuses on tools and policies that are seen as important for dealing with the problem. In this, international actors are considered to be normal agents of aid and resource, and their impact on the lives of people is considered only in terms of their help in mitigating the problems. The possible transformative impact of international actors in relation to people's perspectives on both their lives and the disease is not considered.[1] Here I argue that international actors have an important impact. The impact is evident not only in the distribution of aid or provision of policy tools, such as condoms or abstinence messages, but also in the way people learn to represent themselves in order to be able to benefit from international resources.[2] In other words international actors are much more than just outside help because the perspective of these policy makers feeds into that of those on the ground and influences their actions. Their role in engaging with HIV/AIDS and people's needs should be analysed beyond their typically assumed status as decontextualised international actors. They have to be seen as actors influencing the contexts with which they are linked through policy processes.

One way of assessing such influence is to look at the pathways by which the perspective of international actors is transmitted. In this the language that is used internationally for policy making and implementation processes presents one of the central pathways. To show this I consider the international policy environment in relation to HIV/AIDS as a discourse manifested in a particular language (Escobar 1995). As suggested by Edward Said, by using this language international actors produce a set of representations of the relevant sites and actors of policies external to people's own understanding of themselves (1978: 20–2). This language allows international actors to make sense of people's needs in a context, but in doing so the language gradually becomes the people's representation of themselves. Note that this is not a new claim. The importance of understanding the way a particular language about Africa works is stressed by V.Y. Mudimbe: his work teaches us that the construction of particular representations about Africa in language has been the method used by the Western world in trying to understand the people of the region for a long time (1988, 1994). In his argument he considers and locates linguistic processes within a set of power domains: 'the colonial state, science and Christianity' (1994: 4–5). It is within this set of power relations that the African life is categorised and classified. He argues that 'one can state that they actualize themselves as performances, that is, as institutional exercises regulated by specific rules of method and demanding specialized competences' (1994: 5).[3] The aim of this chapter is to employ this insight to understand the way the international language of the policy makers represents the disease and people to assess its potential impact on the people's perspective in relation to the disease. In order to do this, I take one manifestation of the international policy language used in the Sub-Saharan HIV/AIDS context: the employment of 'civil society' language by the international actors. In the analysis, two questions are raised: What does civil society denote? And what does this denotation do?

The expressions with which I began this chapter point out the employment of the concept of civil society both in the international arena and at the local level. Unpacking the language issue requires us to move beyond a general statement that language matters in shaping representation; it requires engaging with how this happens, that is, with the mechanics of this process. To do this, in the first part of this chapter I elaborate a theoretical position which highlights the way in which definitions of concepts function to name and categorise people's experiences. This approach is located within the post-Wittgensteinian tradition of looking at the performative character of language. Specifically, the orientation of the analysis is based on Ian Hacking's work. His approach not only looks at the relationship between language and action but also locates this relationship within a perspective of power.[4] This is an important step, as it provides a sociological context within which to understand the relationship between language and action. Crucially, Hacking has argued that in social sciences objects and ideas interact: 'ways of classifying human beings interact with the human beings who are classified' (1999: 31). This framework allows me to consider the relationship between the classifier and the classified when looking at the category of civil society. Hacking goes further when he argues that 'classifications do not exist only in empty space of language but in institutions, practices, material interactions with things and other people' (1999: 31). This aspect makes it possible to consider language as one of the mechanisms of power that implicitly transmits power relations. Thus, language becomes transformative through its embeddedness within wider asymmetrical power relations. Once the theoretical lens is set in this way I use it to understand what the definitions of civil society in this policy context indicate by looking at the two international actors quoted at the beginning of the chapter. The choice of these actors is not arbitrary; it is based on their leading role in the international arena for providing policy guidance in the field. Specifically, this part of the chapter looks at the definitions within their domain of articulation. Following this, the discussion moves on to look at how these definitions influence the way people represent their own experiences in the context of HIV/AIDS. The overall aim of the chapter is to respond to the general question of why it matters that *our*[5] definitions are informing action on the ground in the HIV/AIDS pandemic.

Definitions and actions

Following Hacking, it is possible to argue that in the linguistic process there is a link between definitions within policy fora and actions taken by people in relation to that policy. This has two aspects. The international language first constructs the context of the policy implementation as developing countries; this definition then informs the nature and the content of particular policy areas (Hobart 1993; Ferguson 1994; Escobar 1995). Second, this relationship impacts people's everyday experiences on the ground. The first step highlights the importance of asymmetrical power relations where international donors are able to influence local actors through resource relations. The last step, however, is much more difficult to identify while it is produced in this power context. This requires a close examination of the claim that there is a link and of what the status of this link is in terms of action (Giddens 1984: xvi). In order to unpack Hacking's discussion of how language located in power relations produces transformative outcomes, I first look at Ludwig

Wittgenstein's understanding of language.[6] I take this to be an understanding of language as a use analysed from a more sociological lens.[7] In order to link Wittgenstein's more implicit understanding of the social with Hacking's more explicitly sociological analysis, R.M. Hare's view is also introduced.[8] This section will look at the relationship between language and action by highlighting the social context of this process. This will also indicate that power is an important element in this process.

Stuart Hampshire tells us that 'language is a set of signs actually used by intelligent beings to refer to recurrent elements in their experience and in reality' (1960: 11). He suggests that whatever the reason for which the language is used it is always 'a means of singling out, and directing attention to' (1960: 11). In this process definitions are especially active participants to the singling out, since they direct attention according to a particular experience and provide reference points for communication. Ludwig Wittgenstein states that, while the statement that 'to have understood a definition means to have in one's mind an idea of the thing defined, and that is a sample or picture' (*PI* 73),[9] is true, the link between a sample and its general use 'resides in the way the samples are used' (*PI* 73). Therefore, the definition not only provides points of reference for creating this sample, or picture, but also by being used (or acted) in a particular way it establishes how a definition is to be applied in general. In this, reference points are linking a sample with a picture of some general kind explicit in the use. Then the understanding, based on this definition, and the reference points provided in it, identifies what is defined in general. In other words, a definition provides an example to show how the concept is supposed to be applied or used in general. From Hacking's point it is possible to argue that, given the power imbalances between people and the international actors, the use of a definition will be limited within the categories provided by the international actors whereby the object of categorisation has a limited ability to develop use independent of the provided definition. Therefore, by stipulating a definition, the international actors are also stipulating the limits of uses that are appropriate for the policy context. While it is clear that a definition sets out a picture based on a sample of a particular kind, the process provides a general guidance to understanding on the basis of particular reference points chosen by the person defining (using the reference points in a particular way). This then sets the criteria for an understanding of the thing defined for others, 'civil society' in the present case; it is possible to argue that this definition will provide a particular perspective on the issue, to be used as the basis for understanding *this* thing, civil society, in general.[10] This is the first step towards establishing the importance of the link mentioned above.

Wittgenstein's language seems to suggest that the definition provides a certain operational understanding derived from an insider's view of the particular experience. In order to elaborate descriptive context it is possible therefore to ask, following Wittgenstein (*PI* 10), what does *civil society* signify? According to him:

'to signify' is perhaps used in the most straightforward way when the object is marked with the sign. Suppose that the tool A uses in building bears certain marks. When A shows his assistant such a mark, he brings the tool that has the mark on it . . . naming something is like attaching a label to a thing.

(*PI* 15)

Signifying is a process of interpreting the object in a particular manner through attributing a use from the perspective of the signifier. In signifying an object we connect a sign to the object and (already-accepted) uses of the object to the sign. Therefore, considered from this perspective naming has a reference point which is related with the person who names. It is at this juncture that the naming process provides content to the description provided for what is named on the basis of a certain use. In this step it is clear that, in naming a thing as something, a certain descriptive content about use is ascribed.

R.M. Hare's position on descriptive terms helps us to take another step towards its link with action. He suggests that the meaning of a descriptive term is related with rule following, in which following the rule is seen as the condition of general comprehensibility for people who 'understood the language which we are speaking' (Hare 1963: 8). This is consistent with Wittgenstein's example of the tool A uses, since here the assistant knew what was referred to as a tool by A, owing to the prior knowledge of the nature of the tool.[11] In analysing the descriptive nature of a name there is a need, as suggested by Hare, to go beyond the object signified and to understand what it does on the basis of its understood use (also see Hampshire 1989: 93–5).[12] Then, in the present case if we assume that the definitions used in the opening of this chapter are not only providing reference points for understanding civil society but are also indicating a description of this concept in a particular context of HIV/AIDS, what they are naming as civil society needs to be considered according to the uses which are implicit in these descriptions. In other words, the descriptions of civil society providing the substance of the above-mentioned definitions reflect what is expected from *this* or *that* civil society. It then becomes reasonable to pose the following question: do these definitions reflect problems in civil society in a particular country context or are these problems being conceived external to the context and then laid upon the context of a particular country? The context within which they are conceived provides a description according to the particular use in that context. This gives us the second step towards the link to action, that is, descriptions from one context implicitly *move* uses from this context to other contexts.

Hare argues that this relationship between description and rule following leads language users to take anything which resembles, in *some aspects*, the first subject of description and to describe it using similar terms (1963: 12).[13] He says that 'on any occasion of the use of the word "red" the speaker must have some feature of an object in mind as that to which he is drawing attention in using the word' (1963: 14). As a result the speaker becomes the arbiter by using the word in deciding what the similarity is with the description. However, note that Wittgenstein's insistence that uses are already known suggests that deciding takes into consideration *known* uses. Therefore, deciding how to categorise using a term can be considered as deciding as to the similarity between subjects on the basis of their expected use. Hacking's thinking about categories is relevant here, as at this stage descriptions become categories for understanding and analysing. In other words, definitions such as civil society become categories in the policy environment of HIV/AIDS that transfer such *known* uses from the perspective of the international actors to local people.

This last point sets out the third step for us in linking definition to action. Paul Starr suggests that 'categories adopted for institutional purpose' inform action as they mark direction and the form of activities (Starr 1992: 154). But this does not happen in a way of just providing a direction. According to Mary Douglas, 'to denote is to describe' and furthermore 'there is no denotation without classes or without knowing sample members of classes' (Douglas 1992: 246). If we consider civil society from this perspective as a descriptive denotation and attempt to understand what the sources of its articulation are through various definitions, a set of concepts and values (or practices) becomes apparent in these definitions. These may be called a family of concepts and experiences which have particular meaning and value within a particular context. It is in this that civil society denotes a certain kind of political arrangement as well as classes of behaviour. Therefore, the institutionalised definitions presented at the beginning are seen to carry a prescriptive content. They prescribe the correct form of civil society, from the position of the powerful party, for people dealing with HIV/AIDS in Sub-Saharan Africa. It is at this step that the definition becomes influential on action. Here, the important point is that what is defined is far from being a general, or universal, kind. Since to define involves thinking about a category (deciding upon similarity) to understand that which *we* are interested in, the kind of civil society we are looking at will make a lot of difference. The controversial point is not that a definition will have social foundations but rather that the impact of these foundations, once a definition is institutionalised as a denotation, will be transformative.

This follows Hacking's thinking in terms of kind-making. He suggests that different worlds are created 'by very rapidly evolving tradition' (Hacking 1992: 182). He distances the debate of natural kinds in natural sciences from the one that should take place in social sciences. This distinction reveals why definitions in language matter in terms of action. As suggested earlier, Hacking argues that 'the classification of people and their acts can influence people and what they do directly' (1992: 190). This is based on the fact that only people can 'understand what they are called and how they are described, so only people can react to being named and sorted' (Hacking 1992: 190). The idea here is not based on one-way structural impact on people in shaping their identities and lives. The idea is pointing out a dynamic process of what he calls 'a looping effect' (1995). It refers to the realisation that 'entities – people and their acts – of a kind can change in response to being grouped, that the group thereby changes, and hence our characterisation of the group itself has to be revised' (Hacking 1992: 190). In this sense, Hacking is pointing out the impact of categories on people's behaviour subsequent to their exposure to a particular category once this category is institutionalised. Therefore, the relationship between the description and the action implicit in these articulations needs to be linked with the power relations underpinning them. In other words, the locus of institutionalisation of certain definitions within the cognitive world of international actors is located with their vision of social relations. In this sense, definitions employed to deal with the disease in Africa are depicting a particular kind to classify that sort of civil society that institutions of international actors are interested in.[14] Therefore, these definitions have an impact on the way people act and this impact is conditioned according to what is included in the definition and assumed in an expression.[15] These conditionals are transmitted and engaged in the relationship as they establish reference points for communicating within a certain language game, in the Wittgensteinian sense. In the next section I look at civil society as it is employed within a certain international discourse on HIV/AIDS interventions.

Civil society – definition or description?

In this section I will follow the conceptual framework above to trace our understanding of civil society's move from the definitional to the descriptive. I will argue that as a category civil society produces standard operational procedures for organisations which filter reality to make it fit pre-conceived notions. Robert Brandom suggests that 'norms that are explicit in the form of rules presuppose norms implicit in practices' (1994: 20). In this way these pre-conceived notions can be traced back to particular practices or uses within the domain of the policy makers.

Although what civil society means differs depending on the definitional realm in which one is located,[16] in the context of HIV/AIDS in Sub-Saharan Africa its meaning derives from the meaning implicitly contained in the two definitions at the beginning of the chapter employed by two international actors. These are exemplars of the definitional realm we find ourselves in. Thus, it is imperative to understand the institutional realms in which these definitions are produced. Mary Douglas also suggests that 'institutions systematically direct individual memory and channel our perceptions into forms compatible with relations they authorize' (1986: 92). This channelling operates in the form of civil society that is employed in the definitions. They indicate both a form and a basis of production of that form. In the policy realm the latter is observed in the standard procedures established for understanding and acting for these organisations within *the civil society* realm. It is by these processes that the power imbalances, between the international actors and those on the ground, affect their subject, people living with HIV/AIDS.

We can now ask: what is the institutional realm in which civil society definitions are located? The institutional realm includes a conceptual background that creates an ideological imperative, which is based in a string of neo-Tocquevillian traditions,[17] and the imperatives that are based on organisational interests and practical needs. The institutional context of these organisations must be considered within the international development context in which a certain understanding of rich and poor constructs what can be done to help the poor. In this, following Mudimbe and Escobar, it is possible to argue that power domains based on resources and Western knowledge claims construct a paternalistic relationship. This considers participants as poor people who are at the receiving end of the international help (Hobart 1993). Furthermore, this logic is also reflected in the structure of the international financial organisations involved with development in the post-Second World War period. The concrete context of this can be observed in the debates around changing development agendas from structural adjustment-based policies to the Washington Consensus and at present in the Poverty Reduction Strategy Papers and the Millennium Development Goals.[18]

I now look at two organisations that are located in this institutional realm and at how they deploy what we termed the reference points for the sample of a kind of civil society. By looking at the development and the projected deployment field of the definitions by particular organisations we can discern what kind of civil society language is constituted and, thus, denoted.

The document entitled *How to . . . Work with Civil Society to Support Country Strategy Objectives*, produced by the UK Department for International Development (DfID)[19] in 2002, sets out DfID's normative purposes and objectives legitimating its use of civil society. This process relies on basic reference points to reduce the larger realm suggested in the definition to a set of organisational forms of the type we discussed earlier. This is directly recognised by the report. It is suggested that the

> donors seeking to strengthen civil society have to identify clearly their normative purposes, expectations and objectives . . . the definition needs to be accompanied as a broad arena and as a set of particular associational forms, questions that are in turn guided by the normative objectives of the donor agency.
>
> (DfID 2002: 4)

The first point to understand here is the institutional imperatives which are legitimating the use of civil society. This allows us to see why a particular kind is used for the categorisation implicit in the utterance *civil society*. The document suggests that:

civil society can be an important partner in the international development effort and plays a role in the elimination of poverty and the
achievement of the Millennium Development Goals ... civil society
offers citizens and communities the space for debate, association, critical
reflection and action.

(DfID 2002: 2)

Further reasons for thinking about civil society are given: their role in providing citizen voice, in constructing effective and accountable societies, and for
poverty reduction for which civil society is seen as a strong partner with the
state and the market. These ideas, developed in the international fora in the
post-Cold War period, are clearly setting out the interests of the DfID in civil
society.[20] While here civil society is seen as a mechanism to achieve the
poverty-related developmental objectives of the organisation, in a way
as a tool, the ideological characteristics of civil society are used as a set of
justifications for this purpose whereby the overall goal of poverty reduction is
located into a democratic process.

While these ideological points set out important imperatives, the immediate operational needs of the organisation also bring in a set of issues in terms
of the practicalities of recognising and engaging with civil society on a day-
to-day basis. The report comes up with such a diagnostic tool: 'to "map" the
range of civil society organisations in a country, it is useful to distinguish
between organisations according to: Ownership, Accountability, Reasons for
association, Level of operation influence, Level of formality, Operational
aspects' (DfID 2002: 10–11).

Here the general definition of civil society becomes subsumed by looking
at civil society on the basis of organisational forms. Although civil society as
a living space in many cultures is considered more varied than our understanding of it, for DfID's poverty-reduction objectives it is considered under
the familiar organisational forms (DfID 2003). Using the above diagnostic
tools to look at the socio-political conditions in a given context, the DfID
decides whether to engage with civil society or not according to the DfID
country priorities. Once this is decided, there are various ways to engage with
civil society, such as financial mechanisms, and technical support for providing training for internal and external management. In their engagements,
local organisations are then categorised under civil society according to these
assumptions, priorities and interests.

The DfID is not unique. We observe a similar situation in relation to
UNAIDS. According to the Joint United Nations Programme on HIV/AIDS
(UNAIDS) report on the global HIV/AIDS epidemic 2002, 'it has become
commonplace to include multiple ministries, as well as representatives of civil
society and other development partners in high-level political coordination
structures' (UNAIDS 2002b: 176). The normative and prescriptive language
of the following statement is clear: 'an important role for governments is
to clear the way so all sectors of society can contribute to the response',

participating as 'religious, cultural and community groups or associations, employers, trade unions and non-governmental organisations' (UNAIDS 2002b: 176). Such language bolsters the role of civil society for national interventions.

The same report suggests that these multi-sectoral attempts are 'key to building capacity within civil society and enabling people and groups to be active participants, rather than passive targets of, programming' (UNAIDS 2002b: 178). It then goes on to emphasise that this is an important character-istic by outlining the role played by civil society: 'in advocacy, participating in policy and programming design and implementation, and in the provision of services, especially at the community level' (UNAIDS 2002b: 178). These ascribed roles and enabling processes are related to the aims of UNAIDS at large but also related to the international multilateral and bilateral donors' perspective on civil society in channelling their funding towards these activ-ities. It is possible to observe that civil society is again more or less con-structed as an instrumental vehicle for interventions. In this, the role played by civil society in the provision of services in the case of HIV/AIDS is an important issue. In most HIV/AIDS interventions and donor relations, civil society organisations are identified with non-governmental organisations, which are seen as the best way to deliver services by the international organisations.

The conceptual sources of civil society implicit in this language relate to civil society definitions. These are largely based on a division of the insti-tutional realm in a society, by attributing agency to those associational forms which are considered under various rubrics such as: third-sector organisa-tions, non-profit organisations and voluntary sector or non-governmental organisations (Florini 2000; Ottaway and Carothers 2000). These are not merely identifications but they assume particular political relations within which such sectors can exist and are given agency to improve people's lives. The emphasis on the distinct sectoral divide points out a particular under-standing of civil society that is, for example, observable in the discussions of the non-profit sector developed by Lester Salamon and his colleagues. They locate civil society and civil society organisations between the state and the market as a third or non-profit 'sector' in modern society (Salamon *et al.* 1999). It is in this designation of the civil society's location that the concept and its linkage to a larger definitional family provide a prescriptive element to the concept which expresses choices, resolves and straightforward value judgements about the nature of the civil society. Hence, they also carry a prescriptive or normative element into the definition. It is here that we observe what Brandom says when he talks about presupposed 'norms implicit in practices' (1994: 20).[21]

It is also important to recognise that the organisational objectives in both agencies, DfID and UNAIDS, are related to their concerns about effective-ness and efficiency. In order to achieve their aims they link particular expected outcomes to particular organisational forms that they can monitor and evaluate. This, when combined with the particular aspirational under-standing of civil society, leads the utterance of civil society to denote a par-ticular category of organisations that is used interchangeably with *civil soci-ety*. The following example illustrates the way organisational interests and needs inform this process.

At the 2003 International Conference on AIDS and STIs in Africa (ICASA) in Nairobi, UNAIDS and its partners[22] developed a set of prin-ciples, *Coordination of National Responses to HIV/AIDS: Guiding Principles for National Authorities and their Partners*, also known as the *Three Ones*. These are: one agreed HIV/AIDS Action Framework that drives alignment of all partners; one national AIDS authority with a broad-based multi-sectoral mandate; and one agreed country-level monitoring and evaluation system. This was an important exercise to give coherence to the interventions and was largely initiated by UNAIDS and its partners.

In the articulation of the first principle one can observe the perspective and needs of UNAIDS and others in relation to civil society. It states:

> **Affirmation and optimisation** of the growing drive to engage civil society organisations and private sector in service delivery. Key principles to guide this development include:
>
> • mechanism to deal with distribution of skilled human resources, including standards, code of conduct and incentive systems in relation to public service policies etc.
> • measures to retain adequate capacity in the public sector.
> • provision of treatment and care through public and private pro-viders, NGOs and community based organisations with attention to equity and ethical standards, continuity in service delivery and capacity in public regulatory and quality-assurance functions.
> • agreed standards for behavioural change and communication messages.
>
> (UNAIDS 2004a: 2)

In the structure of these overall guidelines, civil society is included as a participant partner in the process of delivering the requirements of the pol-icies. These requirements are informed by the understanding of civil society in relation to the organisational forms we have been discussing. Furthermore, through this new initiative the institutional reference points, implicit in the definitions, which are indicating practices in the experiences of international actors, are becoming much more emphasised as they become explicit rules for policy behaviour. While they elaborate the needs and the objectives of UNAIDS and its partners, they do this on the basis of norms relevant to the context of the international actors rather than to the context of the people living with the disease.

Both the DfID and UNAIDS definitions can be seen as elaborating a way of giving coherence to their understanding in order to engage with a certain reality. In this process the main reference point seems to be the nature of civil society as organisational and social relations mediated and created by people's participation. The second most important reference point is the non-governmental nature of this organisational realm. In considering the UNAIDS definition, we are warned that this is setting out a definition for a particular kind of civil society. However, the same general organisational reference points are still used for understanding civil society. Therefore it is reasonable to assume that they are setting a sample for a general kind in this area.

Following Wittgenstein, it is possible to argue that the process is not merely setting reference points for us, but that the definitions are actually setting the limits of their view (and action) by providing a particular content to civil society, hence blocking out whatever does not fit. Furthermore, the overlap between the organisational forms used as reference points in all definitions suggests that there is a certain shared understanding in the various definitions among the international fora based on these organisational forms and their uses, in Wittgenstein's sense, within the social context of international institutions. Although it is recognised that there may be variations in what is recognised as civil society, for the civil society to be comprehensible, from Hare's perspective, the user of the concept of 'civil society' must have some feature of these definitions in mind. If we consider this situation from Hare's perspective, clearly this shared understanding leads to a certain rule following in identifying what constitutes civil society *out there*. This identification uses the reference points provided in the definitions to refer to what we understand in terms of organisational relations.

Now, this is important for two reasons. At one level the user may be trying to understand civil society using a cognitive map provided by the definitions, in which the definition provides the reference points for her understanding. On a different level, if we are trying to communicate, the communication between two actors becomes comprehensible if they both have the same cognitive map which provides them with the same reference points. Here a certain learning and adapting to a particular cognitive map for use, for those who are at the receiving end of the policies, are also required, and are typically provided, in the present case through capacity building and training schemes. In this context, the similarity of a feature seems to be pointed out by looking at organisational forms to establish the feasibility and reality of civil society for understanding. It is in this establishment of what would be similar in various cases to be recognised as civil society that the definition turns into an active descriptive tool. In some sense it is evident in the definitions that certain organisational forms are prioritised as civil society. These include non-governmental, voluntaristic, international non-governmental organisations that are generally involved in the development context. Through these reference points, the definition implicitly creates a mechanism of calling some organisations 'civil society' and then making any organisation of that form civil society related. In Hacking's sense, civil society becomes a category for understanding a certain reality out there. By using or institutionalising this category, international organisations, in the HIV/AIDS interventions, are not only making reality fit to their perceptions, but are also communicating to people the way to form relations within what is acceptable or authorised for them.

In this section I have engaged in elaborating the link between definition and description and the sources of description as implicitly evident in the language of two organisations and in their engagements. The definitions in fact are descriptive tools for a certain kind of civil society populated by organisational forms that can be used by international actors to achieve their policy aims. The identifiablity of these organisations on the basis of their operational structures seems to be an important point as they become actors with whom international actors can establish relations. In the next section I look at the link between these descriptions and action: how defining civil society is also defining people's own understanding of their positions.

Civil society – description to action?

> We are a group of HIV positive youth and would like to talk about the disease and our experiences. However, we have no funding and it is very difficult in this context to raise our voices when many donor-funded projects get most of the attention.
>
> (Gaborone, Botswana)

> As an organisation we organise sensitisation seminars to inform people but it is very difficult to get men to participate in these meetings and talk about their problems and sexuality.
>
> (Gaborone, Botswana)

> We would like to promote safe-sex messages and provide abstention options to our peer groups but our work is seen as explicit in its nature; therefore we are not allowed to use these posters.
>
> (Gaborone, Botswana)

> By just talking about the disease we assume that we are communicating but we are not.
>
> (Lusaka, Zambia)

> We are very few who are known to be HIV positive; therefore we go where they invite us to talk about our experience, but at the end of the day what we can do is very limited without major changes in the attitudes in the society. Just talking is not going to change the situation.
>
> (Lusaka, Zambia)

These statements are extracts from interviews conducted with civil society activists or workers in Botswana and Zambia. The interviews were trying to understand the way the activists see the role of civil society in the fight against the pandemic. In this, the question was also how they thought about their own location in the debates about the disease. In most of the interviews there is a clear sense of being part of an activity and having an important mission to help people. However, it was also clear that most of the people were articulating their participation in the realm of non-governmental organisations and through their actions. The most revealing expressions in this sense were related to the questions about the impact of their work and the constraints on their interventions. Looking at some snapshots from these responses through the lens provided by Hacking's looping effect makes it possible to analyse the link between civil society as a category and its impact in the way people make sense of their actions. It is important to emphasise at this point that many people recognise themselves as participating in a non-governmental action field first and in a civil society sphere second. In most of the interviews a sense of learning a particular use and gradually being encultured to a particular way of thinking about civil society whereby at the end of the process they can decide about civil society in following certain rules was clearly evident. Although what may seem to be a civil society in terms of public action would exist in many societies in the region, typically discussions of these forms are conceptualised under other ways rather than under one rubric of civil society (Comaroff and Comaroff 1999; Akínrìnádé 2004). In this sense the following discussion is not about whether people have their own sense of civil society or not, but it is about how the category of civil society used in international policy as discussed, above, is influencing their perceptions. This analysis suggests that, in an institutionalised application outside its context of production, language becomes transformative as it transfers meanings and forms of being from the descriptive universe provided by that language. In this part, I would like to elaborate some of these transformative processes in relation to civil society language I have been discussing.

The first of these transformative processes can be seen in the changing nature of what is seen as civil society activity in various social contexts. The definitions employed by the international actors set out particular organisational characteristics as reference points for recognising who can be engaged with as civil society actors. Therefore, they provide criteria to local activists for access to the international policy fora. In other words, these definitions are setting out conditions for their agency, a certain institutional authorisation, as suggested by Mary Douglas. For instance, the group of young people in Gaborone who are living with HIV positive status is an important example of this. The members of the group wanted to go out and talk to people about their conditions and try to encourage them to live positively. However, their main concern was how to establish themselves as an NGO since this would allow them to get funding for their interventions. At the time of the interviews they were waiting to hear from one of the major funders in Botswana.

The donor asked them to reconsider their application as there were a number of groups working on a similar issue. They were also asked to join up with other NGOs working on the same issue of sensitisation. In the group, members were telling me that *We had to change our application three times. We don't have the capacity to fill in these forms. We spent our money to get someone to fill it in; then we had to learn ourselves how to work with these but it stops us doing what we want to do, talk to people about our experience as HIV positive people.* Of course, this can be seen as a positive change as local actors are organised and become recognisable for those who are providing resources and intervention frameworks. In this the conditions of recognition for civil society activism are based on organisational requirements. In return, arguably, these newly formed civil society actors communicate their perspective to the international actors.

The second area of transformation is linked with the first process as a rethinking of needs. As local actors are trying to engage with the definitions provided, there is a process of deflection. Initially this process is a reconstitution of agency of people in relation to the international fora at the expense of an agency located within a particular socio-cultural value system within which the disease is experienced. Then the needs and social concerns that are articulated according to a certain social context are reformulated within the frameworks provided by the institutionalised definitions. Therefore, immediate concerns in terms of HIV/AIDS are conditioned on a successful demonstration of the fulfilment of such requirements. For instance, outside Lusaka, in a hospice the manager was discussing how difficult it is to engage with the problem given its scale and the paperwork that is required to maintain their funding for the project. The hospice was created by outside funding, and caring services in it are provided by Catholic nuns. Their funding was coming from various international sources, and most of the management work was provided by student volunteers from various US medical schools. Here again the funding for the project was a major problem at two levels: (a) one very large donor in Zambia had made it clear to them that since the hospice was outside urban Lusaka (approximately 20 kilometres) it was difficult for them to monitor the project and thus they were unable to fund it; (b) responding to the accountability demands from international donors is taking too much time. One of the nuns stated that while they would provide care for the needy in the compound independently of the donors' funding, it would be difficult to maintain the hospice and other residential services.

In tandem, the articulation of interventions based on local knowledge or existing local mechanisms of social relations is disabled, since the fulfilment of organisational imperatives, such as demonstration of accountability, ownership and legal formalities, goes hand in hand with the possibility of using a limited set of policy tools. This is caused by the performance criteria required by the international institutional imperatives, such as Millennium Development Goals, immanent in the above-discussed definitions of civil society. In Gaborone in a more formalised youth group, the story was different.

Although they have their funding and very good relations with the policy makers, their interventions were closely observed by their funders and the local national AIDS council. They have several programmes, one of which is looking at creating what they call 'youth–adult partnerships' to initiate a conversation in the society; another is using the media to sensitise the community to youth-related issues; and another looks at peer education training. Their poster campaign based on the idea of getting young people to develop messages themselves (youth to youth) was controversial and closely scrutinised by the policy makers. As a result, some of the posters were not used since both the NGO and the funding community were against explicit messages. There were several problems the group has identified in their work: although they have a strong message of 'Get Involved, Be Less Infected', the main problem was to get the youth participating in their projects and activities and to be part of the change. This was partially due to the fact that, once young people got involved and developed their ideas, to see them not being implemented was a disincentive. Another problem is the urban location of the organisation, and thus their message is not very relevant for the rural population. Finally there is the difficulty of demonstrating the impact of their interventions.

The third transformation is an outcome of the earlier changes on the already-existing agency that can be exercised in societies. As a new sphere of civil society is created in relation to the international definitions which allows a new agency for people, more and more already-existing, traditional or conventional spaces for public action and mechanisms of public discussions become neutralised. An activist who is the head of an HIV positive people's organisation, for example, suggested that men do not talk or by and large participate in their work. It was clear to him that in their work men constituted less than 15 per cent of all the participants. When I asked what the reason for this was he said, *Men don't talk about their problems in public. There needs to be a way of finding how to get men but this is not easy and it requires a long-term vision which is not available to us in the funding world.* It was also clear to him that, in order to be included in the debate, groups need to be recognised as a civil society organisation by the national council. While the new value set in relation to civil society recognises certain actors as relevant members of civil society, it also creates what civil society is supposed to be in the context. Given the organisational model used in these particular definitions, arguably the political nature of public debate and civil society actors, as discussed earlier, is mostly concerned with delivery of projects and services. This ignores the importance of political debate and the particularity of social context in relation to HIV/AIDS. The consideration of civil society as part of the international policy system locates the stakes of these organisations, established to engage with this system, to a degree outside their own socio-political context. Disarticulation of local agency to create a new kind of agency, which is beneficial for those who are taking part in that forum, is not reflective overall of positive outcomes for the people who are unable to participate in this new realm of civil society. The disjuncture between these various public spaces, therefore, can be disadvantageous for overall HIV/ AIDS thinking.

As demonstrated above, the commonality in many interviews is the implicit consideration of civil society as a particular organisational form. In many instances these people are working in what they see largely as *non-governmental* organisations. A number of constraints expressed in the above extracts are on the issues of tools of interventions and resources for interventions that are within the NGO realm. This shift from looking at the problems of HIV/AIDS in their everyday lives to looking at the problems of being or becoming an NGO is an important sign of Hacking's *looping effect*. Many people seem to suggest that the possibility of doing something about HIV/ AIDS is referenced to becoming an NGO or an organisational form that is recognisable to the international actors. This situation has been expressed by an organisation of HIV positive people in Lusaka. They were talking about the lack of training and capacity for scaling up their sensitisation programme. They were very clear that the civil society empowerment programmes of international actors were not realistic. Therefore, they wanted to develop their financial and outreach capacity to be able to carry out workshops and sensitisation programmes. I was told, *Well, they come every six months from various organisations and conduct workshops and they disappear. What good that can make. Nobody cares what happens between these trainings.* While they were critical of the international actors, they seemed to identify with the generic organisational format they were given. Most of these tools and resources are considered with reference to the public action as constructed by the international civil society language. Many activists feel that NGOs, and thus civil society, need more resources in financial terms to be able to carry on with their campaigns and address the problems in this field. In most cases outcomes are considered according to the accountability mechanisms that are related to organisational imperatives transmitted via donor relations.

In many cases, objectives to deal with the disease are moderated with organisational concerns. In some ways dealing with the organisational accountability issues as well as adopting particular policy frameworks, around sensitisation, voluntary testing and condom distribution, are seen as moving towards achieving or fulfilling the role of civil society. The most predominant expression of this process, which formalises the international language and interests, can be seen in the above-discussed UNAIDS policy framework, the *Three Ones*. It is a step to centralise the international policy by centralising the set of meanings. Given the imbalances in the power relations between international and local actors, the *Three Ones* become transformative.[23] This process makes sure that the local expressions are using the international perspective as terms of reference in discussing the issues. It is in this that we observe a constitution of a certain understanding of what it is to participate in dealing with the disease in civil society. An activist in Gaborone who has been working with HIV/AIDS programmes for over a decade questioned the impact of what they did in earlier interventions. She questioned the reasons behind certain policy frameworks. It was clear to her that NGOs were really trying very hard to deal with the problem but there were contradictions in many projects and programmes depending on the donors with which various organisation were working. She said, *We did not talk about the concerns of the young but just talked about the condoms and told them to be faithful. Most organisations had chosen to talk about condoms rather than engage with the abstention issue. It is easier to talk about condoms but also you can demonstrate how many of them you have distributed. This was a major mistake.* She also suggested that many of the interventions suffer from design biases due to the location of the projects in urban areas and funding frameworks. Her example is an interesting case of the looping effect: as she has constructed her self-identification with the NGO policy frameworks and interventions over a decade, she has also become aware of the problems and has been trying to influence her donor relations to change their attitudes.

It is possible to argue that through participating in organisational forms people become actors in civil society with a certain agency. Otherwise they would only be considered as infected or affected. It also allows that their actions become meaningful under the definitions provided, contributing to the work of civil society, by becoming activists under a particular description. In this way, in this sort of activism, the signs of the international context that attributes civil society with particular qualities can be observed. This argument is undermined, however, by the outcomes extrapolated from these qualities not being witnessed in the experience of many either working in civil society or at the receiving end of the work. Thus, it is important to pay attention to the disjuncture between civil society as ascribed and what is locally seen as NGOs or as an organisational realm of services.

Why does this matter?

I have so far argued that definitions are related to action since the latter is understood by, or referenced to, the sample depicted in a definition. I have also argued that beyond this linguistic transference of cognitive frameworks, when considered from the institutional perspective, definitions as reference points for understanding are directing policies that become transformative, in Hacking's sense, for it establishes a particular understanding of use based on a particular experience as the way to engage with civil society in general. The concept of civil society employed in the context of international HIV/AIDS interventions was used to elaborate this process by looking at two organisations that have institutionalised a definition of civil society and looking at the impact of this institutionalisation on people who are in some relationship with this international institutional context. But why does this matter, since social relations are always transformative? By way of concluding I respond to this question in this section. Here, I provide two general conclusions: the first is a response as to why it does matter in the context of HIV/AIDS, and the second is why language is an issue.

My analyses of the impact of a particular civil society language can be criticised on several grounds. Several of these could take issue with the arguments that give importance to the existing socio-cultural and political mechanisms. They would consider these mechanisms as part of the problem in creating stigma or maintaining certain social relations that negatively influence the progress in relation to HIV/AIDS. Therefore they consider the new language of civil society as being much more helpful in creating a different space for action. There is no doubt about the influence of existing mechanisms on HIV/AIDS. However, not considering these mechanisms as part of the solution is a step for ineffectiveness in dealing with HIV/AIDS. It can be argued, following Wittgenstein, that, by assimilating various descriptions available to people for action in their context under an international description of civil society, one 'cannot make the uses themselves any more like another . . . they are absolutely unlike' (*PI* 10). One important consequence of this assimilation process is usually seen in relation to people's responses to policy interventions. Sometimes these are constructed as not responding to *our* interventions and at other times as stigmatising. It is important to consider these, following Clifford Geertz (1983), as responses of a particular kind which are responding to many changes and influences including the interventions based on condoms and posters themselves. Or, as Donald Davidson puts it, 'misinterpreting an order is a case of interpreting it' (2001: 45). That said, I am not suggesting that people are misinterpreting what is put to them in terms of HIV/AIDS interventions. I am simply arguing that people are interpreting these in a certain way, which is not generally captured by what is taken to be civil society action from the perspective of the international actors. Therefore, in a way misinterpretation is on the side of the people using the civil society language. The difference between the two interpretations according to some, as discussed earlier, has created the stigma attached to the disease.

Civil society language, with its socio-cultural location, reflects institutional imperatives and interests. It looks at the role of civil society in HIV/AIDS through a particular lens. This ignores the reasons behind contextual interpretations expressed in people's language about HIV/AIDS. The net result of this is a construction of, as Davidson suggests, a simplified contextual agency independent of what is expressed in the language indicating a link between their social context and their action (2001: 61). This process of creating a new language to engage with civil society is exacerbated by negative outcomes. Furthermore by fixing the perspective in civil society language through institutional processes an illusion is created through a looping process: international actors consider actors that are able to participate in their frameworks as representatives of civil society independently of any concrete evidence to the link between this civil society and the way people live through other social forums. In addition it ignores that they define this civil society to which the people are responding.

Another possible critical argument would be that the existing systems do change anyway. Therefore, the influence of the international system mediated by the civil society language should be considered within this process. The argument I have presented in no way suggests that any of these traditional mechanisms are unchanging. Traditions do evolve and change. However, the issue here is where the impetus for change comes from and the nature of the change that introduces a new set of socio-cultural values by setting out new forms of agency while disabling the existing ones. In other words, change as a result of the impact of language needs to be considered within a particular power context. Here, Nelson Goodman's (1978) argument is informative. He argues that worldmaking is always remaking by building on what already exists in the repertoire of the maker. Therefore, self-referentiality within the process of change for cultures presents an important descriptive point in people's lives. In a similar logic the change under the civil society language I have been discussing, that is utilised by international actors, would represent a worldmaking referenced to an *outside* description of culture and social needs. The impact of this mechanism within human reflexivity will mean that the looping effect constructs those who are engaging with the international system in a different manner and pace from that of large parts of the populations. This in turn creates a disjuncture between what these people consider to be the problems of HIV/AIDS and what those people living with the disease experience throughout their everyday lives.

In the end, these conclusions suggest that language matters greatly in the context of HIV/AIDS and that it matters generally in the policy interventions by international actors. From this perspective the theoretical framework presented here has wider implications for understanding international policy prescriptions, their implementation and the relationship between international actors as policy makers and people living with the end results of these policies. My response suggests that language links those who are policy makers and their world, with those who are the target of the policies and their world. However, this is not a mere linking; it is a mechanism through which people construct their identities and perform certain roles. It ultimately constructs the nature of action and thus influences the potential outcomes.

Conclusion
Time to wake up

> To those who are awake there belongs a single and therefore common world, whereas whoever is asleep turns toward a world of his own.
>
> (Heraclitus, in Heidegger 1998: 112)

HIV/AIDS is a complex disease both in its causes and in its consequences. The disease tends to highlight existing social, economic and cultural exclusion patterns in societies. It also creates new patterns of inequalities and injustices. In this, the lack of political voice and participation of those who are impacted by the disease within the policy processes has been instrumental. Furthermore, the disease has highlighted a poverty of policy thinking in relation to the responses to the disease since the early 1980s. Arguably, this poverty of thinking is still evident in the way international HIV/AIDS policies are developed and implemented in resource-poor settings or, in the common parlance, in developing countries. In this context the disease and the way international actors have been responding to it have highlighted enduring colonial attitudes within the international policy environment towards the knowledge claims and the agency of people in their own socio-economic and cultural contexts. The lack of political voice and participation of people in the international politics of HIV/AIDS is producing a new layer of inequality and injustice at a global level. An important aspect of this has been the way international actors consider their role and impact on people living with HIV/AIDS in Sub-Saharan Africa. They have considered their involvement within the boundaries of technical aid and charity for helping people in emergency times. Unfortunately, good intentions do not guarantee good outcomes for people living with the disease. To engage more effectively with those they aim to help, international actors need to become self-reflexive to understand the impact of their policies and their involvement in the lives of people targeted by their policies.

The aim of this book has been to look at the impact of international actors and the nascent global governance of the disease on people and to look at how they can deal with the disease in the future. In doing this, it has so far responded to two of the broad questions that were posed in the Introduction: Where are we going? And is this desirable (Flyvbjerg 2001: 60)? Overall, the responses to these have been 'negative'. It is clear that international actors have an important impact on the way people experience the disease and on their longer-term prospects for dealing with the disease in diverse socio-economic and cultural environments. This impact is not merely related to the technical and financial input that appears to be motivated by the charitable instincts at the international level. International policy on HIV/AIDS frames the realm of interventions and the nature of target groups and their perceived needs in the face of the disease. People living with the disease in diverse socio-economic and cultural contexts are transformed into target populations living with HIV/AIDS. Most contextual differences are ignored by focusing on the existence of the HIV virus in individual bodies. This move allows international actors to devise generalised abstract policies to help these target populations. However, people's experiences of both the disease and the policies demonstrate that there is a considerable gap between this approach and the way people live with the disease. Since international actors are not sensitive to the way people live and the implications of the disease in their everyday lives, policies target more and more what are seen as patient populations or risk groups. These categories provide people with generic identities which are not usually meaningful or relevant to them in their everyday lives. Therefore, when people try to engage with these policies they must do so independently of their everyday lives in order to have access to the resources associated with many international interventions. Also, by attributing agency to NGOs as civil society actors for the implementation of their policies, international actors move themselves one step away from the policy implementation context without distancing themselves from the policy decisions. Here the transformation or the creation of civil society as a service delivery sector within the HIV/AIDS field has important implications for the long-term sustainability of the policy interventions and for the development of local systems. Given the general international development policies influenced by neo-liberal thinking on public services, NGOs act as welfare service delivery agents at present. However, it is doubtful that their work can be taken over by governments since there is no serious long-term investment for the establishment of welfare systems (public services) in most countries. In other words, the long-term impact of international HIV/AIDS interventions based on civil society actors may be limited. In turn, the impact of the present policies on long-term HIV/AIDS interventions is also put in doubt.

By looking at the policies and reactions to them it is possible to consider multiple worlds of HIV/AIDS. In each, one can observe a different kind of assessment of successful policy. One is that which people observe in the media and in the declarations of international organisations and international actors. This view demonstrates a certain urgency to get international resources down to the people to deal with HIV/AIDS. The policy process within this world is very much based on the generic knowledge about HIV/AIDS, how patients engage with these policies, and a generic designation of agency to particular actors such as civil society. The success in this area appears to be measured in terms of getting international actors to agree on action plans and statements and make pledges (however unrealistic these might be). A second world is what happens at the international policy environment once policies move towards implementation. Most of the resources are channelled toward a number of highly prioritised projects in order to demonstrate success and to show what can be done with determination. Thus, policy targets are set to get results at the times of an emergency, and short-term outcomes tend to be targeted. Here quantifiable targets such as the numbers of people tested, the number of sites where ARVs are rolled out, the numbers of condoms distributed, the numbers of training and capacity-building workshops organised and the number of posters that are produced are taken to be the measure of success for implementation purposes. The long-term implications of the disease and of these interventions on the disease are mentioned, but tend not to influence how these policies are implemented at present. This is also due to the gap between the first two worlds, between the declarations and aspirations about what international actors want to do and the available research and financial and technical resources that they can use to actually do things. The third world is that of people's everyday lives in diverse contexts. People's lives are situated in diverse socio-economic and cultural contexts that provide them with multiple identities and diverse spaces for action. Most of the interventions are tangential to their lives, as they are only targeted as patients, and large parts of their lives remain hidden from these interventions unless they are able to think of themselves as patients or as members of a targeted risk group. Their family lives, lives in communities under economic pressures and lives according to particular socio-cultural norms provide them with different ways of understanding the impact of the disease and what they can do about it. Exposure to the international interventions is not easily avoidable for people. They see it on the streets as posters, in NGO campaigns, in hospitals and in clinics. However, there is a gap between what they know about the disease by living in the context of it and what they hear about HIV/AIDS from policy interventions. The success of policies is linked to the extent to which people behave in the way policy makers expect them to behave. In other words, adherence to the policies becomes the measure of success. However, there is no discussion of success in terms of people's everyday perspectives.

These multiple worlds are connected by the policies and the processes creating those policies. This is evident in the way policy success is considered. While the measure of success changes depending on the different worlds, the basis for each type of success is referenced to the aims of the international policies. As I have discussed in the earlier chapters, policies do not reflect the experiences of people with the disease and are by and large framed by the international actors. Therefore, by looking at the policy process, it becomes possible to understand this imbalanced relationship between the international policy context and the people living in the context of the disease. The imbalance points out that many of the policies are not actually making a lot of difference to people's lives in the long term, since they do not really seriously engage with people and their environments. To remedy this requires a questioning whereby international actors think more self-reflexively. They should think about their own position and the implications of their political and organisational characteristics on the policy implementation and on people's lives. The book has begun this questioning by bringing people's perspectives to bear on the international policy processes and its policies. It has also analysed the processes that create this non-reflexive international policy approach. It has argued that the policy processes inherently reproduce imbalanced and unjust policy outcomes where people are adversely incorporated to the international policy context as passive target populations. This reproduction is the source of durable inequalities[1] whereby people are locked into long-term imbalanced resource relations.

The Introduction of the book presented a set of questions and issues which dominate the debate within the international political environment. The Introduction analysed the narrative of global disease and HIV/AIDS as a global disease. This analysis highlighted the nature of what is global about the disease. It argued that it is the political context within which the disease has emerged as an issue which makes it global rather than the people's experiences of the disease in multiple contexts. This analysis provided the first step to understanding the link between the international fora and people living with HIV/AIDS in multiple socio-economic and cultural contexts.

Then Chapter 1 focused on the way the disease had been internationalised. It looked at the processes which have located the disease right at the centre of the international political agenda. It also argued that this process had its own understanding of the disease, with an associated understanding of how to deal with it. It then argued that the existing internationalisation processes con be considered as a governance structure that has emerged in the last decade. The governance here was considered not only as a mechanism of managing relations among the policy actors and policy implementers by establishing systemic values and norms but also as a mechanism that creates its own target groups and field of interventions within multiple country contexts. Thus, it was argued that this productive process creates a homogeneous understanding of the disease independent of people's experiences of the disease in multiple contexts.

The following two chapters (Chapters 2 and 3) looked at the processes that are establishing this governance structure across many countries. In other words they looked at the way particular discourses about HIV/AIDS and its associated policies and policy actors are produced in multiple country contexts. In Chapter 2 the process of institutionalisation was introduced as a productive process within which institutions create and replicate their own norms and values in relation to the systemic behaviour and thinking. It was argued that this is a dynamic process. It works through a number of mechanisms that create and attribute agency to those groups or organisations. These organisations or groups then can participate within the larger institutional system. In this case it was argued that the international organisations dealing with HIV/AIDS policies act as the institutional basis for this process. The institutional concerns about the form of organisations and the form of policy frameworks are based on the concerns of the dominant international policy actors such as the World Bank and UNAIDS and bilateral donors such as USAID in this context. While they might disagree on the exact organisational policy priorities, there seems to be a general understanding about who can participate in the policy discussions and decision making at the level of international actors. In order to highlight the way institutionalisation works, the incorporation of civil society actors into the system was analysed. Their emergence in the last decade in the HIV/AIDS field as policy implementers presents an important example to highlight the way the system works. The chapter analysed the way agency is attributed to NGOs within the international policy environment and what these organisations can actually do with this assumed agency. Here a distinction was clarified between the attributed agency within the international fora and the agency that NGOs are assumed to have in relation to people they work with in particular localities. It argued that while NGOs have agency within the international policy context they gradually lose their local agency to influence people's long-term behaviour. Thus they become extensions of the international policy makers and for their policy implementation aims.

In Chapter 3, the institutionalisation process was analysed by looking at the process of medicalisation. It argued that the justification for policy tools is provided by the medical research. International policy actors use this as another way of institutionalising a particular thinking on HIV/AIDS. Furthermore, in this, people living with the disease or in the context of the disease are reconstructed as patients and target groups whereby they lose their context-specific everyday differences and understanding of the disease and become target populations. The chapter looked at this process of medicalisation in some depth. It looked at the discussions of treatment and highlighted a particular emergency logic which has been driving policy in this field. It also argued that this logic is neutralising or hiding the overall long-term public health needs of the people even if they have access to treatment at present. It argued that without addressing these needs treatment provision today will only be a temporary measure. The chapter then moved on to look at a particular paediatric antibiotic treatment used as a policy tool and the research that justified this policy development at the international level. Overall, the chapter argued that the medicalisation process used as the basis of international policy thinking is also used as a justification mechanism for the institutionalisation of international policy thinking. International actors deploy medical research to claim scientific justification for what they aim to do. Here the claims are justified on the basis of an assumed scientific objectivity and the accuracy attributed to the scientific method that is employed in medical research. However, there is a question about the emphasis put on the accuracy and strength of the method by the international policy actors. The chapter questioned this attribution by introducing a number of evaluative categories such as the question of internal and external validity. It argued that most of the policies that are justified on certain scientific knowledge claims lack, in this context, external validity as generalised policies for use. This is a major problem for the international actors who have pledged recently to develop evidence-based policies (UNAIDS 2006), since it is not clear what amounts to evidence for policy use.

With these processes introduced and analysed, the following two chapters (Chapters 4 and 5) looked at the deeper mechanisms that allow these processes to function and produce their effects within the policy implementation fields. Chapter 4 looked at the claims of the international policy actors that *we know what works*. It carried on from Chapter 3's focus on medicalisation and looked at the preventative medicine-based interventions and their claims to knowledge. The aim of this chapter was to see what the conditions are under which this claim to know is possible and, once the claim is used to support medicine-based policies, to look at what happens to the people's own knowledge of the disease and of themselves. It argued that this claim to know is not an empty gesture but imposes a particular way of knowing and acting once that way of knowing is accepted as the basis of policy interventions. If the expected action or behaviour change is not observed then people's behaviour is categorised as non-adherent. The chapter highlights that the knowledge claim and its associated policies act as a transformative mechanism for people in their everyday lives. The transformation is framed according to the international policy makers' expectations and requirements. In this way the institutionalisation process becomes a reality at the everyday level of people's lives as they are exposed to the prevention messages and their lives are measured according to how far they comply with these messages or not. In this way people are extracted from their own socio-economic and cultural contexts and relocated as target populations within the international policy context. The knowledge claim and the way it functions are located within Western thinking as a deep-seated norm which directs Western behaviour and action.

The following chapter (Chapter 5) then looked at language. In particular it looked at the policy language as a transformative mechanism which drives the institutionalisation process. Most of what we know of what works and which agents are relevant for what works is expressed in the policy language. These claims are not just expressed orally but are written down as the basis of the policy and influence the way of developing the policy. Therefore, the language of the policies is implicitly expressing what we think works. The chapter looked at how this process influences the way people act and how it then transforms what they can do in their socio-economic and cultural contexts. The civil society language that is explicit in the policy documents was analysed. The policy documents first set out the civil society and NGOs as the rights agents and partners for their interventions. In this they implicitly also describe what they consider to be the relevant civil society for them. These descriptions gradually turn into prescriptions as international policy makers also state that these are the conditions for them to recognise organisations as civil society groups for their partnering arrangements. These descriptions are not value or norm neutral, particularly considered from within the larger international development context of PRSPs and neo-liberal concerns over public expenditure. It is clear that the language of civil society reflects particular thinking about the role of civil society in this context. The aim is to have civil society as a service delivery arm of the international policy context. Once these views are implemented as actual policies, one can observe that existing civil society and community groups start to use the same language to define themselves and their work. In other words, the vibrant civil society observed within the HIV/AIDS field is not a random occurrence, but an effect of the institutionalisation of local civil society into the international policy environment.

> The road to hell is paved with good intentions.
>
> (attributed to Samuel Johnson)

Earlier chapters have analysed where we are going by way of looking at where we are at present in relation to international HIV/AIDS policies. Given that the direction appears undesirable there remains the question of what should be done (Flyvbjerg 2001: 60). In this section, I engage with this question by building on the earlier parts of the book that provide pathways to address it. Before doing that I would first like to take the following objection seriously, since one often hears it when the existing interventions and policy actors are critically analysed. At the end of my analysis those who are involved in international policy processes and others who are involved with civil society groups and policy implementation might sceptically raise the following issue: 'This analysis is fine, but what do we do in the face of the emergency? People are dying. We can't just get depressed and not do anything. We should be doing whatever we can do under the circumstances.'

   This is a familiar assertion against the assumed inaction that follows from critical analysis of what goes on. It asserts that *doing something is better than doing nothing*. This logic then constructs any critical questioning of actions at present as a move towards inaction and, thus, as a turning *away from those people who need our help*. I counter that not every action – however well meant – is good independent of its consequences for those people whom we are trying to help. Furthermore this logic has two important implications for the social sciences and for policy application in this area. One, it focuses research on HIV/AIDS in a particular way: social science research becomes focused mostly on the technical policy issues in implementation. As a result, research becomes a mechanism for policy evaluation located with the service delivery actors. One important outcome of this is that research frames tend to become subsumed under policy interests and the funding timeframes of international donors. In other words, there is little time or interest for in-depth research to understand the socio-economic and cultural conditions of people in various locations over time. Two, it facilitates the emergence of a gap between consideration of policy implementation and the conditions under which policies are produced. In other words, this logic allows actors involved in the policy context to be non-reflexive, since justification for their actions is provided with the assertion discussed that doing something is better than doing nothing. Research into international actors' behaviour in this context becomes discounted as irrelevant to action in the field. This turns the institutional systems within which policies are produced into a natural given that is hard to change. Thus, it is argued that *we need to work under these constraints and this is the best we can do*. It appears that this logic is another effect of an institutionalisation which asserts its centrality for what can be done in the field of HIV/AIDS interventions. This book doesn't claim to provide a simple answer or choice in this matter. Instead, it provides a number of pathways out of this logic.

This book has provided a set of analytical tools with which to understand the relationships between various actors and the way the policy process engages with people in the field of policy implementation. The analysis based on these tools demonstrated that the fundamental issues or problems associated with HIV/AIDS interventions are not technical problems. They are problems about the assumptions, perceptions and grounds on which policy actors locate their policy decisions and interventions.[2] In other words, in order to deal with the policy problems or with the poverty of thinking, policy analysis should look beyond immediate policy concerns and engage with the grounds of policy decisions. These analytical tools also valorise people's experiences of policies in the context of the disease. As people's experiences demonstrate different kinds of problems and issues important for their context, the generic formulation of policies for the target populations is seriously questioned. There are two central outcomes from these discussions. First, the various processes of institutionalisation and medicalisation described in the chapters highlight the fact that policy processes are not neutral. The theoretical discussion provides methodological steps for resituating policy actors and policies according to the consequences of their actions as they are experienced by people in the field of implementation. It is clear that policies have histories with associated values and norms for behaviour. It has been argued that these histories locate people as patients or target groups in an important power imbalance. Policy actors follow these embedded values and norms, informing their intentionality as the natural way of acting in relation to those targeted. People are constructed for the policy purposes as passive recipients of services. By looking at the knowledge claims and language use as mechanisms for influencing behaviour rather than as neutral processes for communication, it has been possible to raise questions about the role of international actors and the assumptions dominating their thinking. Second, the discussions in the chapters on medicalisation and knowledge have demonstrated that it is not only with the policy process and policy actors that a problem lies in terms of the international policy. There are also serious questions about the content of the policies which is based on the knowledge claims of these actors. In other words, there are serious doubts about what is claimed to be known about the disease and the way of dealing with the disease in various contexts. It has been argued here that the knowledge claims in fact work as a depoliticising and disempowering mechanism for people living with the disease. People's experiences and knowledge of the disease become irrelevant to policy considerations. In this, prioritisation of a particular scientific method and particular research approaches are used to legitimate the knowledge claims and, subsequently, policies based on them. While some of these methods and approaches produce information about the disease in experimental settings (this can be seen as speculative knowledge) it is not clear whether this produces knowledge for use outside the experimental context, for use in general policy implementations. There appears to be a lack of contextual knowledge (grounds for external validity) to be able to turn the information from research into knowledge for use within particular socio-cultural and economic contexts.[3]

The analytical discussions in this book are not about inaction. By critically questioning the justification provided for various policies, the role of policy actors and their knowledge claims has been reconsidered. As a result, a number of problems in relation to the asserted roles of actors and knowledge claims informing policies have been highlighted. Furthermore, the questioning destabilises the justification provided by the assertion that *doing something is important*. For the existence of these problems in the international policy formulation demands responsibility from the international actors for their actions independent of their declared good intentions. Overall, the analysis suggests that, in *trying to do something* without actually engaging with the policy actors, policy frames and their contents maintain the existing inequalities. While something needs to be done in times of need, this is not mutually exclusive with questioning the role of international actors and analysing how these may be exacerbating the situation.

The theoretical discussions provided in this book open up a set of questions for research to inform policy in the field:[4] What do people think about HIV/AIDS? What are the sources of their thinking about the disease? How do they react to other diseases? Are there differences in their reaction to HIV/AIDS and, if so, why? What are the influences motivating their behaviour in relation to the disease? What are the different ways sex and sexualities are considered? What does this mean for particular socio-cultural groups? How do young people negotiate sex? What socio-cultural significance does sex have for young people? What are the structures of gender relations? Do various masculinities influence people's responses to HIV/AIDS? How do these gender identities influence behaviour? Are local civil society groups the answer? Do they have resources to deal with the pandemic? Have their interventions provided positive changes in their communities? Can the small-scale localised interventions by civil society groups be scaled up? Can everyone who needs it be on treatment? For how long can they afford to be on treatment? How many people can access treatment? Who decides who gets treatment? How sustainable are the donor-led treatment programmes? What happens to prevention if all the resources are channelled to treatment? What are the medical behaviour patterns in different communities? How do they use drugs? What determines their drug consumption patterns? How do they react to long-term generalised drug use? What happens when they develop fatigue to medical interventions? Can developing countries sustain both prevention and treatment-based interventions at the same time? Are there financial and human resources available to support these interventions in the long term? How will they cope with people developing resistance to drugs? Will there be second- and third-line drugs for treatment available in developing countries? How would these be delivered? What happens if there is underproduction of international provision of drugs and condoms? Will there be employment, housing and education to support people who are becoming *healthier* with treatment? Do people living with HIV know what the long-term implications are of treatment? Are there any changes in the socio-economic context of people to motivate them toward healthier life choices? What are the healthier life options for so many in different socio-cultural and economic contexts? Has there been a change in developmental interventions to create less vulnerability for people? Is there political will in the international fora beyond the rhetoric of charity? Has the way international actors produce and provide drugs for treatment in developing countries changed? Is the pandemic an emergency? Can an emergency last over two decades? Does this emergency thinking, prevalent among the international policy makers, compromise what can be done for the long term? Does it compromise what we want to know in order to develop policies? Has the emergency thinking created a particular model of intervention? What has the role of international actors been in this pandemic? Do they provide know-how for interventions? Do their generalised policies effectively engage with communities? Do they really know how people change behaviour in the long term and whether that behaviour change can be transgenerational? If the policies do not have transgenerational impact, what are the mechanisms for dealing with the next cycle of disease and its spread? Do they know how HIV/AIDS and interventions influence different gender and age groups? What are the implications of the disease on different sexualities? Do they know why people have sex? What are the traditional ways of change in different communities and societies? How far are the existing policy interventions relevant for these channels of change? What happens if the expected behaviour-change patterns do not overlap with existing socio-cultural pathways for change? Are people aware of resource constraints on existing policies? Do they know how the disease interacts with child bearing and socio-cultural aspirations to have children? How far have the experts looked at the long-term implications of existing policy interventions? How do the international organisations consider their

own impact on the disease and people living with the disease? Do international actors really care?

All of these questions and many more are significant for understanding the
context within which the disease is experienced and responded to by people.
They are also significant for policy development and the subsequent interventions by various policy actors. However, producing knowledge that is based
on these questions requires persistent and long-term research which cannot
be produced under the emergency logic that drives the international policy
process. It also requires the questioning of deep-seated assumptions and
beliefs that are based on Western rationality models and their impact on the
way policies are produced. Thus, these questions challenge the international
policy thinking in its emergency logic and in its socio-cultural conditions. The
challenge provides a number of pathways that can facilitate a change in the
system. These pathways can be looked at under two headings: issues about
policy processes and policy content.

The international actors have to rethink their basic characteristics and the
decision-making processes that produce their policies. At present, they do
not consider people who are affected by their policies as relevant parties to
the process other than as a population in need. Some argue that there has
been an increased emphasis on participation among the international
donors and organisations to address this problem. While the language of
participation is widespread, and at times attached to the discussions
of human rights, an analysis of language similar to that in Chapter 5
suggests that this emphasis remains rhetorical (see also Kapoor 2005).
Most participatory processes require people to participate with existing
international policy discussions and existing methods of service delivery.
Participation policies are limited within funding timeframes and constrained
by existing policy frameworks. They do not create deliberative processes
whereby people can question the overall policy frameworks and the role of
actors assumed within these. As a result, participatory processes become a
technical tool for further institutionalisation of the international policy
thinking. They are used to legitimate the existing policy thinking and demonstrate that people were consulted (Uvin 2004). It is not clear, for instance,
what happens when young people argue that abstinence does not work for
sexually active people and that there have to be different kinds of interventions and messages for them. Does this change the policy framework? It
appears not. Participation in the policy discussions and framing is rare.
Another important issue here is the way the participation language changes
the way people are looked at. By participating in consultations by NGOs or
international donors, people are considered to have become active, doing
something for themselves and for their communities. This attitude ignores
that people are already living and doing something about the disease, given
that they are exposed to it in their everyday lives, independently of the
international policy interventions. Given that HIV/AIDS highlights complex social issues within which people live, this attitude treats people's

everyday lives as passive, where people are seen as expecting to have help from the outside.

The perspective on HIV/AIDS will have to change from one that considers HIV/AIDS as one among a set of questions in the international developmental policy context, where international actors bring their understanding to bear on the problem to implement ready-made policies. The discussion needs to start from the experiences of those who are living in the context of the disease and their long-term needs in their own contexts. If international actors are serious about their commitment to deal with the disease they need to ask themselves: where are the people living with HIV/AIDS and their contexts in all these processes? This in turn brings in the issue of representation at all levels of policy for those who are affected by these policies. The demand requires the establishment of clear accountability mechanisms and procedures for demanding responsibility from the international actors on the basis of people's experiences of policies in both the short and the long term. Furthermore, the question of *who participates* is central. These demands cannot be ignored by merely pointing out the participation of NGOs in the policy processes. Given the discussions in the earlier chapters on the incorporation of these into the international policy processes, there are serious questions about whether they can claim to represent people at all. Their claims are constrained by the service delivery role which is attributed to them. NGOs' ability to help people voice their needs is also hampered by the often-mentioned implicit code of conduct among NGOs which stops them from publicly questioning or criticising any other NGO's work. The norm that *NGOs don't complain about other NGOs* transforms them into a sector with their own interests independent of people's voices and needs. Given such issues, people need public spaces to be able to demand responsibility from all these actors for their policies and their impact on their lives. People should be able to question, for instance, changing policy fashions and why they are supposed to be following these changes or why they should be expected to switch between various policy tools without questions being asked of international expertise on the issue. In this way, a process could be initiated of questioning at the international level which might motivate the self-reflexivity of the actors, beyond their assumed good intentions.

It is clear that HIV/AIDS is complex in its causes and consequences. The complexity is linked with people's everyday lives. The analyses provided in the book and questions that are raised in it challenge the attitude of looking at HIV/AIDS as one of the agenda items within general international development discussions,[5] which can only be addressed by focusing on certain issues in the development. This book's analyses argue that the impact of international actors on people's lives will have to be looked at in their entirety in order to be able to adequately understand some of the complex issues related to HIV/AIDS. Rather than compartmentalising HIV/AIDS policies to limited interventions that are justified on medical grounds, policies have to be analysed within the context of existing general developmental interventions.

In particular, there is a necessity for understanding the long-term impact and sustainability of these interventions. People not only live within the context of HIV/AIDS as patients or target groups, but they have been living through long cycles of developmental interventions that have determined and influenced their livelihood for a long time. Their experience of the disease is also located within this larger context (see Cheru 2002; Whiteside 2006). The structuring of resources and their distribution within communities has been influenced by multiple interventions by international donors. The dominance of particular views on development, ranging from infrastructural interventions to more recent interventions based on neo-liberal thinking, has important implications for the way people live. Given that international development policies are constantly restructuring the role of states, their involvement in the public provision of welfare goods, such as health and education, and people's economic livelihoods, the impact of these on HIV/AIDS has to be assessed. Furthermore, while international actors are trying to deal with the HIV/AIDS emergency, it is clear that some of these other developmental interventions, which are also implemented by the same actors, can hamper the impact of these interventions. It is also clear that, while some of the earlier international developmental policies and interventions might have had an important role in creating the circumstances under which HIV spread, the cleavage today between policies of international development and the pledges and aspirations underpinning the HIV/AIDS policies demonstrates that international actors do not link these areas together. It is imperative at this stage to consider international developmental interventions and their impact on the basis of HIV/AIDS and its impact on people, rather than the other way round. There is a need for international actors to think about the question: what have they changed in their overall developmental policy thinking and its implementation as a result of HIV/AIDS? People's experiences of disease within particular socio-economic and cultural contexts that are exercised by decades of international development interventions question the wisdom in many of these interventions. They also point out that, unless the logic of the international actors is changed, the long-term combined implications of international development and HIV/AIDS will make people even more vulnerable. To deal with HIV/AIDS, independent of the extant neo-liberal common sense in development, there has to be long-term investment in building welfare systems and public social security with special reference to health infrastructure and education that can be sustained over the long term. Funding HIV/AIDS and funding and creating the right environment for these infrastructural investments should not be mutually exclusive; far from it, they need to happen at the same time.

This process requires international actors, including international policy experts, to acknowledge that people are not passive in their lives and that they have agency in terms of their lives. This agency is independent of our knowledge claims and does not depend on people transforming themselves into what experts expect them to be for dealing with their poverty or with the disease. This does not mean that experts' knowledge has nothing to say about the disease or how to deal with it. It only makes the point that for this knowledge to be useful it has to engage with what people know about themselves without neutralising the latter as a non-scientific or a policy-irrelevant socio-cultural obstacle. The knowledge of experts may be necessary but it is not sufficient for evidence to be used for policy applications in particular contexts.

This brings in the third challenge of the analyses provided in this book. Recently a number of publications by UNAIDS have emphasised and highlighted the importance of evidence-based policy (2005a, 2006). This is an effect of the growing focus on evidence-based policy both in the developed countries and among international donors. For instance, according to the UNAIDS policy position paper *Intensifying HIV Prevention*, among the main principles of effective HIV prevention are: 'programmes must be differentiated and locally adapted; prevention actions must be evidence-informed based on what is known and proven to be effective and investment to expand the evidence base should be strengthened' (2005b: 17). While it is important to have evidence for policy, it is not very clear what is meant by evidence. If we follow what has been already used for policy-making purposes as evidence in the international context, then, given the discussions in Chapters 4 and 5, there are serious questions about this understanding of evidence. Another central question here is: what is the evidence for? The analyses in the above chapters show that what is established as evidence has particular problems. While it may be seen as evidence for particular knowledge in an experimental context, its status as evidence for use in different contexts is highly questionable. What makes evidence an evidence for use is linked with a complex set of questions, some of which are posed earlier in this section in relation to the external validity of a knowledge claimed.

Here we also have two other complications since the knowledge claimed relies on a set of categories that are used as analytical interpretive tools to turn the knowledge into policy, as discussed in Chapter 4. These are also influenced by who decides what the context of use is for particular knowledge. In other words, not only does the context of evidence production have central importance, but also the context of its interpretation has importance for a claim that there is an evidence for use. In the context of international HIV/AIDS policies the claims of international policy actors are prioritised over people's knowledge based on their experiences.[6] Furthermore, social research looking at people's experiences is also marginalised, owing to its methodologies (Hemmings 2005). Tim Allen, for instance, argues that:

> 'data' are given much greater emphasis, and 'anecdotes' tend to be set aside as perhaps interesting, but largely irrelevant when it comes to policy. A fetish for numbers is not unusual, but seems to be extreme with respect to HIV/AIDS.
>
> (2006: 8)

There is a link between this discussion and the way successful policies are decided, as discussed earlier. Attributing success according to a common policy target agreed at the international level, or to interventions which can produce quantifiable short-term outcomes, and using these success stories as evidence for generalisable policies is highly questionable. The status of success stories as evidence does not clinch the argument in terms of the sustainability of such success once it is removed from its context, and the lack of available people's perspectives on the policies makes the link from success to evidence even more questionable. The idea of evidence as an objective and neutral fact out there waiting to be discovered needs to be questioned. It clearly is not neutral, since the boundaries of what amounts to evidence are decided according to assumptions held within international policy circles. Unless international experts and policy makers rethink what is meant by evidence and try to understand what amounts to evidence for use in context, the introduction of the idea of evidence-based policy acts as yet another fig leaf and asserts what international actors think is relevant. The best evidence for use is found within people's everyday lives, communities and the way they conduct their lives in them. However, given the priorities of the international policy actors it appears that there is no time to engage with this, partially because they are dealing with an emergency and partially because there are no resources provided to support long-term in-depth engagement with communities to understand the local responses to some of the important questions posed earlier.

In the end there is no doubt that the people who are participating in the international policy discussions and contributing to the efforts of international organisations have good intentions. International organisations are attempting to address people's needs with the utmost urgency. However, given the points discussed above and in the book as a whole, the question of 'Do international actors really care?' still remains. It poses a challenge for international organisations, experts and other actors who participate in the policy processes. The question contests that HIV/AIDS can be addressed under the existing international approach in which care is a function of charity. In the charitable attitudes there is an inherent imbalance. It is up to the will of the charitable party to do *this* or *that* independently of what needs to be done according to the people in need. If international actors are really caring, they have to go beyond charity and reflect on the issues raised above in relation to their own actions and the implications of these on the people. This move requires a different kind of caring that is about being open to people's lives, their needs and their hopes for the future in the way they see them. In other words, if international actors do care about people it is time to stop assuming that they know what is best for people now and in the future, and to be prepared to help people even if the people's demands do not agree with the international actors' assumptions about the good life and with their policy interests.

Notes

Introduction

1 As soon as HIV/AIDS was identified it was related to particular social relations and their political struggle within the larger political debate in the United States of America. However, the disease was difficult to accept initially even for the gay communities (Shilts 1987). Once people began to realise that the federal and local authorities were not responding to the crisis and they were alone, the debate turned to look for ways of people taking the initiative themselves to address the crisis (Perrow and Guillen 1990). Rapidly HIV/AIDS became an issue for gay people's politics.

2 The experience with the disease in the early 1980s in the US was taking place within an intensely political context, with the establishment of self-help groups like Gay Men's Health Crisis in 1982 and the emergence of People with AIDS Coalition in 1983, leading to participation of people living with AIDS from San Francisco in the Fifth National Lesbian/Gay Health Conference in Denver, which had the Second National Forum on AIDS and brought people's voices into the debate in radical fashion. This meeting produced the principles known as the Denver Principles. People were asking for their rights to health and care independent of the prejudices policy makers had in relation to their sexualities. The activism was further radicalised by the establishment of AIDS Coalition to Unleash Power (ACT UP) in 1987. Within a few weeks of their establishment ACT UP targeted directly the Federal Food and Drug Administration (FDA). Their demand was the release of drugs 'that might help save our lives'. According to Bastos, after ten years of activism the movement moved into a new phase around 1991 with the increased specialisation through the activist organisations (1999: 470).

1 Governance of HIV/AIDS

1 As discussed in the Introduction, the statistical estimates have been challenged as inaccurate and also, given the ranges that are indicated by UNAIDS, there is a certain scope for error. However, this does not necessarily point to the existence of a less severe pandemic. The numbers here are used just to indicate the scope of the problem.

2 Another is the Thai organisation Population and Community Development Association (PDA), which, founded by Mechai Viravaidya in 1974 to deal with development and birth control issues, allowed AIDS activism to be taken on without too much trouble. Their long-standing relationship with government also allowed them to lobby the government to engage with the issue whereby they were able to bring Buddhist monks into their project to disseminate information around the country.

3 In a way this can also be seen as a paradoxical situation for the WHO at the time, considering that in the early 1980s WHO still considered homosexuality as a mental disorder.

4 The WTO regulations required all member states to comply with the patenting laws of the US by 2005. This had important implications for the production of generic drugs. In particular the Indian government's decision to comply with them in 2005 created questions in terms of treatment in developing countries if they are not able to produce second- or third-line treatment drugs in the future.

5 For the full text see: http://www.accessmed-msf.org/prod/publications.asp?scntid=17122001173935&contenttype=PARA&.

6 The treatment-based activism in South Africa presents a very dynamic and political engagement with the government of South Africa whose views on HIV/AIDS have been controversial. The Treatment Action Campaign over a long campaign managed to move the government to provide comprehensive treatment across the country (see Heywood 2002 and Gomez-Pablos 2001). However, this activism and effectiveness should be seen within the particular political context of post-apartheid South Africa; it is difficult to generalise this to the rest of the region.

7 UNAIDS breaks down this international contribution as follows: the US provides 30 per cent (US$514 million), the United Kingdom 14 per cent (US$300 million), the UN agencies 27 per cent, Canada, Germany, Japan and Italy together another 9 per cent, 13 per cent from other OECD countries, and 7 per cent from foundations such as Bill and Melinda Gates, Ford, Marie Stopes, Kaiser, the Open Society and Rockefeller (UNAIDS 2002b: 167).

8 Of the overall amount, US$1.9 billion is spent on prevention, with the rest allocated to care- and support-related expenditure. The funds allocated to prevention amount to the main expenditure; out of total funds contributed, 57 per cent of the US, 67 per cent of the UK and 80 per cent of the foundations' contributions were committed to prevention. The Working Group estimated that US$1.5 billion would be needed by 2005 (GHPWG 2003: 10).

9 Here language game is used in Ludwig Wittgenstein's sense. A 'language game is meant to bring into prominence the fact that the speaking of language is part of an activity, or form of life' (1977: 11). Also see Seckinelgin (2002).

10 Without spending too much time discussing definitional problems, I take civil society to mean civil society organisation – NGOs and community organisations. This is the way the term is commonly used by international policy makers (see Seckinelgin 2002).

11 http://www.unaids.org/en/about+unaids/cosponsors.asp

2   Constructing agency in the time of an epidemic

1 This is called organisational isomorphism by DiMaggio and Powell (1983).

2 See for example de Graff (1987) and the more critical Tvedt (1998), Hilhorst (2003) and Michael (2004).

3 Arguably this situation is due to the tradition of action research which is located closer to the organisations and to the aspirational positive qualities generally attributed to these sorts of organisations, particularly after the Cold War. See Uvin and Miller (1994); Ottaway and Carothers (2000).

4 This line of discussion follows from Barnett and Finnemore (1999: 701). Also see Ruggie (1998) and Wendt (1998).

5 There is an extensive literature on this debate, particularly on regimes and environmental regimes. See Hasenclever *et al.* (1997); Haas (1990); Hurrell and Woods (1995); Keohane (1984); Krasner (1983); Ruggie (1998); Wendt (1998); and Young (1989).

6 This is related to the preference given to states as actors in the realist and neo-liberal theories of international relations (see Barnett and Finnemore 1999; Wendt 1999). The logic of these theoretical positions is linked with what Meyer and Jepperson call 'the realist imagery' (Meyer and Jepperson 2000: 101).

7 For instance Alexis de Tocqueville's *Democracy in America* is an important study that demonstrates the institutionalisation processes constructing a particular set of political and social relations culminating in voluntary organisations. However, this view is neutralised by neo-Tocquevillians who take the organisational form created at the end of this process as the substance of civil society and voluntarism in general (de Tocqueville 1998; Putnam 1993).

8 Hilhorst's position on various domains of knowledge used in overcoming a conflict can be considered from this perspective. It is discussed in the next section.

9 In this line of thinking different scientific disciplines like medicine and anthropology can be taken as presenting different worlds with the institutionalised values and particular rationalities that they have. It also means that engaging with these disciplines requires thinking within these institutionalised values and rationalities.

10 Finnemore and Sikkink's discussion of norm entrepreneurs is also relevant for this (Finnemore and Sikkink 1998: 896–9).

11 Tvedt raises a similar concern by looking at the claims of comparative advantage attributed to NGOs (Tvedt 1998: 131).

12 This argument would question attempts to classify a generalised perspective on NGOs focusing on development, environment, etc. according to their functions in service delivery and advocacy. It would argue that these attempts are still looking for a generalised understanding of NGOs and their agency.

13 Douglas argues: 'let no one take comfort in the thought that primitives think through their institutions while moderns take the big decisions individually. That very thought is an example of letting institutions do the thinking' (Douglas 1986: 124).

14 See also Powell (1991: 190); Scott (1991: 175).

15 This process is divided into various analytical categories by DiMaggio and Powell: coercive, mimetic and normative. It is possible to see each of these playing a role in the process and enforcing the impact of each other in creating isomorphism (DiMaggio and Powell 1991: 67–71).

16 I am reading 'free to push' as 'free to choose to push'.

17 This understanding of free agents is related to what Meyer calls modern 'autochthonous' actors that are abstracted from a culture (Meyer 1988).

18 See Anscombe 1957 in particular.

19 A particular way of seeing civil society, and a search for this kind of organisation, is probably one way of explaining large unspent funding at times with MAP/UNAIDS. It is clear that, in order to be able to access funding, organisations will have to have a particular form, as otherwise they cannot get access to funding.

20 A sign of this can be seen in the debates on provision of treatment. It is packaged as an economic imperative to maintain certain developmental goals and achievements.

21 See DiMaggio and Powell 1991: 67–70.

22 Also see Glasius 2002.

23 This, of course, means that the questions are generally related to states' role and the functioning of the international state system and social relations within this system in the international fora.

24 More transnational views associated with David Held and Richard Falk would attribute a much more central role to non-state actors in the system but this is very difficult to demonstrate empirically. It is also argued that the quality and depth of this influence very much depend on the issue area and the relations between actors that are constructed in that field (see Coleman 2001 and Van Rooy 1998). This also

holds true for the main thrust of Keck and Sikkink's discussions on international networks (1998).

25 This creates an accountability and responsibility gap on the side of the international actors as, strictly speaking, from a formal international relations perspective, people do not have direct political links with international actors. Their relations are mediated by their individual national governments.

26 DiMaggio and Powell (1991: 70).

27 www.pactworld.org

28 http://www.pactworld.org/reach/aps/Lesotho/Lesotho_APS_05-05.doc

29 http://www.whitehouse.gov/infocus/hivaids/index.html

30 http://www.whitehouse.gov/news/releases/2004/06/20040623-1.html

31 This is also in line with the way Meyer and Jepperson discuss the agency in modern society (Meyer and Jepperson 2000).

32 Such as The AIDS Support Organisation (TASO) and Traditional and Modern Health Practitioners Together Against AIDS and Other Disease (THETA) in Uganda, AVEGA 'AGAHOZO' in Rwanda, and Thandizani: Community Based HIV/AIDS Prevention Care in Zambia or Partners in Health in Haiti and in Peru. See Farmer 1999 and Farmer *et al.* 2001.

3 Medicalisation

1 C. Helman links the rise of this process to a number of issues including 'the Cartesian conceptualization of the body as a machine, stripped from its social and cultural context and a regard for medical technology as a means to tame uncontrolled and unpredictable social phenomena' (1994).

2 'Once a society is so organized that medicine can transform people into patients because they are unborn, newborn, menopausal, or at some other "age of risk" the population inevitably loses some of its autonomy to its healers' (Illich 1977: 86).

3 It is also argued that policy makers prefer medical solutions since they are 'less elusive than the economic and political measures' (Rosenberg 1988: 26). However, this view seems to ignore an important link between medicalisation and political and economic policy orientations, in particular those in non-Western contexts where people are treated as populations subject to development interventions for their own good.

4 As argued by Baldwin (2005) in the domestic context, the international response has also followed a historical path which is in accordance with the general behaviour of international organisations dealing with diseases.

5 This is also recognised by UNAIDS: 'Twenty-five years into the epidemic, the global response to AIDS must be transformed from an episodic, crisis-management approach to strategic response that recognises the need for long-term commitment' (2006: 17).

6 While I am focusing here on treatment policy and the way it has been articulated, the medical frame of reference is also the basis of the prevention policies. I will look at these in the next chapter.

7 Horton (2003: 223-8).

8 It is noted that, 'though the number exceeds 100,000 today, it is still a far cry from 8 million who are thought to require such therapy (Wainberg 2005: 747).

9 Some of the initiatives in this context are discussed in an earlier section.

10 The aim is to attack the virus to stop its life cycle by which it replicates itself within the human cell by using chemicals and proteins. For HIV type 1 there are four classes of drugs: 'nucleoside and nucleotide analogues, which act as DNA-chain terminators and inhibit reverse transcription of the viral RNA genome into DNA, a crucial event occurring at an early stage of viral life cycle; nonnucleoside reverse-transcriptase inhibitors, which bind and inhibit reverse transcriptase, the viral

enzyme that conducts reverse transcription; protease inhibitors, which target the viral protease, the enzyme required for cleavage of precursor proteins, permitting the final assembly of the inner core of viral particles; and enter inhibitors, which block the penetration of HIV virions into their target cells' (Clavel and Hance 2004: 1023).

11 The commonly prescribed HAART regimen consists of two nucleoside reverse transcriptase inhibitors (NRTI) and either a protease inhibitor (PI) or a non-nucleoside reverse transcriptase inhibitor (NNRTI) (Clavel and Hance 2004). According to WHO, in resource-poor settings the 'first line regimen would consist of 2 nucleoside and non-nucleoside or abacavir or a protease inhibitor' (WHO 2006).

12 Recent evidence suggests that there is still ongoing low-level HIV replication even when plasma HIV RNA is below the current level of detection. This makes it clear that ARVs can be used to manage the disease (Meech 2006) rather than entirely cure the infection (Frenkel and Mullins 2001).

13 Though not so much in the north, owing to long-running problems with the guerrillas.

14 Again a sceptic might argue that this is a question of availability. If the cost of treatment gradually goes down and international actors make good their funding commitments, in addition to the national government's allocation of more funds for health interventions, there is no reason to think that people would not receive treatment as long as they need.

15 The same is also suggested for Botswana and the way international funding is structured in that country.

16 Given that there has been a gradual cost reduction for treatment.

17 In the 'Results' section of the paper the discussion highlights the importance of attending the clinic for observation and the receipt of the trial drug: 'in a total 89% of scheduled clinic visits before death or last seen alive up to and including week 96 were attended (89.7% trimoxazole, 88.5% placebo)' and furthermore '245 (46%) children did not miss any scheduled clinic visits (122 co-trimoxazole, 123 placebo)' (Chintu *et al.* 2004: 1868). In this 193 children allocated to the trial drug and 184 in the placebo group spent more than 90 per cent of their follow-up time supplied with the trial drug, while 60 and 59 children respectively 'spent more than 31 consecutive days without being supplied such treatment at some stage during the trial' (ibid.). Overall 25 children received antiretroviral treatment during the trial (11 were in the placebo group). During the trial '74 (28%) children died in the co-trimoxazole group and 112 (42%) died in the placebo group' (Chintu *et al.* 2004: 1869). Among these only 92 (49%) of them died in hospital and in some cases (15%) it was not possible to establish the cause of death even if they died in hospital. According to the authors, 'pneumonia was the only clinical diagnosis that was more frequent in those allocated placebo than in those allocated trial drug' (Chintu *et al.* 2004: 1869).

18 Cartwright argues that this is done to 'finesse our lack of knowledge about what other reasons might be responsible for probabilistic dependency between a treatment and an outcome' (Cartwright 2007: 36).

19 See Horton (2003: 49).

20 'Pneumonia was the only clinical diagnosis that was more frequent in those allocated placebo than in those allocated to the treatment' (Chintu *et al.* 2004: 1869).

21 Revised guidelines require these procedures (see WHO *et al.* 2004).

22 On the issue of care see also Chimwaza and Watkins (2004).

23 Horton (2003: 362).

24 Horton argues that 'what medicine has achieved is the creation of a powerful means to acquire evidence, but at the cost of frequently devaluing the evidence gathered during the patient's encounter with a doctor' (2003: 49).

4 What do we need to know for HIV/AIDS interventions in Africa?

1 Peter Piot's comments were part of his presentation in the African Union Summit, World Forum on Health and Development, on 10 July 2003. He repeated his claim in a public lecture at LSE in 2005.

2 Julian Lob-Levyt's comments were also part of his presentation in the African Union Summit, World Forum on Health and Development, on 10 July 2003.

3 In this way it is also argued that policy makers prefer medical solutions as they are 'less elusive than the economic and political measures' (Rosenberg 1988: 26). However, this seems to ignore an important link between medicalisation and political and economic policy orientations, particularly in non-Western contexts where people are treated as populations subject to development interventions for their own good.

4 See, for instance, Suzette Heald's study of Botswana (Heald 2006).

5 This process, according to Michel Foucault, 'tended to individualize bodies, diseases, symptoms, lives and deaths' (1977: 144).

6 For instance, in 2002 both in Rwanda and Uganda it was clear that there was a massive drive to test people, and the justification for this was based on providing people with a knowledge of their health which would influence their risk behaviour. In 2005 most of the VCT discussion had shifted to the VCTs in the context of ARV provision since without tests it is not possible to provide drugs.

7 Here, I take 'proven' to mean what we know but also what we know on a scientific basis. This trope is employed in this report (GHPWG 2003) and in the UNAIDS report several times.

8 The basis for this forecast is challenged by Landon Myer and his colleagues in a letter sent to the *British Medical Journal* in 2001. They argued that the gap is much larger and the real number is more likely to be around 13 billion condoms per year; see *British Medical Journal* (2001), 323 (20 October): 937.

9 These categories are generic to the framework. For instance the category of prisoners is a difficult one because there is a strong social stigma attached to same-sex intercourse. In the event of finding people having sex in the overcrowded post-genocide prisons in Rwanda, it is not rare to see other prisoners giving out severe punishment to the caught people. Thus, it is not easy to distribute condoms in prisons. The distribution had to be packaged as a prevention for having sex outside the prison while prisoners are used as workers in the fields or on building or road works.

10 Here I am referring to the research conducted in Kenya, Trinidad and Tobago, and Tanzania by the Efficacy Testing Group (ETG) in 2000. This research has been widely used as the scientific support in the documents that are discussed for VCT interventions.

11 1957, para. 29. She refers to Aristotle on this, according to whom 'one does not deliberate about acquired skill; the description of what one is doing, which one completely understands, is at a distance from the details of one's movements, which one does not consider at all'.

12 Though this claim is debatable, given that the number of condoms distributed is assumed to be a reliable measure of the effectiveness of VCT. This measure is potentially flawed, however, because it is difficult to assess actual condom use (on this see for instance Bracher *et al.* 2004).

13 In what follows all the names have been changed for reasons of anonymity. The locations of the stories remain accurate. Interviews were conducted at various points between January 2002 and June 2005.

14 These are analytical divisions. In real life these areas are intimately linked in complex processes. The sub-headings for each case are an analytical divide for clarity.

Each case can offer practical knowledge for non-action in relation to the policies from various positions and can be located under all three sub-headings.

15 The questions that were asked by me during these conversations are within parentheses.

16 On this see also Miller 2003.

17 On this also see Peltzer *et al.* 2006.

18 Of course, this is a complex problem. If the people have no energy themselves owing to the disease or there are no carers who can also deal with their fields, the introduction of new crops will not yield the expected results in relation to food security.

19 In this VCT project the definition of a couple is two people who define themselves as together, but do not necessarily cohabit. There was also a suggestion that the project does not keep those people who don't stay in couples in its VCT programmes.

20 However, one can argue about whether she is suggesting that in doing one can see what was the intention and then infer its description, which would then still be based on what we know.

21 It is clear that this practical knowledge cannot be entirely independent of speculative categories. The point is that the speculative base and categories would be related to the person's own context or, in other words, categories of herself.

22 For Wittgenstein and Anscombe I will follow the established convention and cite paragraphs rather than pages.

23 This is what is called 'concepts have memories' by Hacking (2003: 37).

24 The results of such a divide between a world-maker's view of the situation and people's own perceptions are demonstrated in Uvin's important study of the development industry in Rwanda. See Uvin (1998).

5 Language as a transformative mechanism

1 Cathy Campbell's work points out this lack in the research field (Campbell 2003; also see Seckinelgin 2002).

2 D.C. Dorward's work on Tiv is very interesting in this area. It highlights how local colonised people considered the colonial discourse and developed a particular way of dealing with it (1974).

3 On this Philip Curtin's work is also informative (Curtin 1965). Timothy Mitchell's *Colonising Egypt* is another interesting work looking at the impact of colonial rule in creating an imagery of the locals by using classifications and categories based on its own interest and concerns (1991).

4 Ian Hacking has recently suggested that his work combines Ludwig Wittgenstein's thinking on language with Michel Foucault's discussions of power (Hacking 2005).

5 *Our* does not indicate a belief on my side but indicates a location from the perspective of international actors and donors in this context.

6 This is an important step, as looking at Hacking we are not given too many insights for the mechanism behind his argument.

7 This reading of Wittgenstein is also supported by Nicolas Greenwood Onuf's work in international relations. Onuf's work emphasises the way Wittgenstein 'sought to convey the sense of the term "rule" by examining its use' (Onuf 1989: 47). Onuf's interpretation of Wittgenstein and his language theory is also influential on Karin Fierke's work in critical international security studies (1998). Also, more generally on language F.V. Kratochwil's work on rules and norms in international relations is relevant, as it looks at the way norms and rules direct action in the international field (1989).

8 The interpretation of Wittgenstein here is also parallel to Robert Brandom's

understanding of later Wittgenstein. He considers this period as an attempt to understand the 'normative significance of intentional content' (Brandom 1994: 14).

9 References to Ludwig Wittgenstein's *Philosophical Investigations* (*PI*) (1997 [1958]) will follow the established convention of using paragraph numbers for referencing.

10 Karin Fierke also seems to be using a similar interpretation to suggest that language use is possible on the basis of a certain agreement on the meaning of that particular use (1998: 25).

11 However, Wittgenstein counters a possible reduction of a description to a statement 'that this word signifies this object' (*PI* 10). This is an important restriction, as he argues that 'the use of these words, for the rest, is already known' (*PI* 10).

12 This interpretation is also evident in the work of Vendulka Kubalkova, N. Onuf and P. Kowert. They suggest that 'the person shouting "fire" believes that a series of empirical generalizations cover the situation. Flickering light, intense heat, voluminous smoke, or crackling noises generally mean fire' (1998: 14–15).

13 Here one could question what is meant by some aspects, though it is reasonable to assume that they refer to those reference points which are set by some definition of the first subject. Onuf also follows this line of argument while discussing constructivism in international relations (1998: 64).

14 John M. Janzen's work is interesting on the introduction of colonial medicine and its impact on the way disease had been managed in 'Lower Zaire'. It is suggested that availability of two different sets of medical practices that are ideologically competing with each other have collided in the minds and practices of the sufferers. In this sufferers have played with the language of the colonial medicine to create a manoeuvring space for themselves (Janzen 1978). The power context of the introduction of colonial medicine is an important aspect of the transformation of traditional medicine as discussed in Janzen's work (also see Curtin 1992; Ngubane 1992; MacCormack 1992).

15 Also see Susan Reynolds Whyte's work where she looks at the way AIDS awareness campaigns have been interpreted by people in eastern Uganda (1997: 203–23).

16 There are various debates and discussions on civil society and its use (Keane 1988; Cohen and Arato 1994; Colas 1997).

17 See Putnam *et al.* 1992 and Taylor 1990.

18 For in-depth analysis of these see Maxwell 2003; Craig and Porter 2003; Bradshaw and Linneker 2003; and Crawford 2003.

19 The history of the DfID goes back to 1929 when the UK government recognised its responsibility for the development of its colonies on a permanent basis. This was recognised by the Colonial Development Act at the time. In order to deal with the technical issues within the aid programme, in 1961 a Department of Technical Co-operation was established. This was followed by the establishment of the Ministry of Overseas Development, as a separate ministry, in 1964. In this way the UK government joined together its overseas aid relations that were managed under various government departments. However this ministry was dissolved in 1970 and its functions were added to the portfolio of the Department of Foreign and Commonwealth Affairs. In this department a subsection handled this portfolio, Overseas Development Administration (ODA). In 1997 the ODA, once more, was replaced by the Department for International Development, headed by a secretary of state with Cabinet rank (DfID 2005).

20 According to Jonathan Skinner, DfID occupies a space within '"colonial governmentality" with its "rational administration", assumes control over the development of the native population, frequently employing the classic mechanisms of bureaucratisation, documentation, rationalisation and registration' (2003: 99–100).

21 According to Mudimbe, 'an interpretation of the relation between a lived experience and an oral or written narrative witnessing to it can be a reduction to a theoretical synthetic unit' (Mudimbe 1994: 192). Here the above-mentioned discussions of civil society based on sectoral divides are one such synthetic unit.

22 Partners consist of officials from national coordinating bodies and relevant ministries of African nations, major funding mechanisms, multilateral and bilateral agencies, NGOs and the private sector focused on the need to further clarify roles and relationships at the country level. The DfID is also a partner of UNAIDS through its HIV/AIDS programmes.

23 By 2002 around 36 African countries out of 44 countries had established national AIDS councils, while none had managed to allocate 15 per cent of their budgets to health; only four of them (Benin, Botswana, Burundi and Namibia) had legislation against stigma and social discrimination (UNAIDS 2002a).

Conclusion: time to wake up

1 This term comes from Charles Tilly's work. He argues that, 'since all social relations involve fleeting, fluctuating inequalities, let us concentrate on durable inequalities, those that last from one social interaction to the next, with special attention to those that persist over whole careers, lifetimes, and organizational histories' (1999: 6).

2 This view uses the logic of Martin Heidegger's discussion on *The Question concerning Technology*. He argues that 'the manufacture and utilization of equipment, tools, and machines, the manufactured and used things themselves, the needs and ends they serve, all belong to what technology is' (1977: 4).

3 Stuart Hampshire argues that 'Speculation is not knowledge, although it may suggest paths to the investigations that produce knowledge' (2005: viii).

4 Some might argue that some of these questions are already being studied. This might be true. But they still are far from being included in the policy discussions.

5 It is common to hear for instance how countries are losing their developmental gains that they had achieved in the decades before they were hit by HIV/AIDS. Here the discussions highlight the importance of saving productive lives to be able to maintain these developmental gains. There is no doubt that this is an important consideration, but the basis of helping people should be their fundamental human right to health. The interventions should be looking at how to sustain people's long-term health needs and livelihoods rather than how to maintain global-market-oriented developmental gains (which may or may not produce equal access to health and long-term benefits for everyone in the given society).

6 Here another useful way of seeing this is to look at Michel Foucault's concept of subjugated knowledge. He argues that there are 'whole series of knowledges that have been disqualified as nonconceptual knowledges, as insufficiently elaborated knowledges: naïve knowledges, hierarchically inferior knowledges, knowledges that are below the required level of erudition or scientificity', and he adds that 'it is the reappearance of what people know at a local level, of these disqualified knowledges, that made the critique possible' (2003: 7–8).

Bibliography

Acharya, A. (2004) 'How ideas spread: whose norms matter? Norm localization and institutional change in Asian regionalism', *International Organization*, 58 (Spring).

Adih, W.K. and Alexander, C.S. (1999) 'Determinants of condom use to prevent HIV infection among youth in Ghana', *Journal of Adolescent Health*, 24: 63–72.

Agnew, C.R. (2000) 'Behavioural and normative beliefs about condom use: comparing measurement alternatives within the theory of reasoned action', in P. Norman, C. Abraham and M. Conner (eds), *Understanding and Changing Health Behaviour*, pp. 115–36, Amsterdam: Harwood Academic Publishers.

Akínrínádé, S. (2004) 'On the evolution of civil society in Nigeria', in M. Glasius, D. Lewis and H. Seckinelgin (eds), *Exploring Civil Society: Political and Cultural Contexts*, London: Routledge.

Alden, D. and Miller, J.C. (2000) 'Out of Africa: the slave trade and the transmission of smallpox to Brazil, 1560–1831', in R.I. Rotberg (ed.), *Health and Disease in Human History*, Cambridge, MA: MIT Press.

Allen, T. (2006) 'AIDS and evidence: interrogating some Ugandan myths', *Journal of Biosocial Science*, 38: 7–28.

Altman, D. (2002) 'Sexual politics and international relations', in L. Odysseos and H. Seckinelgin (eds), *Gendering the International*, New York: Palgrave.

Anang, F.T. (1994) 'Evaluating the role and impact of foreign NGOs in Ghana', in E. Sandberg (ed.), *The Changing Politics of Non-Governmental Organizations and African States*, Westport, CT: Praeger.

Anscombe , G.E.M. (1957) *Intention*, Oxford: Blackwell.

Armstrong, D. (1993) 'Public health spaces and the fabrication of identity', *Sociology*, 27: 393–410.

Arno, S. and Feiden, K.L. (1992) *Against the Odds: The Story of AIDS Drug Development, Politics and Profits*, New York: HarperCollins.

Arnold, D. (1996) 'Introduction: tropical medicine before Manson', in D. Arnold (ed.), *Warm Climates and Western Medicine*, Atlanta, GA: Rodopi.

Attaran, A., Freeberg, K.A. and Hirsch, M. (2001) 'Dead wrong on AIDS', *Washington Post*, 15 June.

Attawell, K. and Mundy, J. (2003) *Provision of Antiretroviral Therapy in Resource-Limited Settings: A Review of Experience up to August 2003*, London: DfID Health Systems Resource Centre.

Baldwin, P. (2005) *Disease and Democracy: The Industrialized World Faces AIDS*, Berkeley, CA: University of California Press.

Balotta, C., Berlusconi, A., Pan, A., Violin, M., Riva, C., Colombo, M.C., Gori, A., Papagno, L., Corvasce, S., Mazzucchelli, R., Facchi, G., Velleca, R., Saporetti, G., Galli, M., Rusconi, S. and Moroni, M. (2000) 'Prevalence of transmitted nucleoside analogue-resistant HIV-1 strains and pre-existing mutations in polreverse transcriptease and protease region: outcome after treatment in recently infected individuals', *Antiretroviral Therapy*, 5: 7–14.

Barnett, M.N. and Finnemore, M. (1999) 'The politics, power and pathologies of international organizations, *International Organization*, 53: 4.

Barnett, T. and Whiteside, A. (2002) *AIDS in the Twenty-first Century*, London: Palgrave.

Barnett, T. and Whiteside, A. (2006) *AIDS in the 21st Century: Disease and Globalisation*, 2nd edn, London: Palgrave Macmillan.

Barsky, A.J. (1988) 'The paradox of health', *New England Journal of Health*, 318.

Bastos, C. (1999) *Global Responses to AIDS: Science in Emergency*, Bloomington, IN: Indiana University Press.

Bawani, M. (2003) All Africa News Agency, 23/24 June, www.wfn.org/2003/07/msg00017.html-27k.

Baylies, C., Chgabala, T. and Mkandawire, F. (2000) 'AIDS in Kanyama: contested sexual practice and the gendered dynamics of community interventions', in C. Baylies and J. Bujra (eds), *AIDS, Sexuality and Gender in Africa*, pp. 96–113, London: Routledge.

Becker, M.H. (1993) 'A medical sociologist looks at health promotion', *Journal of Health and Social Behaviour*, 34(1): 1–6.

Bilton, T., Bonnett, K., Jones, P., Lawson, T., Skinner, D., Stanworth, M. and Webster, A. (1996) *Introductory Sociology*, 3rd edn, London: Macmillan.

Boli, J. and Thomas, G.M. (eds) (1999) *Constructing World Culture: International Nongovernmental Organizations since 1875*, Stanford, CA: Stanford University Press.

Boomgaard, P. (1996) 'Dutch medicine in Asia, 1600–1900', in D. Arnold (ed.), *Warm Climates and Western Medicine*, Atlanta, GA: Rodopi.

Booth, K.M. (2004) *Local Women, Global Science: Fighting AIDS in Kenya*, Bloomington, IN: Indiana University Press.

Boseley, S. (2004) 'Antibiotic hope for children with AIDS', *Guardian*, 19 November.

Boyer, P. (1990) *Tradition as Truth and Communication*, Cambridge: Cambridge University Press.

Bozzette, S.A., Ake, C.F., Tam, H.K., Chang, S.W. and Louis, T.A. (2006) 'Cardiovascular and cerebrovascular events in patients treated for human immunodeficiency virus infection', *New England Journal of Medicine*, 348(8): 702–10.

Bracher, M., Santow, G. and Watkins, S.C. (2004) 'Assessing the potential of condom use to prevent the spread of HIV: a microsimulation study', *Studies in Family Planning*, 35(1): 48–64.

Bradshaw, S. and Linneker, B. (2003) 'Civil society response to poverty reduction strategies in Nicaragua', *Progress in Development Studies*, 3(2).

Brandom, R.B. (1994) *Making It Explicit: Reasoning, Representing and Discursive Commitment*, Cambridge, MA: Harvard University Press.

Brett, T. (2000) 'Understanding organisations and institutions', in D. Robinson, T. Hewitt and J. Harriss (eds), *Managing Development: Understanding Interorganizational Relationships*, London: Sage.

Brundtland, G.H. (2001) Fourth Meeting of the Global Roll Back Malaria Partner-ship, http://www.who.int/directorgeneral/spe. . .h/20010418_RBMeetingwashington .en.html.

Butchart, A. (1998) *The Anatomy of Power: European Constructions of the African Body*, London: Zed Books.

Campbell, C. (2003) *'Letting Them Die': Why HIV/AIDS Prevention Programmes Fail*, London: James Currey.

Caron, M., Auclair, M., Vigouroux, C., Glorian, M., Forest, C. and Capeau, J. (2001) 'The HIV protease inhibitor indinavir impairs sterol regulatory element-binding protein-1 intranuclear localization, inhibits preadipocyte differentiation, and induces insulin resistance', *Diabetes*, 50: 1378–88.

Carr, A. (2002) 'Improvement of analysis and reporting of adverse events associated with antiretroviral therapy', *Lancet*, 360: 81–5.

Cartwright, N. (2007) *Hunting Causes and Using Them: Approaches in Philosophy and Economics*, Cambridge: Cambridge University Press.

Chabbott, C. (1999) 'Development INGOs', in J. Boli and G.M. Thomas, *Construct-ing World Culture: International Nongovernmental Organisations since 1875*, Stanford, CA: Stanford University Press.

Chambers, R. (1993) *Challenging the Profession: Frontiers for Rural Development*, London: Intermediate Technology Publications.

Chandhoke, N. (2002) 'The limits of global civil society', in M. Glasius, M. Kaldor and H. Anheier (eds), *Global Civil Society Yearbook 2002*, Oxford: Oxford University Press.

Chatterjee, P. (2006) *The Politics of the Governed: Reflections on Popular Politics in Most of the World*, New Delhi: Permanent Black.

Cheru, F. (2002) 'Debt, adjustment and the politics of effective response to HIV/ AIDS in Africa', *Third World Quarterly*, 23(2): 299–312.

Chimwaza, A.F. and Watkins, S.C. (2004) 'Giving care to people with symptoms of AIDS in rural Sub-Saharan Africa', *AIDS Care*, 16(7): 795–807.

Chintu, C., Bhat, G.J., Walker, A.S., Mulenga, V., Sinyinza, F., Lsihimpi, K., Farrelly, I., Kaganson, N., Zumla, A., Gillespie, S.H., Nunn, A.J. and Gibb, D.M., on behalf of the CHAP trail team (2004) 'Co-trimoxazole as prophylaxis against opportunistic infections in HIV-infected Zambian children (CHAP): a double-blind randomised placebo-controlled trial', *Lancet*, 364: 1865–71.

Chodoff, P. (2002) 'The medicalization of the human condition', *Psychiatric Service*, 53: 627–8, http://ps.psychiatryonline.org/cgi/content/full/53/5/627.

Clark, J. (1991) *Democratizing Development: The Role of Voluntary Organisations*, London: Earthscan.

Clavel, F. and Hance, A.J. (2004) 'HIV drug resistance', *New England Journal of Medicine*, 350(10): 1023–35.

Cohen, J.L. and Arato, A. (1994) *Civil Society and Political Theory*, Cambridge, MA: MIT Press.

Colas, D. (1997) *Civil Society and Fanaticism: Conjoined Histories*, Stanford, CA: Stanford University Press.

Coleman, W.D. (2001) 'Policy networks, non-state actors and internationalized policy-making: a case study of agricultural trade', in D. Josselin and W. Wallace (eds), *Non-State Actors in World Politics*, London: Palgrave.

Comaroff, J.L. and Comaroff, J. (1999) *Civil Society and the Political Imagination in Africa*, Chicago, IL: University of Chicago Press.

Conrad, P. (1975) 'The discovery of hyperkinesis: notes on the medicalization of deviant behaviour', *Social Problem*, 23: 12–21.

Conrad, P. (1992) 'Medicalization and social control', *Annual Review of Sociology*, 18: 209–32.

Cooper, D. (1998) *Governing out of Order: Space, Law and the Politics of Belonging*, London: Rivers Oram Press.

Correia-Afonso, J. (1990) *Intrepid Itinerant: Manuel Godinho and His Journey from India to Portugal in 1663*, Bombay: Oxford University Press.

Craig, D. and Porter, D. (2003) 'Poverty Reduction Strategy Papers: a new convergence', *World Development*, 31(1).

Crawford, G. (2003) 'Partnership or power? Deconstructing the "Partnership for Governance Reform" in Indonesia', *Third World Quarterly*, 24(1).

Crawford, R. (2000) 'The ritual of health promotion', in S.J. Williams, J. Gabe and M. Calnan (eds), *Health, Medicine and Society: Key Theories, Future Agendas*, London: Routledge.

Crush, J. (ed.) (1995) *Power of Development*, London: Routledge.

Curtin, D. (1996) 'Disease and imperialism', in D. Arnold (ed.), *Warm Climates and Western Medicine*, Atlanta, GA: Rodopi.

Curtin, P.D. (1965) *The Image of Africa: British Ideas and Action 1780–1850*, London: Macmillan.

Curtin, P.D. (1992) 'Medical knowledge and urban planning in colonial tropical Africa', in S. Feierman and J.M. Janzen (eds), *The Social Basis of Health and Healing in Africa*, Berkeley, CA: University of California Press.

D'Adesky, A.-C. (2004) *Moving Mountains: The Race to Treat Global AIDS*, London: Verso.

D'Aquila, R.T., Johnson, V.A., Welles, S.L., Japour, A.J., Kuritzkes, D.R., DeGruttola, V., Reichelderfer, P.S., Coombs, R.W., Crumpacker, C.S., Kahn, J.O. and Richman, D.D. (1995) 'Zidovudine resistance and HIV-1 disease progression during antiretroviral therapy', *Annals of Internal Medicine*, 122(6): 401–8.

Davidson, D. (1980a) 'Freedom to act', in D. Davidson, *Essays on Actions and Events*, Oxford: Oxford University Press.

Davidson, D. (1980b) 'Psychology as philosophy: comments and replies', in D. Davidson, *Essays on Actions and Events*, Oxford: Oxford University Press.

Davidson, D. (2001) *Essays on Actions and Events*, Oxford: Oxford University Press.

Deeks, S.G., Wrin, T., Liegler, T., Hoh, R., Hayden, M., Barbour, J., Hellman, N.S., Petropoulos, C.J., McCune, J.M., Hellerstein, M.K. and Grant, R.M. (2001) 'Virologic and immunologic consequences of discontinuing combination antiretroviral-drug therapy in HIV-infected patients with detectable viremia', *New England Journal of Medicine*, 344(7): 472–80.

Desmond, N., Allen, C.F., Clift, S., Justine, B., Mzugu, J., Plummer, M.L., Watson-Jones, D. and Ross, D.A. (2005) 'A typology of groups at risk of HIV/STI in a gold mining town in north-western Tanzania', *Social Science and Medicine*, 60: 1739–49.

DfID (UK Department for International Development) (2002) *How to . . . Work with Civil Society to Support Country Strategy Objectives*, London: DfID.

DfID (2003) *Departmental Report 2003*, London: DfID.

DfID (2005) *About DfID: History*, http://www.dfid.gov.uk/aboutdfid/history.asp.

DiMaggio, P.J. and Powell, W.W. (1983) 'The iron cage revisited: institutional isomorphism and collective rationality in organizational fields', *American Sociological Review*, 48 (April).

DiMaggio, P.J. and Powell, W.W. (1991) 'The iron cage revisited: institutional isomorphism and collective rationality', in W.W. Powell and P.J. DiMaggio (eds), *The New Institutionalism in Organizational Analysis*, Chicago, IL: University of Chicago Press.

Domek, G.J. (2006) 'Social consequences of antiretroviral therapy: preparing for the unexpected futures of HIV-positive children', *Lancet*, 367: 1367–9.

Dorward, D.C. (1974) 'Ethnography and administration: a study of Anglo-Tiv "working misunderstanding"', *Journal of African History*, 15(3): 457–77.

Douglas, M. (1986) *How Institutions Think*, Syracuse, NY: Syracuse University Press.

Douglas, M. (1992) 'Rightness of categories', in M. Douglas and D. Hull, *How Classification Works: Nelson Goodman among the Social Sciences*, Edinburgh: Edinburgh University Press.

Easterly, W. (2002) *The Elusive Quest for Growth: Economist's Adventures and Misadventures in the Tropics*, Cambridge, MA: MIT Press.

Edwards, M. and Hulme, D. (eds) (1992) *Making a Difference: NGOs and Development in a Changing World*, London, Earthscan.

Edwards, M. and Hulme, D. (eds) (1996) *Beyond the Magic Bullet: NGO Performance and Accountability in the Post-Cold War World*, Bloomfield, CT, Kumarian Press.

Epstein, S. (1996) *Impure Science: Aids, Activism, and the Politics of Knowledge*, Berkeley, CA: University of California.

Escobar, A. (1995) *Encountering Development: The Making of the Third World*, Princeton, NJ: Princeton University Press.

ETG (Voluntary HIV-1 Counselling and Testing Efficacy Testing Groups) (2000) 'Efficacy of voluntary HIV-1 counselling and testing in individuals and couples in Kenya, Tanzania and Trinidad: a random trial', *Lancet*, 8 July, 356: 103–12.

Farley, J. (1991) *Bilharzia: A History of Imperial Tropical Medicine*, Cambridge: Cambridge University Press.

Farmer, P. (1993) *AIDS and Accusation: Haiti and the Geography of Blame*, Berkeley, CA: University of California Press.

Farmer, P. (1999) *Infections and Inequalities: The Modern Plagues*, Berkeley, CA: University of California Press.

Farmer, P. (2003) *Pathologies of Power: Health, Human Rights and the New War on the Poor*, Berkeley, CA: University of California Press.

Farmer, P., Léandre, Fernet, Mukherjee, Joia S., Claude, Marie Sidonise, Nevil, Patrice, Smith-Fawzi, Mary C., Koenig, Serena P., Castro, Arachu, Becerra, Mercedes C., Sachs, Jeffrey, Attaran, Amir and Kim, Jim Yong (2001) 'Community-based approaches to HIV treatment in resource-poor settings', *Lancet*, 358.

Farrington, J. and Bebbington, A., with Wellard, K. and Lewis, D. (1993) *NGOs and the State in Asia: Rethinking Roles in Sustainable Agricultural Development*, London: Routledge.

Ferguson, J. (1990) *The Anti-Politics Machine: Development, Depoliticization and Bureaucratic Power in Lesotho*, Cambridge: Cambridge University Press.

Ferguson, J. (1994) *The Anti-Politics Machine*, Minneapolis, MN: University of Minnesota.

Ferguson, J. (1999) *Expectations of Modernity: Myths and Meanings of Urban Life on the Zambian Copperbelt*, Berkeley, CA: University of California Press.

Ferradini, L., Jeannin, A., Pinoges, L., Izopet, J., Odhiambo, D., Mankhambo, L., Karungi, G., Szumilin, E., Balandine, S., Fedida, G., Carrieri, M.P., Spire, B., Ford, N., Tassie, J., Guerin, P.J. and Brasher, C. (2006) 'Scaling up of highly active antiretroviral therapy in rural district of Malawi: an effectiveness assessment', *Lancet*, 367: 1335–69.

Fierke, K.M. (1998) *Changing Games, Changing Strategies: Critical Investigations in Security*, Manchester: Manchester University Press.

Finnemore, M. (1996) 'Norms, culture and world politics: insights from sociology's institutionalism', *International Organization*, 50(2).

Finnemore, M. and Sikkink, K. (1998) 'International norm dynamics and political change', *International Organization*, 52(4).

Florini, A.M. (ed.) (2000) *The Third Force: The Rise of Transnational Civil Society*, Washington, DC: Carnegie Endowment for International Peace.

Flyvbjerg, B. (2001) *Making Social Science Matter: Why Social Inquiry Fails and How It Can Succeed Again*, Cambridge: Cambridge University Press.

Ford, N. (1994) 'Cultural and developmental factors underlying the global pattern of the transmission of HIV/AIDS', in D.R. Phillips and Y. Verhasselt (eds), *Health and Development*, London: Routledge.

Foster, S. and Lucas, S. (1991) *Socioeconomic aspects of HIV and AIDS in Developing Countries* (Department of Public Health and Public Policy), London: London School of Hygiene and Tropical Medicine.

Foucault, M. (1977) *Discipline and Punish: The Birth of the Prison*, New York: Vintage Books.

Foucault, M. (1978) *The History of Sexuality*, vol. 1: *An Introduction*, London: Random House.

Foucault, M. (1990) *The History of Sexuality*, vol. 1: *An Introduction*, London: Penguin.

Foucault, M. (2000) 'Governmentality', in M. Foucault, *Power: Essential Works*, 3, ed. J.D. Faubion. New York: New Press.

Foucault, M. (2003) *Society Must Be Defended*, trans. D. Macey, London: Penguin, Allen Lane.

Fowler, A. (1988) *Non-Governmental Organisations in Africa: Achieving Comparative Advantage in Relief and Micro-Development*, Discussion Paper 249, Brighton: Institute of Development Studies, Sussex University.

Fowler, A. (1997) *Striking a Balance: A Guide to Enhancing the Effectiveness of Non-Governmental Organisations in International Development*, London: Earthscan.

Fredberg, K.A., Losina, E., Weinstein, M.C., Paltiel, A.D., Cohen, C.J., Seage, G., Craven, D.E., Zhang, H., Kimmel, A.D. and Goldie, S.J. (2001) 'The cost effectiveness of combination antiretroviral therapy for HIV disease', *New England Journal of Medicine*, 344(11): 824–31.

Frenkel, L.M. and Mullins, J.I. (2001) 'Should patients with drug-resistant HIV-1 continue to receive antiretroviral therapy?', *New England Journal of Medicine*, 344(7): 520–1.

Friedland, R. and Alford, R.R. (1991) 'Bringing society back in: symbols, practices, and institutions contradictions', in W.W. Powell and P.J. DiMaggio (eds), *The New Institutionalism in Organizational Analysis*, Chicago, IL: University of Chicago Press.

Gallant, J.E., DeJesus, E., Arribas, J.R., Pozniak, A.L., Gazzard, B., Campo, R.E., Lu, B., McColl, D., Chuck, S., Enejosa, J., Toole, J.J. and Cheng, A.K. for the Study 934 Group (2006) 'Tenofovir DF, emtricitabine, and efavirenz vs. zidovudine, lamivudine, and efavirenz for HIV', *New England Journal of Medicine*, 354(3): 251–60.

Geertz, C. (1983) *Local Knowledge: Further Essays in Interpretive Anthropology*, New York: Basic Books.

GHPWG (Global HIV Prevention Working Group) (2003) *Access to HIV Prevention: Closing the Gap*, www.gatesfoundation.org or www.kaisernetwork.org.

Giddens, A. (1984) *The Constitution of Society*, Cambridge: Polity Press.

Glasius, M. (2002) 'Expertise in the court of justice: global civil society influence on the statute for an international criminal court', in M. Glasius, M. Kaldor and H. Anheier (eds), *Global Civil Society Yearbook 2002*, Oxford: Oxford University Press.

Global Fund (2006) Current funding rounds, http://www.theglobalfund.org/en/apply/current/.

Gochman, D.S. (ed.) (1988) *Health Behaviour: Emerging Research Perspectives*, New York: Plenum Press.

Gomez-Pablos, A. (2001) 'South Africa in AIDS drug fight', 9 March, http://www.cnn.com/2001/WORLD/europe/03/09/inside.europe/.

Goodman, N. (1978) *Ways of Worldmaking*, Indianapolis, IN: Hackett Publishers.

Gordenker, L. and Weiss, T.G. (1996) 'Pluralizing global governance: analytical approaches and dimensions', in L. Gordenker and T.G. Weiss (eds), *NGOs, the UN and Global Governance*, Boulder, CO: Lynne Rienner.

Gordenker, L., Coate, R.A., Jonsson, C. and Soderholm, P. (1995) *International Cooperation in Response to AIDS*, London: Pinter.

Graff, M. de (1987) 'Context, constraint or control? Zimbabwean NGOs and their environment', *Development Policy Review*, 5.

Grant, R.M., Hecht, F.M., Warmerdam, M., Liu, L., Liegler, T., Petropoulos, C.J., Hellmann, N.S., Chesney, M., Busch, M.P. and Kahn, J.O. (2002) 'Time trends in primary HIV-1 drug resistance among recently infected persons', *Journal of the American Medical Association (JAMA)*, 288: 181–8.

Gray, A., Karim, S.S.A. and Gengiah, T.N. (2006) 'Ritonavir/saquinavir safety concerns curtail antiretroviral therapy options for tuberculosis–HIV co-infected patients in resource constrained settings', *AIDS*, 20(2): 302–3.

Grinspoon, S. and Carr, A. (2005) 'Cardiovascular risk and body-fat abnormalities in HIV-infected adults', *New England Journal of Medicine*, 352(1): 48–62.

Gulick, R.M., Mellors, J.W., Havlir, D., Eron, J.J., Gonzalez, C., McMahon, D., Richman, D.D., Valentine, F.T., Jonas, L., Meibohm, A., Emini, E.A., Chodakewitz, J.A., Deutsch, P., Holder, D., Schleif, W.A. and Condra, J.H. (1997) 'Treatment with indinavir, zidovudine, and lamiduvine in adults with human immunodeficiency virus infection and prior antiretroviral therapy', *New England Journal of Medicine*, 337: 734–9.

Gupta, S., McPherson, S., Sellers, T., Chamreun, C.S., Choudhary, B.N. and Levene, J. (2006) 'Assessing and evaluating community organizations' capacity for working in HIV/AIDS: responses in India, Ecuador and Cambodia', *Journal of International Development*, 18: 595–8.

Guzzini, S. (2005) The concept of power: a constructivist analysis, *Millennium*, 33(3): 495–523.

Haas, E. (1990) *When Knowledge Is Power*, Berkeley, CA: University of California Press.

Hacking, I. (1992) 'World-making by kind-making: child abuse for example', in M. Douglas and S. Hall, *How Classification Works: Nelson Goodman among the Social Sciences*, Edinburgh: Edinburgh University Press.

Hacking, I. (1995) 'The looping effects of human kinds', in D. Sperber, D. Premack and A. Premack (eds), *In Causal Cognition: An Interdisciplinary Approach*, Oxford: Oxford University Press.

Hacking, I. (1998) *Mad Travellers: Reflections on the Reality of Transient Mental Illnesses*, Charlottesville, VA: University Press of Virginia.

Hacking, I. (1999) *The Social Construction of What?*, London: Harvard University Press.

Hacking, I. (2003) *Historical Ontology*, Boston, MA: Harvard University Press.

Hacking, I. (2005) 'Dialogue with Ian Hacking: Forum for European Philosophy', LSE (February).

Hammer, S.M. (2005) 'Management of newly diagnosed HIV infection', *New England Journal of Medicine*, 353(16), 1702–9.

Hammer, S.M., Squires, K.E., Hughes, M.D., Grimes, J.M., Demeter, L.M., Currier, J.S., Eron, J.J., Feinberg, J.E., Balfour, H.H., Deyton, L.R., Chodakewitz, J.A., Fischl, M.A., Phair, J.P., Pedneault, L., Nguyen, B.-Y. and Cook, J.C. (AIDS Clinical Trials Group 320 Study Team) (1997) 'A controlled trial of two nucleoside analogues plus indinavir in persons with human immunodeficiency virus infection and CD4 cell counts of 200 per cubic millimetre or less', *New England Journal of Medicine*, 337: 725–33.

Hampshire, S. (1960) *Thought and Action*, Oxford: Chatto & Windus.

Hampshire, S. (1989) *Innocence and Experience*, London: Penguin.

Hampshire, S. (2005) *Spinoza and Spinozism*, Oxford: Oxford University Press.

Hare, R.M. (1963) *Freedom and Reason*, Oxford: Oxford University Press.

Harper, M. (1989) 'AIDS in Africa: plague or propaganda?', *West Africa* (7–13 November): 2072–3.

Harriss, J. (2001) *Depoliticizing Development: The World Bank and Social Capital*, London: Anthem Press.

Hartwig, K.A., Eng, E., Daniel, M., Ricketts, T. and Quinn, S.C. (2005) 'AIDS and "shared sovereignty" in Tanzania from 1987 to 2000: a case study', *Social Sciences and Medicine*, 60: 1613–24.

Hasenclever, A., Mayer, P. and Rittberger, V. (1997) *Theories of International Regimes*, Cambridge: Cambridge University Press.

Havlir, D.V. and Hammer, S.M. (2005) 'Patents versus patients? Antiretroviral therapy in India', *New England Journal of Medicine*, 353(8): 749–51.

Haynes, D.M. (1996) 'Social status and imperial service: tropical medicine and the British medical profession in the nineteenth century', in D. Arnold (ed.), *Warm Climates and Western Medicine*, Atlanta, GA: Rodopi.

Heald, S. (2006) 'Abstain or die: the development of HIV/AIDS policy in Botswana', *Journal of Biosocial Science*, 38: 29–41.

Heap, S. (2000) *NGOs Engaging with Business: A World of Difference and a Difference to the World*, Oxford: INTRAC.

Hearn, J. (2000) 'Aiding democracy? Donors and civil society in South Africa', *Third World Quarterly*, 21(5): 815–30.

Heidegger, M. (1977) *The Question concerning Technology and Other Essays*, New York: Harper Torchbooks.

Heidegger, M. (1998) 'On the essence of ground', in M. Heidegger, *Pathmarks*, ed. W. MacNeill, Cambridge: Cambridge University Press.

Helman, C. (1994) *Culture, Health and Illness: Introduction for Health Professionals*, 3rd edn, Oxford: Butterworth-Heinemann.

Hemmings, C.P. (2005) 'Rethinking medical anthropology: how anthropology is failing medicine', *Anthropology and Medicine*, 12(2): 91–103.

Herring, S.J. and Krieger, A.C. (2006) 'Acute respiratory manifestations of the abacavir hypersensitivity reaction', *AIDS*, 20(2): 301–2.

Heywood, M. (2002) 'Treatment Action Campaign', in M. Glasius, M. Kaldor and H. Anheier (eds), *Global Civil Society Yearbook 2002*, pp. 128–9, Oxford: Oxford University Press.

Hilhorst, D. (2003) *The Real World of NGOs: Discourses, Diversity and Development*, London: Zed Books.

Hirsch, M.S. (2002) 'HIV drug resistance: a chink in the armor', *New England Journal of Medicine*, 347(6): 438–9.

Hobart, M. (1993) 'Introduction: the growth of ignorance?', in M. Hobart (ed.), *An Anthropological Critique of Development: The Growth of Ignorance*, London: Routledge.

Hobsbawm, E.J. (1987) *The Age of Empire*, New York: Penguin.

Holzscheiter, A. (2005) 'Discourse as capability: non-state actors' capital in global governance', *Millennium: Journal of International Studies*, 33(3): 723–46.

Hooper, E. (1999) *The River: A Journey to the Source of HIV and AIDS*, New York: Little, Brown.

Horton, R. (2003) *Second Opinion: Doctors and Diseases – Wretched Arguments at the Sickbed*, London: Granta Books.

Hulme, D. and Edwards, M. (eds) (1997) *NGOs, States and Donors: Too Close for Comfort?*, London: Macmillan.

Hunt, N.R. (1999) *A Colonial Lexicon of Birth Ritual, Medicalization and Mobility in the Congo*, Berkeley, CA: University of California Press.

Hunter, S. (2003) *Who Cares: AIDS in Africa*, New York: Palgrave.

Hurrell, A. and Woods, N. (1995) 'Globalisation and inequality', *Millennium*, 24(3).

IFMSA (International Federation of Medical Students Associations) (2001) WHO Civil Society Initiative, http://www.tripodent.nl/Jtroon/Aug01column3.htm.

Illich, I. (1977) *Limits of Medicine: Medical Nemesis – the Expropriation of Health*, Harmondsworth: Penguin.

Ivarature, H. (2000) 'The institutionalization and "medicalization" of family planning in Tonga', *Asia-Pacific Population Journal*, 15(2), 35–52.

James, D. (2002) 'To take the information down to the people: life skills and HIV/AIDS peer-educators in the Durban area', *African Studies*, 61(1): 169–91.

Janzen, J.M. (1978) *The Quest for Therapy in Lower Zaire*, Berkeley, CA: University of California Press.

Jepperson, R.L. (1991) 'Institutions, institutional effects and institutionalism', in W.W. Powell and P.J. DiMaggio (eds), *The New Institutionalism in Organizational Analysis*, Chicago, IL: University of Chicago Press.

Josselin, D. and Wallace, W. (2001) 'Non-state actors in world politics: the lessons', in D. Josselin and W. Wallace, *Non-State Actors in World Politics*, London: Palgrave.

Kaler, A. (2003) '"My girlfriends could fill a yanu-yanu bus": rural Malawian men's claims about their own serostatus', *Demographic Research*, Special Collections 1, www.demograhic-research.org, pp. 350–70.

Kapoor, I. (2005) 'Participatory development, complicity and desire', *Third World Quarterly*, 26(8): 1203–20.

Karnik, N.S. (2001) 'Locating HIV/AIDS and India: cautionary notes on the globalization of categories', *Science, Technology and Human Values*, 26(3): 322–48.

Keane, J. (1988) *Democracy and Civil Society: On the Predicaments of European Socialism, the Prospects for Democracy and the Problem of Controlling Social and Political Power*, London: Verso.

Keck, M.E. and Sikkink, K. (1998) *Activists beyond Borders: Advocacy Networks in International Politics*, Ithaca, NY: Cornell University Press.

Keohane, R.O. (1984) *After Hegemony*, Princeton, NJ: Princeton University Press.

Korten, D. (1990) *Getting to the 21st Century: Voluntary Action and the Global Agenda*, Hartford, CT: Kumarian Press.

Krahmann, E. (2003) 'National, regional, and global governance: one phenomenon or many?', *Global Governance*, 9.

Kramer, L. (1987) 'Taking responsibility for our lives: does the gay community have a death wish?', *New York Native* (29 June): 37–40, 66–7.

Krasner, S.D. (1983) *International Regimes*, Ithaca, NY: Cornell University Press.

Kratochwil, F.V. (1989) *Rules, Norms and Decisions: On the Conditions of Practical and Legal Reasoning in International Relations and Domestic Affairs*, Cambridge: Cambridge University Press.

Kubalkova, V., Onuf, N. and Kowert, P. (eds) (1998) *International Relations in a Constructed World*, New York: M.E. Sharpe.

Lalezari, J.P., Henry, K., O'Hearn, M., Montaner, J.S.G., Piliero, P.J., Trottier, B., Walmsley, S., Cohen, C., Kuritzkes, D.R., Eron, Jr, J.J., Chung, J., DeMasi, R., Donatacci, L., Drobnes, C., Delehanty, J. and Salgo, M. for the TORO 1 Study Group (2003) 'Enfuvirtide, an HIV-1 fusion inhibitor, for drug-resistant HIV infection in North and South America', *New England Journal of Medicine*, 348(22): 2175–86.

Laxminarayan, R., Mills, A.J., Breman, J.G., Measham, A.R., Alleyne, G., Claeson, M., Jha, P., Musgrove, P., Chow, J., Shahid-Salles, S. and Jamison, D.T. (2006) 'Advancement of global health: key messages from the Disease Control Priorities Project', *Lancet*, 367: 1193–208.

Levine, P. (2003) *Prostitution, Race and Politics: Policing Venereal Disease in the British Empire*, London: Routledge.

Lewis, D. (2001) *The Management of Non-Governmental Development Organizations*, London: Routledge.

Liddell, C., Barrett, L. and Bydawell, M. (2005) 'Indigenous representations of illness and AIDS in Sub-Saharan Africa', *Social Science and Medicine*, 60: 691–700.

Little, S.J., Daar, E.S., D'Aquila, R.T., Keiser, P.H., Connick, E., Whitcomb, J.M., Hellman, N.S., Petropoulos, C.J., Sutton, L., Pitt, J.A., Rosenberg, E.S., Koup, R.A., Walker, B.D. and Richman, D.D. (1999) 'Reduced antiretroviral drug susceptibility among patients with primary HIV infection', *Journal of American Medical Association (JAMA)*, 282: 1142–9.

Little, S.J., Holte, S., Routy, J.P., Daar, E.S., Markowitz, M., Collier, A.C., Koup, R.A., Mellors, J.W., Connick, E., Conway, B., Kilby, M., Wang, L., Whitcomb, J.M., Hellman, N.S. and Richman, D.D. (2002) 'Antiretroviral-drug resistance among patients recently infected with HIV', *New England Journal of Medicine*, 347(6): 385–94.

Lock, M. and Scheper-Hughes, N. (1996) 'A critical-interpretive approach in medical anthropology: rituals and routines of discipline and dissent', in C.F. Sargent and T.M. Johnson (eds), *Handbook of Medical Anthropology: Contemporary Theory and Method*, Westport, CT: Praeger.

Long, N. (2001) *Development Sociology: Actor Perspectives*, London: Routledge.

Long, N. and Long, A. (1992) *Battlefields of Knowledge: The Interlocking of Theory and Practice in Social Research and Development*, London: Routledge.

Luginaah, I., Elkins, D., Maticka-Tyndale, E., Landry, T. and Mathui, M. (2005) 'Challenges of a pandemic: HIV/AIDS-related problems affecting Kenyan widows', *Social Science and Medicine*, 60: 1219–28.

McCaa, R. (2000) 'Spanish and Nahuatl views on smallpox and demographic catastrophe in Mexico', in R.I. Rotberg (ed.), *Health and Disease in Human History*, Cambridge, MA: MIT Press.

MacCormack, C.P. (1992) 'Health care and the concept of legitimacy in Sierra Leone', in S. Feierman and J.M. Janzen (eds), *The Social Basis of Health and Healing in Africa*, Berkeley, CA: University of California Press.

Mallon, P.W., Miller, J., Cooper, D.A. and Carr, A. (2003) 'Prospective evaluation of the effects of antiretroviral therapy on body composition in HIV-1-infected men starting therapy', *AIDS*, 17: 971–9.

Mann, J. (1999) 'The future of the global AIDS movement', *Harvard AIDS Review*, Spring, http://www.aids.harvard.edu/publications/har/spring_1999/spring99-7.html.

Mann, J.M., Francis, H., Quinn, T., Asila, P.K., Bosenge, N., Nzilambi, N., Bila, K., Tamfum, M., Ruti, K. and Piot, P. (1986) 'Surveillance for AIDS in a Central African city: Kinshasa, Zaire', *Journal of the American Medical Association*, 225 (20 July): 3255–9.

Marcus, G.E. and Fischer, M.J. (1999) *Anthropology as Cultural Critique: An Experimental Moment in the Human Sciences*, Chicago, IL: University of Chicago Press.

Martinez, E., Arnaiz, J.A., Podzamcer, D., Dalmau, D., Ribera, E., Domingo, P., Knobel, H., Riera, M., Pedrol, E., Force, L., Llibre, J.M., Segura, F., Richart, C., Cortes, C., Javaloyas, M., Aranda, M., Cruceta, A., de Lazzari, E. and Gatell, J.M. for the Nevirapine, Efavirenz and Abacovir (NEFA) Study Team (2006) 'Substitution of neirapine, efavirenz, or abacavir for protease inhibitors in patients with human immunodeficiency virus infection', *New England Journal of Medicine*, 349(11): 1036–46.

Maxwell, S. (2003) 'Heaven or hubris: reflections on the new "New Poverty Agenda"', *Development Policy Review*, 21(1).

Meech, R. (2006) *Antiretroviral Therapy for HIV and AIDS: The Aim of Antiretroviral Therapy*, Medic8® Family Health Guide, http://www.medic8.com/healthguide/articles/antiretroviraltx.htm (12 July 2006).

Mermin, J., Ekwaru, J.P., Liechty, C.A., Were, W., Downing, R., Ransom, R., Weidle, P., Lule, J., Coutinha, A. and Solberg, P. (2006) 'Effect of co-trimoxazole prophylaxis, antiretroviral therapy, and insecticide-treated bednets on the frequency of malaria in HIV-1-infected adults in Uganda: a prospective cohort study', *Lancet*, 367: 1256–61.

Meyer, J.W. (1988) 'Society without culture: a nineteenth-century legacy', in F. Ramirez (ed.), *Rethinking the Nineteenth Century*, New York: Greenwood Press.

Meyer, J.W. and Rowan, B. (1977) 'Institutionalized organizations: formal structure as myth and ceremony', *American Journal of Sociology*, 83: 340–63.

Meyer, J.W. and Rowan, B. (1991) 'Institutionalized organizations: formal structure as myth and ceremony', in W.W. Powell and P.J. DiMaggio (eds), *The New Institutionalism in Organizational Analysis*, Chicago, IL: University of Chicago Press.

Meyer, J.W. and Jepperson, R.L. (2000) 'The "actors" of modern society: the cultural construction of social agency', *Sociological Theory*, 18(1).

Michael, S. (2004) *Undermining Development: The Absence of Power among Local NGOs in Africa*, Oxford: James Currey.

Miller, C.M.N. (2003) 'Concern regarding the HIV/AIDS epidemic and individual childbearing evidence from rural Malawi', *Demographic Research*, Special Collections 1, www.demograhic-research.org, pp. 319–48.

Mitchell, Timothy (1991) *Colonising Egypt*, Berkeley, CA: University of California Press.

Mitchell, T. (1995) 'The object of development', in J. Crush (ed.), *Power of Development*, London: Routledge.

Moe, T. (1987) 'Interests, institutions, and positive theory: the politics of the NLRB', in *Studies in American Political Development*, 2, New Haven, CT: Yale University Press.

Morrison, D.M., Baker, S.A. and Gillmore, M.R. (2000) 'Using the theory of reasoned action to predict condom use among high-risk heterosexual teens', in P. Norman, C. Abraham and M. Conner (eds), *Understanding and Changing Health Behaviour*, pp. 27–50, Amsterdam: Harwood Academic Publishers.

Mudimbe, V.Y. (1988) *The Invention of Africa*, Bloomington, IN: Indiana University Press.

Mudimbe, V.Y. (1994) *The Idea of Africa*, Bloomington, IN: Indiana University Press.

Najam, A. (1996) 'Understanding the third sector: revisiting the prince, the merchant and the citizen', *Nonprofit Management and Leadership*, 7(2).

Najam, A. (1999) 'Citizen organisations as policy entrepreneurs', in D. Lewis (ed.), *International Perspectives on Voluntary Action: Reshaping the Third Sector*, London: Earthscan.

Nelson, P. (2000) 'Whose civil society? Whose governance? Decisonmaking and practice in the new agenda at the Inter-American Development Bank and the World Bank', *Global Governance*, 6: 405–31.

Ngubane, H. (1992) 'Clinical practice and organisation of indigenous healers in South Africa', in S. Feierman and J.M. Janzen (eds), *The Social Basis of Health and Healing in Africa*, Berkeley, CA: University of California Press.

Noehrenberg, E. (2004) 'Accelerating Access to AIDS Medicines Initiative: a public/private sector partnership to save lives', *Health and Social Issues*, www.sustdev.org/getfile.php?id=71.

Onuf, N.G. (1989) *World of Our Making: Rules and Rule in Social Theory and International Relations*, Columbia, SC: University of South Carolina Press.

Onuf, N. (1998) 'Constructivism: a user's manual', in V. Kubalkova, N. Onuf and P. Kowert (eds), *International Relations in a Constructed World*, New York: M.E. Sharpe.

Osborne, M.A. (1996) 'Resurrecting Hippocrates: hygienic sciences and the French scientific expeditions to Egypt, Morea and Algeria', in D. Arnold (ed.), *Warm Climates and Western Medicine*, Atlanta, GA: Rodopi.

Ostrom, E. (1986) 'An agenda for the study of institutions', *Public Choice*, 48: 3–25.

Ostrom, V. (1993) 'Opportunity, diversity, and complexity', in V. Ostrom, D. Feeny and H. Picht (eds), *Rethinking Institutional Analysis and Development: Issues, Alternatives, and Choices*, San Francisco, CA: ICS Press.

Ottaway, M. and Carothers, T. (eds) (2000) *Funding Virtue: Civil Society Aid and Democracy Promotion*, Washington, DC: Carnegie Endowment for International Peace.

Palella, F.J., Delaney, K.M., Moorman, A.C., Loveless, M.O., Fuhrer, J., Satten, G.A.,

Aschman, D.J. and Holmberg, S.D. for HIV Outpatient Study Investigators (1998) 'Declining morbidity and mortality among patients with advanced human immunodeficiency virus infection', *New England Journal of Medicine*, 338(13): 853–60.

Panos Institute (1988) *AIDS and the Third World*. London: Panos Institute.

Parker, R. (2001) 'Sexuality, culture and power in HIV/AIDS research', *Annual Review of Anthropology*, 30.

Patterson, T.J.S. (1974) 'The transmission of Indian surgical techniques to Europe at the end of the eighteenth century', *Proceedings of the XXIII International Congress of the History of Medicine*, 2 vols, London: Wellcome Institute.

Patton, C. (1996) *Fatal Advice: How Safe-Sex Education Went Wrong*, Durham, NC: Duke University Press.

Pearson, M.N. (1996) 'First contacts between Indian and European medical systems: Goa in the sixteenth century', in D. Arnold (ed.), *Warm Climates and Western Medicine*. Atlanta, GA: Rodopi.

Peltzer, K., Pengpid, S. and Mashego, T.B. (2006) *Youth Sexuality in the Context of HIV/AIDS in South Africa*, New York: Nova Science Publishers.

Perrow, C. and Guillen, M.F. (1990) *The AIDS Disaster: The Failure of Organizations in New York and the Nation*, New Haven, CT: Yale University Press.

Piot, P. (1996) 'AIDS experts caution about hope for cure', http://www.cnn.com/WORLD/9607/07/aids.conference/index.html.

Piscitelli, S.C. and Gallicano, K.D. (2001) 'Interactions among drugs for HIV and opportunistic infections', *New England Journal of Medicine*, 344(13): 984–96.

Poku, N.K. (2002) 'Poverty, debt and Africa's HIV/AIDS crisis', *International Affairs*, 78(3) (July): 531–46.

Pottier, J., Bicker, A. and Sillitoe, P. (eds) (2003) *Negotiating Local Knowledge: Power and Identity in Development*, London: Pluto Press.

Powell, W.W. (1991) 'Expanding the scope of institutional analysis', in W.W. Powell and P.J. DiMaggio (eds), *The New Institutionalism in Organizational Analysis*, Chicago, IL: University of Chicago Press.

Preda, A. (2005) *AIDS, Rhetoric and Medical Knowledge*, Cambridge, Cambridge University Press.

Price-Smith, A.T. (2002) *The Health of Nations: Infectious Disease, Environmental Change, and their Effects on National Security and Development*, Cambridge, MA: MIT Press.

Putnam, D.P. (1993) *Making Democracy Work: Civic Traditions in Modern Italy*, Princeton, NJ: Princeton University Press.

Putnam, R., Leonardi, R. and Nanetti, R.Y. (1992) *Making Democracy Work*, Princeton, NJ: Princeton University Press.

Quarles van Ufford, P. (1993) 'Knowledge and ignorance in the practices of development policy', in M. Hobart (ed.), *An Anthropological Critique of Development: The Growth of Ignorance*, London: Routledge.

Richards, P. (1993) 'Cultivation: knowledge or performance', in M. Hobart (ed.), *An Anthropological Critique of Development: The Growth of Ignorance*, London: Routledge.

Robinson, D., Hewitt, T. and Harriss, J. (eds) (2000) *Managing Development: Understanding Inter-organizational Relationships*, London: Sage.

Rose, N. (1996) 'Governing "advanced" liberal democracies', in A. Barry, T. Osborne and N. Rose (eds), *Foucault and Political Reason*, London: UCL.

Rosenberg, C.E. (1988) 'Disease and social order in America: perceptions and expectations', in E. Fee and D.M. Fox (eds), *AIDS: The Burdens of History*, Berkeley, CA: University of California Press.

Ruggie, J. (1998) 'What makes the world hang together', *International Organization*, 52(3).

Sahley, C. (1995) *Strengthening the Capacity of NGOs: Cases of Small Enterprise Development Agencies in Africa*, INTRAC Management and Policy Series No. 4, Oxford: International NGO Training and Research Centre.

Sahlins, M. (1976) *Culture and Practical Reason*, Chicago, IL: University of Chicago Press.

Said, E. (1978) *Orientalism: Western Concepts of the Orient*, New York: Routledge & Kegan Paul.

Salamon, L., Sokolowski, S.W. and Associates (1999) *Global Civil Society: Dimensions of the Nonprofit Sector*, vol. I, Boulder, CO: Kumarian Press.

Sandberg, E. (1994) 'The changing politics of non-governmental organizations and African states', in E. Sandberg (ed.), *The Changing Politics of Non-Governmental Organizations and African States*, Westport, CT: Praeger.

Schoepf, B.G. (2001) 'International AIDS research in anthropology: taking a critical perspective on the crisis', *Annual Review of Anthropology*, 30.

Scott, W.R. (1991) 'Unpacking institutional arguments', in W.W. Powell and P.J. DiMaggio (eds), *The New Institutionalism in Organizational Analysis*, Chicago, IL: University of Chicago Press.

Seckinelgin, H. (2002) 'Time to stop and think: HIV/AIDS, global civil society and people's politics', in M. Glasius, M. Kaldor and H. Anheier (eds), *Global Civil Society Yearbook 2002*, Oxford: Oxford University Press.

Sepkowitz, K.A. (2006) 'One disease, two epidemics: AIDS at 25', *New England Journal of Medicine*, 354(23): 2411–14.

Setel, P.W. (1999) *A Plague of Paradoxes: AIDS, Culture and Demography in Northern Tanzania*, Chicago, IL: University of Chicago Press.

Shadlen, K. (2007, forthcoming) 'The political economy of AIDS treatment: intellectual property and the transformation of generic supply', *International Studies Quarterly*, 51(4), December.

Shand, A. (2005) 'Rejoinder: in defence of medical anthropology', *Anthropology and Medicine*, 12(2): 105–13.

Shelton, J.D., Halperin, D.T. and Wilson, D. (2006) 'Has global HIV incidence peaked?', *Lancet*, 367: 1120–2.

Shepsle, K.A. (1986) 'Institutional equilibrium and equilibrium institutions', in H. Weisburg (ed.), *Political Science: The Science of Politics*, New York: Agathon.

Shilts, R. (1987) *And the Band Played On: People, Politics, and the AIDS Epidemic*, New York: St Martin's Press.

Sikwibele, A., Shonga, C. and Baylies, C. (2000) 'AIDS in Kapulanga, Mongu: poverty, neglect and gendered patterns of blame', in C. Baylies and J. Bujra (eds), *AIDS, Sexuality and Gender in Africa*, pp. 59–75, London: Routledge.

Skinner, J. (2003) 'Anti-social "social development"? Governmentality, indigenousness and the DFID approach on Montserrat', in J. Pottier, A. Bicker and P. Sillitoe (eds), *Negotiating Local Knowledge*, London: Pluto Press.

Sklar, P. and Masur, H. (2003) 'HIV infection and cardiovascular disease: is there really a link?', *New England Journal of Medicine*, 349(21): 2065–7.

Skolnik, P.R. (2003) 'HIV therapy: what do we know, and when do we know it?', *New England Journal of Medicine*, 349(24): 2351–2.

Slack, C., Stobie, M., Milford, C., Lindegger, G., Wasswnaar, D., Strode, A. and IJsselmuiden, C. (2005) 'Provision of HIV treatment in HIV preventive vaccine trials: a developing country perspective', *Social Science and Medicine*, 60: 1197–208.

Smillie, I. (1995) 'Naming the rose: what is an NGO?', in I. Smillie, *The Alms Bazaar: Altruism under Fire – Nonprofit Organisations and International Development*, London: Intermediate Technology.

Smith, P.K. and Watkins, S.C. (2005) 'Perceptions of risk and strategies for prevention: responses to HIV/AIDS in rural Malawi', *Social Science and Medicine*, 60: 649–60.

Starr, P. (1992) 'Social categories and claims in the liberal state', in M. Douglas and S. Hall, *How Classification Works: Nelson Goodman among the Social Sciences*, Edinburgh: Edinburgh University Press.

Stebbing, J., Gazzard, B. and Douek, D.C. (2004) 'Where does HIV live?' *New England Journal of Medicine*, 350(8): 1872–80.

Stevens, W., Kaye, S. and Corrah, T. (2004) 'Antiretroviral therapy in Africa', *British Medical Journal*, 328: 280–2.

Sullivan, J.L. and Luzuriaga, K. (2001) 'The changing face of paediatric HIV-1 infection', *New England Journal of Medicine*, 345(21): 1568–9.

Sweat, M., Gregorich, S., Sangiwa, G., Furlonge, C., Balmer, D., Kamenga, C., Grinstead, O. and Coates, T. (2000) 'Cost-effectiveness of voluntary HIV-1 counselling and testing in reducing sexual transmission of HIV-1 in Kenya and Tanzania', *Lancet*, 356: 113–21.

Taylor, C. (1990) 'Modes of civil society', *Public Culture*, 3.

Tendler, J. (1982) *Turning Private Voluntary Organisations into Development Agencies: Questions for Evaluation*, Program Evaluation Discussion Paper 12, Washington, DC: United States Agency for International Development.

Therkildsen, O. and Semboja, J. (1995) *Service Provision under Stress in East Africa: The State, NGOs and People's Organizations in Kenya, Tanzania and Uganda*, London: James Currey.

Thomas, Jr, C.F. and Limper, A.H. (2004) 'Pneumocystis Pneumonia', *New England Journal of Medicine*, 350(24): 2487–99.

Tilly, C. (1999) *Durable Inequality*, Berkeley, CA: University of California Press.

Timberg, C. (2006) 'How AIDS in Africa was overstated', *Washington Post*, 6 April.

Tocqueville, A. de (1998) *Democracy in America*, trans. G. Lawrence, New York: Harper Perennial.

Treichler, P. (1999) *How to Have Theory in an Epidemic: Cultural Chronicles of AIDS*, Durham, NC: Duke University Press.

Tully, J. (2002) 'Political philosophy as a critical activity', *Political Theory*, 30(4): 533–55.

Turner, C.F., Miller, H.G. and Moses, L.E. (eds) (1989) *AIDS: Sexual Behaviour and Intravenous Drug Use*, Washington, DC: National Academy Press.

Tvedt, T. (1998) *Angels of Mercy or Development Diplomats?*, Oxford: James Currey.

TWN (Third World Network) (2002) People's Health Assembly 2000, http://www.twnside.org.sg/title/pha2000.htm (accessed 12 April 2002).

UNAIDS (1999) 'About UNAIDS? Governance', http://www.unaidsorg/en/about+unaids/what+is+unaids.asp (accessed 10 December 2005).

UNAIDS (2002a) *Leadership for Better Health*, Geneva: UNAIDS.

UNAIDS (2002b) *Report on the Global HIV/AIDS Epidemic: 2002*, Geneva: UNAIDS.

UNAIDS (2004a) *Coordination of National Responses to HIV/AIDS: Guiding Principles for National Authorities and their Partners*, Geneva: UNAIDS.

UNAIDS (2004b) *Three Ones*, http://www.unaids.org/en/about+unaids/what+is+unaids/unaids+at+country+level/the+three+ones.asp.

UNAIDS (2004c) *Report on the Global AIDS Epidemic*, Geneva: UNAIDS.

UNAIDS (2005a) *AIDS Epidemic: Update December 2005*, Geneva: UNAIDS.

UNAIDS (2005b) *Intensifying HIV Prevention: UNAIDS Policy Position Paper*, Geneva: UNAIDS.

UNAIDS (2006) *Report on the Global AIDS Epidemic*, Geneva: UNAIDS.

Uvin, P. (1998) *Aiding Violence: The Development Enterprise in Rwanda*, Bloomfield, CT: Kumarian Press.

Uvin, P. (2004) *Human Rights and Development*, Bloomfield, CT: Kumarian Press.

Uvin, P. and Miller, D. (1994) *Scaling Up: Thinking through the Issues*, Providence, RI: World Hunger Program.

Vakil, A. (1997) 'Confronting the classification problem: toward a taxonomy of NGOs', *World Development*, 25(12).

Van de Perre, P. (2000) 'HIV voluntary counselling and testing in community health services', *Lancet*, 356: 86–7.

Van Rooy, A. (1998) *Civil Society and the Aid Industry*, London: Earthscan.

Verweij, M. (1999) 'Medicalization as a moral problem for preventive medicine', *Bioethics*, 13: 89–113.

Vitebsky, P. (1993) 'Is death the same everywhere? Contexts of knowing and doubting', in M. Hobart (ed.), *An Anthropological Critique of Development: The Growth of Ignorance*, London: Routledge.

Wainberg, M.A. (2005) 'Generic HIV drugs: enlightened policy for global health', *New England Journal of Medicine*, 352(8): 747–50.

Wakabi, W. (2006) 'Condoms still contentious in Uganda's struggle over AIDS', *Lancet*, 367: 1387–8.

Washington Post (2006) Editorial: 'Assessing AIDS', 10 April.

Watkins, S.C., Zulu, E.M., Kohler, H.P. and Behrman, J.R. (2003) 'Introduction onto social interactions and HIV/SIDS in rural Africa', *Demographic Research*, Special Collections 1, www.demograhic-research.org, pp. 2–28.

Watney, S. (1994) *Practices of Freedom: Selected Writings on HIV/AIDS*, London: Rivers Oram Press.

Wendt, A. (1998) 'Constructing international politics', *Review of International Studies*, 24(4).

Wendt, A. (1999) *Social Theory of International Politics*, Cambridge: Cambridge University Press.

Whiteside, A. (2006) 'Development: failures of vision and imagination', *International Affairs*, 82(2): 327–44.

WHO (2001) 'Provisional WHO/UNAIDS Secretariat recommendations on the use of cotrimoxazole prophylaxis in adults and children living with HIV/AIDS in Africa', *African Health Systems*, 1(1): 30–1.

WHO (2006) *Antiretroviral Therapy (ART)*, http://www.who.int/hiv/topics/arv/en (12 July 2006).

WHO, UNAIDS and UNICEF (2004) Joint WHO/UNAIDS/UNICEF statement on use of cotrimoxazole as prophylaxis in HIV exposed and HIV infected children, http://data.unaids.org/Media/Press-Statements01/PS_Cotrimoxazole_22Nov04_en.pdf.

Whyte, S.R. (1997) *Questioning Misfortune: The Pragmatics of Uncertainty in Eastern Uganda*, Cambridge: Cambridge University Press.

Wilkin, T., Glesby, M. and Gulick, R.M. (2006) 'Changing antiretroviral therapy: why, when, and how', HIV InSite Knowledge Base Chapter, http://hivinsite.ucsf.edu/InSite?page=kb-03-02-06 (12 July 2006).

Williamson, O.E. (1985) *The Economic Institutions of Capitalism*, New York: Free Press.

Wittgenstein, L. (1997) *Philosophical Investigations*, London: Blackwell.

Wood, G.D. (1997) 'States without citizens: the problem of the franchise state', in D. Hulme and M. Edwards (eds), *NGOs, States and Donors: Too Close for Comfort?*, London: Macmillan.

Woods, N. (2006) *The Globalizers: The IMF, the World Bank and their Borrowers*, Ithaca, NY: Cornell University Press.

Worboys, M. (1996) 'Germs, malaria and the invention of Mansonian tropical medicine: from "disease in the tropics" to "tropical diseases"', in D. Arnold (ed.), *Warm Climates and Western Medicine*, Atlanta, GA: Rodopi.

World Bank (2003) *Local Government Responses to HIV/AIDS: Handbook*, Washington, DC: World Bank.

World Bank (2004) *The Multi-Country HIV/AIDS Program for Africa*, http://www.worldbank.org/afr/aids/map.htm   and   http://worldbank.org/afr/aids/map_eligibility.htm.

Wyatt, C.M., Arons, R.R., Klotman, P.E. and Klotman, M.E. (2006) 'Acute renal failure in hospitalized patients with HIV: risk factors and impact on in-hospital mortality', *AIDS*, 20(4): 561–5.

Yerly, S., Vora, S., Rizzardi, P., Chave, J.-P., Vernazza, P.L., Flepp, M., Telenti, A., Battegay, M., Veuthey, A.-L., Bru, J.-P., Rickenbach, M., Hirschel, B., Perrin, L. and the Swiss HIV Cohort Study (2001) 'Acute HIV infection: impact on the spread of HIV and transmission of drug resistance', *AIDS*, 15: 2287–92.

Young, O. (1989) 'The politics of international regime formation: managing natural resources and environment', *International Organization*, 43(3).

Zola, I.K. (1972) 'Medicine as an institution of social control', *Sociological Review*, 20: 487–504.

Zola, I.K. (1983) *Socio-Medical Inquiries: Recollections, Reflections and Reconsiderations*, Philadelphia, PA: Temple University Press.

Zola, I.K. (1991) 'Bringing our bodies and ourselves back in: reflections on a past, present and future "medical sociology"', *Journal of Health and Social Behaviour*, 32(1): 1–16.

Zucker, L.G. (1991) 'The role of institutionalization in cultural persistence', in W.W. Powell and P.J. DiMaggio (eds), *The New Institutionalism in Organizational Analysis*, Chicago, IL: University of Chicago Press.

Index

Miller, J.C. 13
Mitchell, Timothy 167n3
monitoring 136
morality 39, 74
mother-to-child transmission 22, 29, 38, 102
MSF *see* Médecins Sans Frontières
Mudimbe, V.Y. 127, 133, 169n21
Multi-Country HIV/AIDS Program for Africa (MAP) 60, 62, 163n19
multi-sectoral approaches 38, 42, 59, 135, 136
multiple drug therapy 26–7, 79–80, 83
Mung'esi, Zebulon 23
Mutshewa, Bawani 109
Myer, Landon 166n8

Namibia 32, 169n23
naming 130
National AIDS Councils 32, 62, 169n23
Natsios, Andrew 29
neo-liberalism 49, 147, 152, 158
new institutional economics 48
Ngele, David Chizao 108–9
non-governmental organisations (NGOs) 10, 23, 37, 126, 137, 142; agency 44–8, 53–9, 147, 150; capability 57, 58, 59, 60–1, 65, 69; Global Programme on AIDS 25; governance structure 34, 36, 42; increase in numbers 32; institutional values 59–65; institutionalisation 44–7, 48–53, 58–9, 61–5, 67–8, 69–70; international policy documents 44; limitation of role 157; local initiatives 24; organisational characteristics 41–2; participatory processes 156; policy frameworks 143; service delivery 135, 147, 157; UNAIDS Three Ones principles 136; volunteers 116; *see also* international organisations
non-profit sector 135
norms 43, 64, 132, 135; gender 112; institutionalisation 49, 50, 51, 149; international relations 167n7; policy histories 153; socio-cultural 108, 109, 148
nutrition 112

Onuf, Nicolas Greenwood 167n7, 168n12, 168n13
orphans 39
Osborne, M.A. 15

Parker, R. 122
participation 35, 37, 156, 157
Partners in Health 59
partnerships 42
patent rights 27–8, 162n4
patriarchy 76
PDA *see* Population and Community Development Association
peer education 40, 109, 115, 141
people living with HIV/AIDS (PLWHA) 40–1, 82
people with AIDS (PWAs) 24, 25
People's Health Assembly 9–10
PEPFAR *see* President's Emergency Plan for AIDS Relief
Perez de Cuellar, Javier 25
pharmaceutical companies 26, 27, 28, 29, 84
Philippines 57
Piot, Peter 26, 96, 166n1
plague 12
PLWHA *see* people living with HIV/AIDS
policy 8, 98, 146, 157–60; antiretroviral therapy 78–84; civil society role 36–7, 42, 135; co-trimoxazole research 89; convergence 1; evaluation 6; evidence-based 151, 159–60; governance concept 34; implementation 2, 5–6, 22, 43, 93, 97, 121, 148, 152–3; ineffectiveness 148–9; institutionalisation 150; international documents 37–8, 44; knowledge claims 3–4, 98–100, 121, 122–3, 124, 151, 153–4; language issues 127, 145, 151–2; medicalisation 73, 77, 78, 93–4, 150; NGO agency 59, 69, 147; non-compliance with 114; participatory processes 156–7; preventative medicine 97; state decision-making 63–4; sustainability 147; targets 66, 148; vertical-health 16–17; *see also* interventions
politics 9, 10; global politics of health 11; of medicine 14–18; politicisation of HIV/AIDS issues 17–18
Population and Community Development Association (PDA) 161n2
poster campaigns 110, 138, 141
poverty 17, 41, 92, 112–13; civil society role in poverty reduction 134; disease-induced 8, 9; gender issues 111; influence on treatment process 81, 82

eBooks – at www.eBookstore.tandf.co.uk

A library at your fingertips!

eBooks are electronic versions of printed books. You can store them on your PC/laptop or browse them online.

They have advantages for anyone needing rapid access to a wide variety of published, copyright information.

eBooks can help your research by enabling you to bookmark chapters, annotate text and use instant searches to find specific words or phrases. Several eBook files would fit on even a small laptop or PDA.

NEW: Save money by eSubscribing: cheap, online access to any eBook for as long as you need it.

Annual subscription packages

We now offer special low-cost bulk subscriptions to packages of eBooks in certain subject areas. These are available to libraries or to individuals.

For more information please contact webmaster.ebooks@tandf.co.uk

We're continually developing the eBook concept, so keep up to date by visiting the website.

www.eBookstore.tandf.co.uk